70   39.95
      60B

JOB
DISPLACEMENT

JOB DISPLACEMENT

CONSEQUENCES

and

IMPLICATIONS FOR POLICY

EDITED BY
John T. Addison

 WAYNE STATE UNIVERSITY PRESS   DETROIT

Copyright © 1991 by Wayne State University Press,
Detroit, Michigan 48202. All rights are reserved.
No part of this book may be reproduced without formal
permission.
Manufactured in the United States of America.
95 94 93 92 91   5 4 3 2 1

Library of Congress Cataloging-in-Publication Data

Job displacement : consequences and implications for policy / edited
    by John T. Addison.
        p.   cm. — (Labor economics and policy series)
    Includes bibliographical references and index.
    ISBN 0-8143-2285-9 (alk. paper)
    1. Displaced workers—United States.   2. Displaced workers—
Government policy—United States.   I. Addison, John T.
II. Series.
HD5708.55.U6J63   1991
331.13'704—dc20   90-22623

Designer: Joanne E. Kinney

Contents

Contributors

John T. Addison	Professor of Economics, University of South Carolina
Daniel S. Hamermesh	Professor of Economics, Michigan State University, and Research Associate, National Bureau of Economic Research
Lori Gladstein Kletzer	Assistant Professor of Economics, Williams College
Douglas L. Kruse	Assistant Professor of Economics, Rutgers University
Duane E. Leigh	Professor of Economics, Washington State University
Michael J. Podgursky	Associate Professor of Economics, University of Massachusetts at Amherst
Pedro Portugal	Assistant Professor of Economics, Universidade do Porto
Christopher J. Ruhm	Assistant Professor of Economics, Boston University
Adam Seitchik	Assistant Professor of Economics, Wellesley College
Paul L. Swaim	Assistant Professor of Economics, University of Massachusetts at Amherst

Acknowledgments

The genesis of this volume owes much to the encouragement of Professor John D. Owen of Wayne State University whom I should like to thank personally. As editor, I am of course indebted most of all to the contributors, each of whom demonstrated an uncanny ability to meet deadlines without any sacrifice in rigor. To them my sincere thanks. I also owe a debt of gratitude to my fellow European and colleague Pedro Portugal for helpful discussions over the course of the project. Finally, I am happy to acknowledge the organizing skill and typing of Georgene Dance.

CHAPTER ONE

Overview

JOHN T. ADDISON

I believe that we as a nation owe an obligation, as well as a helping hand, to those who pay the price of economic re- adjustment.

Ronald Reagan

I. Introduction

This text gathers within one volume the results of a major series of empirical investigations into the worker displacement phenomenon. The essays assembled here are long on analysis and short on description. This mix rather differentiates the volume from other treatments. That said, it would be idle to pretend that we have uncovered the philosopher's stone in any policy prescriptive sense or necessarily covered the entire range of issues raised by worker dislocation. What *is* provided here is a modern framework for analysis and policy evaluation.

In this opening chapter, we provide a detailed overview of the individual essays, set a contextual framework for the more policy-oriented material, and offer a modicum of interpretation. Inevitably in an environment in which policy implementation precedes hard analysis, and has its own dynamics, there will be some criticism of past and present policy initiatives. But such criticism is secondary in importance to the task of setting down what has been learned from substantive analyses of worker dislocation and what remains unknown. As noted earlier there is no policy blueprint but there are very clear implications for policy in what follows.

9

II. Nature and Effects of Displacement

Although the problem of job displacement has much exercised policy-makers in recent years—the history and evolution of policy is charted in section III—continuing controversy attaches to definitional issues. This identification question is brought out very clearly in Adam Seitchik's opening contribution: "Who Are Displaced Workers?" Seitchik notes not only the disparity between eligibility criteria for job displacement assistance under policy instruments (he cites the example of Title III of the Job Training Partnership Act, as amended in 1988) and more conceptually grounded definitions, but also the sheer diversity of the latter. Thus, for example, should displaced workers be so categorized on the basis of declining employment in their industry, occupation, or region of job loss; for reasons that have to do with the consequences of job loss; or reflecting other restrictions such as extent of predisplacement tenure, age of the job loser, and source of job loss? Clearly, different definitions produce different displaced worker counts and may prejudge the nature of the displaced worker problem.

Having entered these caveats, Seitchik next proceeds to document the strengths and limitations of the main sources of information on displaced workers; principally, the Panel Study of Income Dynamics (PSID), the National Longitudinal Survey (NLS), and, most recently, the Displaced Worker Survey (DWS) conducted as a supplement to the Current Population Survey (CPS). Special attention should be paid to this discussion because of the empirical focus of chapters 3, 6, 7 on the PSID and chapters 4, 5, and 8 on the Displaced Worker Survey. Briefly put, no single data set is without blemish. The major advantage of the Displaced Worker Survey over the two other nationally representative data bases is sample size; for example, the number of households interviewed is approximately 58,000. Moreover, it contains fairly extensive information on the nature of the lost job and postdisplacement labor market experience that supplements the detailed demographic and economic variables provided in the regular CPS. Shortcomings of the Displaced Worker Survey include possible recall bias, given the five-year retrospective nature of this survey; some ambiguity as to whether workers are in fact permanently as opposed to temporarily laid off; subjective responses to the source of job loss question in the survey; some fuzziness as to the unemployment duration measure (see chapter 5); and the difficulty of using the survey as a longitudinal vehicle because of sample rotation.

The two longitudinal surveys, for their part, have the advantage of

10

allowing the observer to distinguish between instances of temporary versus permanent layoff, the ability to track earnings and unemployment development through time, as well as facilitating the construction of a control group. (Given the rotation problem in the DWS, most studies of earnings development focus on changes in *relative* earnings over the five-year sample period[s]). That being said, both the PSID and the NLS produce rather small samples of dislocated workers and lump together various types of job loss; for example, the PSID groups layoffs with firings and, potentially more serious, the NLS groups layoffs, plant closings, and seasonal job cessations. Moreover, they lack the richness of detail provided by the DWS in combination with the regular CPS.

The balance of Seitchik's contribution is given over to an investigation of the size and characteristics of the displaced worker population, the characteristics of the jobs lost, and the process of labor market adjustment in the wake of displacement. Seitchik draws almost exclusively on the 1984 and 1986 Displaced Worker Surveys, although in charting reemployment earnings an attempt is made to estimate the impact of earnings losses from displacement on family income using data from the annual work experience supplement to the March CPS. In presenting a variety of cross tabulations, Seitchik sets the scene for the subsequent, more analytical treatments of the effects of displacement on earnings and unemployment.

Some of the more striking results from the cross tabulations may be itemized as follows. First, the annual displacement rate in the United States, expressed as a fraction of the civilian labor force aged twenty and above, amounts to approximately 1% to 3%. Second, displaced workers appear representative of the U.S. labor force in terms of age, race, and marital and family status, although they are somewhat less well educated than the labor force as a whole. Third, roughly 50% of workers receive some indication of their impending displacement and one out of every seven displaced workers is able to quit prior to officially being laid off. (Note that the DWS contains information on whether the worker received official notice of layoff or otherwise anticipated the coming job loss, but does not differentiate between formal communication and expectation of a layoff. This distinction can now be pursued on the basis of the 1988 DWS, and grouped notice intervals are provided *for those receiving written notice*). Fourth, 53% of the displaced had less than three years of accrued tenure on the lost job and 84% had less than ten years' tenure, although plant shutdowns affected an older and more tenured labor force than "slack work." Fifth, job loss disproportionately affects those in mining, construction, and manufacturing and, in occupational terms, is

11

skewed toward industrial blue-collar jobs. Sixth, displacement should not be viewed as a "rust belt" phenomenon. Although Midwest states have a higher percentage of all displaced workers than any other regional grouping, they contain a roughly corresponding fraction of the labor force. Seventh, the reemployment rate among all workers displaced over the full five years of the 1984 and 1986 surveys stood at 66.9% and 61.6%, respectively. In both survey years, reemployment rates were higher among workers displaced via plant closings than other sources of job loss. Eighth, using (censored and uncensored) data from the 1986 DWS, the mean length of unemployment spell between displacement and survey date was 27.1 weeks for the unemployed, 21.1 weeks for the reemployed, and 51.8 weeks for those currently out of the labor force. Exactly equal percentages (31.4%) of job losers, irrespective of their current employment status, reported less than 5 weeks and more than six months of unemployment. Ninth, although the majority of reemployed workers earn less in real terms on the new job than on the predisplacement job, there is wide variation in earnings development; for example, 43% of those reemployed in January 1986 enjoyed higher real earnings on the new job while 30% received less than three-fourths of their previous wage. Similar variation is observed in the impact of earnings losses on family income. Finally, an examination of the characteristics of workers suffering major dislocation suggests that unskilled blue-collar workers, women, older workers, and those with educational deficits are more prone to experience long-term unemployment, while those with higher tenure on the lost job and occupying blue-collar unskilled jobs at displacement are more likely to record pronounced earnings losses. Further analysis of the correlates of major dislocation clearly requires the use of multivariate techniques.

In chapter 3, Daniel Hamermesh examines the relation between wages and the probability of plant closings with a view to determining the size of wage concessions necessary to keep plants from closing. As a by-product of this exercise, he also obtains an estimate of the constant output elasticity of demand for labor.

Hamermesh's model is set within a contract theoretic framework: workers and firms are envisaged as being involved in a long-term employment relationship. Workers contract with their employers for a package that includes a probability that the job will exist and a wage premium over their next best alternative. It is the latter that bonds the worker to the firm. Notice that although insurance is implicit in the model it may still be in the interests of the parties to sever the employment relation if market circumstances worsen the workers' prospects in the firm sufficiently. In other words, complete insurance may be too costly to the worker side.

Workers are viewed as initially sorting themselves into firms offering different degrees of employment risk. As is conventional, it is assumed that there will be a positive relationship between the observed probability that a plant will close and the wage rate. Employers offering a lower degree of job security will, then, have to pay a higher wage in order to attract labor, which is assumed to be homogeneous. To fully understand the model it is important to note that the wage premium for a higher observed probability that a plant will close is captured in the worker's reservation wage. Thus, Hamermesh writes that the market will produce a compensating differential in the reservation wage at different firms that is positively related to the ex ante expected probability that the firm will close. The reservation wage, including the compensating differential, provides a benchmark value against which workers evaluate their wages once they have joined the firm. Note finally that the bonding process referred to earlier is produced by instantaneous firm-specific training on induction. This raises the worker's wage above his or her next best alternative and also the firm's interest in keeping the worker because it is assumed that the training raises the worker's marginal revenue product more than it does the wage.

Hamermesh seeks to establish the equilibrium relationship between the wage rate—more particularly, the excess of wages over the reservation wage—and the probability that a plant will close. The components of this equilibrium relation are the firm's probabilistic shutdown frontier and the worker's utility function. The firm's shutdown frontier traces the relation between the negotiated wage rate and the likelihood that the plant will close. The firm confronts a known distribution of random prices. Exogenous shocks shift the distribution of prices. Given a particular set of exogenous conditions or index of demand, at the start of each period the firm draws from the known distribution of stochastic prices and decides whether or not to close down. Product prices must be sufficiently high in relation to the wage to enable the firm to meet some critical level of profits. Satisfying the profit constraint implies a higher probability of closure for higher wages, so that for a given distribution of stochastic prices the shutdown frontier is positively sloped in p-W space, where p denotes the probability of closure and W the wage rate measure. As noted earlier, changes in the distribution of prices generated by exogenous shocks serve to shift the shutdown frontier: favorable demand realizations shifting it to the right (making the probability of closure less likely and raising the wage) and unfavorable demand shocks shifting it to the left. In other words, for a given wage, a positive shock to the market will produce a reduced risk of closure, and conversely.

Turning to the worker side, the individual is assumed to choose between a higher wage and a reduced risk that the firm will close. Workers' expected utility is a function of the excess of the wage over their next best alternative and the probability of closure. For a given level of utility the worker's indifference curve is again positively sloped in p-W space. But, consistent with conventional analysis, since the worker is assumed to be less willing to trade off security for wages as the probability of closure increases, the indifference curve(s) is concave with respect to the wage rate measure. Clearly combinations of wage rates and risks of plant closing that lie on indifference curves closer to the origin of the p-W map will be inferior to those farther away from the origin, because at each wage rate along the former the risk of losing the job will be higher.

Equilibrium thus obtains at the point of tangency of the firm's shutdown frontier for a given demand realization and the worker's indifference curve. Given the variety of ex post demand realizations, the object is to obtain the slope of the locus of equilibrium combinations of (the measure of) wages and closure probabilities. Hamermesh argues that this equilibrium locus will have a negative slope in p-W space, having assumed a linear probabilistic shutdown frontier for the firm and having incorporated a conventional measure of relative risk aversion into the worker's utility function.

In estimating form, therefore, his model points to a *negative* relation between probability of closure and the excess of wages over reservation wages (the bigger the demand shock the smaller the wage measure) *and* a positive relation between the reservation wage and the probability of closure to capture the existence of compensating differentials. In addition, Hamermesh introduces a tenure variable and proxies for degree of risk aversion. These variables shift the equilibrium locus. On the reasoning that tenure picks up firm-specific training, which in turn introduces a gap between marginal product and the wage—one which increases over much of the range of observed tenure—the impact of any given wage on the probability of closure is correspondingly reduced. Similarly, higher (lower) degrees of risk aversion lower (raise) the equilibrium locus.

Using PSID data, the model is estimated over a sample of displaced ($n = 114$) and nondisplaced ($n = 2,433$) workers. The dependent variable in Hamermesh's analysis is of course a dummy indicating whether or not the worker was displaced. Weighted probit analysis is employed. It is reported that shocks that increase the probability of displacement also significantly reduce the wage increase. Specifically, each 1% reduction in wages is associated with an increase in the probability of plant closing of .00034. (The slope of the equilibrium locus is thus −.034.) Given that the mean probability of plant closure is 2.3%, a 1% decrease is associated with a 1.5% increase in the likelihood of closure (.034 ÷ .023). But if this result is in conformity with the predictions of the model, the finding of a negative coefficient for the reservation wage argument is not. In other words, there is no evidence of compensating differentials for the ex ante risk of closure, which finding Hamermesh interprets as reflecting the dominance of the income effect of higher earnings on the demand for security. The proxies for risk in the model perform poorly, although the (quadratic) tenure argument is significantly negative as expected.

Having obtained his preferred estimate of the slope of the equilibrium locus, Hamermesh next proceeds to compute an analogue to the firm's elasticity of demand for labor and, more importantly, the magnitude of wage reduction required to keep the plant open in the face of unfavorable demand realizations. The former exercise requires computation of the inverse of the slope of the equilibrium locus, suitably modified to take account of nonparallel shifts in the shutdown frontier. Using a second-order approximation to the equilibrium locus, he obtains an estimate of the constant output elasticity of demand for labor of −.37, well in line with those obtained using industry, or yet more aggregative, data.

Proceeding with the second-order approximation, Hamermesh calculates that a 34.97% reduction in wages would be required to offset fully a negative demand shock that increases the overall probability of plant closure by one percentage point. Note that we would not expect to observe such reductions in wages because this solution would not lie on the (negatively sloped) equilibrium locus. Note also that, for this data set, a one percentage point upward movement in the overall risk parameter translates into more than a 40% increase in the risk that a particular plant will close since it will be recalled that the overall probability of a closure is only 2.3%. Nevertheless, these values are still very large, suggesting that workers who accept small cuts in wages as a means of staving off the closure of their plant are unlikely to be successful. Alternatively put, Hamermesh argues that it will often be logical and indeed socially optimal for workers to resist wage concessions.

We noted earlier that the latter estimates should not be taken to mean that workers do not make concessions, since the estimates of the equilibrium locus clearly indicate that some wage cuts are accepted in response to negative demand shocks. Indeed, most of the impact of a demand shock is apparently taken up by reductions in wage growth rather than in plant closings. Thus, the research trail turns to a more detailed examination of the circumstances of plant closure. Relevant considerations here include the role of information asymmetries, the scale of the worker losses from displacement, and of course the modeling of the concession bargaining process itself. In the interim, Hamermesh has provided us with an important preliminary analysis of plant closings (his model is not intended to apply to layoffs) that, while not denying that assistance be provided workers, recognizes explicitly the frailty of legislative exercises seeking to place constraints on plant closings.

Attention shifts in chapter 4 to the wage losses sustained by displaced workers in the wake of redundancy. In an analysis that is notable for its close attention to detail and careful handling of DWS data, Lori Gladstein Kletzer focuses on the sacrifice of firm-specific training investments. She also pays attention to the impact of industry and occupation variables. The backdrop to Kletzer's analysis is concern with the conventional earnings function (originally developed by Jacob Mincer). Here, when earnings are related to tenure on the current job, to total labor market experience, and to other explanatory variables, the coefficient on current tenure is supposed to capture the earnings payoff of nonportable, firm-specific, training investments, while the coefficient on labor market experience the returns to portable, general training, investments. Such an earnings function estimated for the predisplacement job has been used to compute the sacrifice in firm specific training investments brought about by the premature termination of the employment relation. Yet, modern theoretical developments have suggested that the tenure coefficient compounds a number of distinct elements, the effect of which is to overstate considerably the contribution of firm-specific training to earnings growth and hence to computed earnings losses. To fix ideas, consider first unobserved differences in ability between individuals. If more able individuals both earn more and stay on the job longer, then the contribution of tenure to earnings development will clearly be overstated. Next, consider the role of good jobs and good job matches; if workers in good jobs or in good job matches stay longer on their jobs and earn more, then once again the tenure coefficient will yield an upwardly biased estimate of the return to firm-specific training. In these circumstances the error term in the conventional earnings function can no longer be assumed to be orthogonal to tenure (and experience) and must be modeled explicitly. We note parenthetically that the coefficient on total labor market experience will no longer pick up a

pure return to general training investments because the longer the exposure of the worker to the labor market the greater will be the likelihood
that he or she will obtain a better job match.

Arguing that the postdisplacement earnings of displaced workers
will be less influenced by heterogeneity bias—if the job/match component on the old job is uncorrelated with the job/match component on the
new job, then previous job tenure in the postdisplacement wage equation will be correlated only with ability—Kletzer observes that one can
make reasonable inferences about the transferability of supposedly specific skills by examining the coefficient on predisplacement tenure in the
postdisplacement wage equation. That coefficient will of course still
include a component that is a return to unobserved ability. Differences
between the predisplacement tenure coefficients in the two wage equations will reflect the loss of job/match effects and specific skills. The
composition of the bias in predisplacement earnings will of course influence the determination of postdisplacement earnings.

Kletzer's data are drawn from the displaced worker surveys for 1984
and 1986. Her sample comprises workers aged twenty to sixty years (at
displacement) who were displaced from full-time nonagricultural jobs
over the full five years preceding each survey date. Displacement is
defined in terms of job loss by reason of plant closings, abolition of shift
or position, and slack work. The overall sample comprises some 6,042
workers of whom 3,765 were reemployed at the survey date, the balance
representing those currently unemployed or out of the labor force.

Kletzer splits the sample by gender and by broad occupational status
(blue collar/white collar). Prior to providing detailed regression results,
she offers cross tabulations of the ratio of post- to predisplacement
earnings for each of her four groups (see also chapter 2). These reveal
inter alia that there are sizable differences in the distribution of earnings
loss: being larger for blue-collar workers than for white-collar workers
(for whom the change in earnings distribution is skewed toward earnings
gains) and larger for women than for men. This descriptive exercise also
reveals that workers displaced from relatively high wage industries do
not necessarily experience large earnings reduction. An interesting feature of the cross tabulations is a detailed breakdown of the industrial
pattern of postdisplacement employment, including return rates.

With these preliminaries behind her, Kletzer turns to her detailed
regression analysis. She focuses on the postdisplacement earnings function in which the key variables are tenure on the predisplacement job,
predisplacement industry and occupation, and changes in industry and
occupation. (The regressions also include arguments for race, skill level,

education, experience, and working hours status.) Separate earnings regressions are provided for each of the four gender/occupation subgroups. More accurately, three sets of regressions are provided for each: ordinary least squares (OLS) and two selectivity adjusted estimates, to take account of selection into reemployment status, first without and then with correction for unobserved individual heterogeneity among the displaced.

The most notable result of the OLS equations is the significantly positive sign on predisplacement tenure in the postdisplacement wage equation. Recall that this coefficient picks up *both* individual heterogeneity and transferable skills. Not surprisingly the coefficient is smaller than that reported in the predisplacement equation since the latter includes job-specific factors, namely, job/match heterogeneity and nontransferable skills. The gap between the coefficients represents the loss of such job-specific factors and it varies considerably across the four gender/ occupational groups, being greatest for blue-collar males and smallest for blue-collar women, and generally increasing in predisplacement tenure. Kletzer associates the higher losses of blue-collar males with the greater specificity of their training. For females the explanation is symmetric—for reasons of choice and/or discrimination, women have lower firm-specific assets—but it should also be recalled that blue-collar females have larger reductions in actual earnings than any other group.

The next stage in the analysis is to allow for the selection of workers into reemployment. Using the standard Heckman two-stage procedure, Kletzer reports evidence of negative selection; that is, those currently unemployed are predicted to have higher earnings than their reemployed counterparts. Correcting for selection bias does not materially affect the coefficient on previous tenure in the postdisplacement wage equation. Not for that matter does Kletzer's subsequent correction for unobserved individual heterogeneity—by including the residual from the *predisplacement* wage equation as a separate regressor—substantially alter the tenure coefficients, although it is universally positive and significant.

Kletzer's inclusion of the predisplacement industry (five dummies) is an interesting wrinkle. She reports evidence of continuing industry wage differentials for blue-collar workers, although not for the other groups. Specifically, workers displaced from mining, durable goods manufacturing, and transportation and public utilities continue to earn positive wage differentials relative to services (the omitted category). These are the very same industries that are associated with positive wage differentials in the predisplacement wage equation (reflecting an unmeasured mix of efficiency wages, monopoly rents, and *perhaps* compensating wage differentials). Kletzer argues that this outcome may be the result of workers displaced from high-wage industries finding reemployment in the same industries, possibly because they return to the same job. Here, probit equations, used to construct the selection argument, reveal that blue-collar men displaced from high-wage industries are less likely to be reemployed. Put another way, they have higher reservation wages. But once reemployed they continue to earn positive wage differentials relative to comparable workers displaced from other sectors. The argument that such workers are recalled is consistent with Kletzer's finding from her industry reemployment cross tabulations that blue-collar males exhibit the strongest tendency to stay in mining and manufacturing—in all cases the return percentages exceed .34.

Turning to the effect of changes in (two-digit) industry and occupations, both factors are associated with reduced earnings across all gender/occupational groups. The losses associated with industry and occupational shifts are always greater for blue-collar than for white-collar workers.

This summary does not do justice to the full range of arguments in Kletzer's chapter, which will repay detailed scrutiny. Some of the subsidiary findings include the powerful depressing effect of higher unemployment rates on reemployment probabilities and the important role of education and jobs skills in mitigating earnings losses. *Kletzer concludes that the appropriate focus for displaced worker policy is toward the individual and job characteristics associated with earnings losses rather than categorical programs, a theme that is reiterated in the subsequent essays.*

Kletzer's principal finding that earnings losses attributed to the sacrifice of firm-specific training investments are much smaller than is implied by simply equating the coefficient on tenure in the predisplacement job with a return to such training is of crucial importance (see also Addison and Portugal 1989a, 1989b). But this does not imply that the losses are trivial, especially when one adds in the negative effect on earnings of changes in industry and occupation. For the future, more work is required on whether the private costs of displacement stemming from lost firm-specific training investments translate into social costs by, for example, producing a suboptimal quantity of firm specific training system wide. Elements that need to be addressed in this inquiry include the presence of rents on the previous job, the degree to which displacement is or can be anticipated, and the pattern of earnings throught time. *On the basis of our current knowledge, however, there is no case for establishing a system of compensation payments based on tenure.*

Unemployment duration in the wake of displacement is the focus of chapter 5. Here, Paul Swaim and Michael Podgursky examine the escape rate from unemployment through time, the role of individual and other variables in influencing the expected duration of joblessness, and the presence of structural elements in displaced worker unemployment. Like Kletzer, they employ data from the 1984 and 1986 Displaced Worker Surveys, impose much the same set of restrictions on the data, and present separate results for the same population subgroups.

An extremely useful set of cross tabulations of weeks of joblessness by gender and occupation, and of worker characteristics by weeks of joblessness, precede the authors' analytical material. These reveal not only the diverse unemployment experience of the displaced—many displaced workers experience little or no unemployment, while a significant minority suffer long spells of joblessness—but also challenge certain stylized hypotheses concerning the long-term unemployed displaced worker population. First, unemployed workers of longer duration are not simply those with (absolutely) high reservation wages who have chosen to search longer for more attractive job offers. This is because earnings losses, as proxied by the reemployment wage ratio, generally rise with duration of unemployment. Second, the longer-term unemployed are not primarily older workers. Third, although changes in (three-digit) industry and occupation in the wake of redundancy produce somewhat longer spells of joblessness on average, displaced workers in general are not immobile across jobless duration intervals.

Having entered a number of caveats as to the nature of the unemployment duration variable in the displaced worker survey and problems of recall bias (see also chapter 2), Swaim and Podgursky turn to their model. The probability of an ongoing spell of unemployment ending during a particular week is a product of the probability of receiving at least one job offer in that week and the probability of the maximum offered wage exceeding the worker's reservation wage. Variables subsequently employed in estimating the model proxy the frequency with which job offers are received and the level of the worker's reservation wage relative to the distribution of offered wages.

Swaim and Podgursky estimate three parametric hazard models (lognormal, log-logistic, and Weibull) depicting the instantaneous escape rates from unemployment through time. The shape parameter from these distributions summarizes changes in the hazard rate over time and hence signals the presence or otherwise of duration dependence.

The particular form of hazard function they ultimately select has been widely used in the unemployment literature and is known as a Weibull proportional hazards model. This model implies that two individuals with different characteristics will have hazard rates that differ by the same proportionate amount over the life of the unemployment spell. The proportional hazards model further assumes that individuals with identical characteristics will have identical hazard functions. Unobserved differences between individuals, however, could produce spurious negative duration dependence since those members of the group with higher exit probabilities will of course account for a smaller share of the sample as unemployment duration lengthens. In recognition of this problem, Swaim and Podgursky seek to generalize their model to allow for unobserved individual heterogeneity. They accomplish this by adding an error term to the hazard function and then specifying a specific distribution for that error term. Empirical estimations are carried out for both this model and the original Weibull distribution.

The independent variables employed in the authors' regression analysis are meant to proxy the frequency with which job offers are received and the level of the worker's reservation wage relative to the distribution of offered wages. Variables expected to increase the probabilities of remaining jobless from one week to the next (and hence to increase the duration of unemployment) are race, age, tenure on the previous job, industry unionization rate, eligibility for unemployment insurance (UI) benefits, and the area unemployment rate at the time of displacement. Variables expected to increase the escape rate from unemployment, and hence reduce unemployment duration, are education, marital status (being married), layoff by reason of plant shutdown, and advance notification of impending redundancy. (Also included are a number of other arguments for which the authors have no strong priors as to net outcome.) Note that this is a reduced form model because neither the arrival rate of job offers nor the reservation wage vis-à-vis the offered wage is explicitly modeled.

In implementing the model across the four gender/occupation subgroups, age, education, race, tenure, union membership, plant shutdowns, and area unemployment rates emerge as the most consistently significant variables. Schooling, race, plant shutdowns, and area unemployment rates have particularly strong effects on unemployment duration. The results for blue-collar male workers indicate that each additional year of schooling reduces expected duration by 11.5%; that blacks have expected jobless spells that are 143% longer than comparable workers; that workers displaced by plant shutdowns have an expected jobless spell that is 37% shorter than that occasioned by other sources of job loss (which the authors construe as indicating the absence of a waiting-for-recall effect); and that a one percentage point increase in area

21

unemployment rates produces a lengthening of jobless spells of some 11%. Other results worthy of note include the tendency for duration to rise with tenure on the lost job and union status, the failure of advance notification significantly to reduce duration (although the authors enter the caveat that their proportional hazards model does not allow for the possibility than notice most affects the escape rate from unemployment early in the jobless spell), and the general insignificance of UI eligibility.

The magnitude of the estimated shape parameter suggests monotonically declining hazard rates and hence negative duration dependence (that is, the longer the observed spell of unemployment, the more likely the worker to remain unemployed). The authors thus see scope for a policy that seeks to intervene early in the jobless spell so as to stop the illness from worsening. However, the modified Weibull distribution outperforms the simple Weibull, meaning that unobserved heterogeneity is present in the duration data. So there is a problem. *If policy is to intervene early in the duration spell, who is one to target ex ante?* We will further address this apparent dilemma below.

Nevertheless, whether produced by duration dependence or unobserved heterogeneity, the decline in the reemployment rate as weeks of joblessness increase does produce a highly skewed distribution of completed spell lengths of unemployment across all four gender/occupation groups. Mean spell durations are on the order of 50% higher than the median, and there also exists a high risk of protracted unemployment. These results imply that *the long-term unemployed worker thus confronts poor reemployment prospects.*

Finally, Swaim and Podgursky question whether displaced workers in any sense suffer from structural unemployment. They take the position that both frictional/turnover and structural elements are present. In particular, while it is conceded that the high unemployment of women, older workers, and some UI eligibles may reflect lower search costs/ higher reservation wages, they see no scope for a similar explanation with respect to the higher unemployment of blacks, those with low educational credentials, and workers living in areas of high unemployment. Can the latter reasonably be expected to adopt job search strategies that promote their long-term unemployment?

In the light of their structuralist interpretation, Swaim and Podgursky question whether existing income maintenance programs provide sufficient support for truly dislocated workers while recommending the targeting of manpower programs toward blue-collar workers, those with educational deficits, minorities, and communities with above average rates of unemployment. They add that, subject to the caveat concerning the impact of unobserved heterogeneity, prompt adjustment assistance may be of no small importance.

The analyses of earnings and unemployment development contained in chapters 4 and 5 do not discuss the time profile of displacement-induced changes in the two variables. The difficulty of using the DWS longitudinally in part explains this focus on "relative" wage changes and the length of the spell of joblessness immediately following the occurrence of displacement. Important questions that still need to be addressed, therefore, are the "representativeness" of the results and the persistence of observed displacement-induced effects through time. How do the earnings of the displaced compare with those of the nondisplaced, and to what extent does unobserved heterogeneity underpin earnings and unemployment development? These are the concerns that motivate Christopher Ruhm's essay in chapter 6 of this volume.

In his intriguing analysis of panel data from the PSID, Ruhm attempts to construct a control group that is more representative of displaced workers than is the sample of all nondisplaced workers with whom the displaced are being compared. (For an alternative approach, see Madden 1988.) The goal is to distinguish between "true" displacement effects and unobserved heterogeneity among job losers compared to those who do not lose their jobs. To this end, Ruhm constructs a comparison group of yet-to-be displaced workers. Individuals are first classified as displaced or nondisplaced in each of five base years 1971 through 1975. Approximately 68% of workers were not displaced in any of the five base years. Each type of worker is followed for the two years preceding and the four years subsequent to the base period. The control group is made up of those individuals who are eventually displaced, that is, outside of the base year frame. Specifically, a displaced worker is assigned to the control group if his dislocation occurs one year later than the end of the observation period for the base period displaced. Thus, for example, if 1971 is the base year, the worker displaced in that year is followed for four years after job loss (up to 1975) and the corresponding heterogeneity controls for such base year separations are workers who lose their jobs in 1976. (This is a controversial procedure, not least because workers from some of the earlier base periods who are again displaced *two* years after the end of the observation period could enter the control group; that is, populate both the base period sample and the control sample.) Ruhm's total sample thus comprises base year displaced workers and nondisplaced (largely never displaced) workers and yet-to-be displaced workers outside of the observation period for the former. It follows that his time frame is the interval 1969 to 1980.

23

Restrictions imposed include confining the sample to those aged between twenty-one and sixty-five years and to those who are economically active during at least part of the observation period.

Ruhm considers in turn predisplacement employment conditions, postdisplacement unemployment, and the pattern of wage changes. Beginning with predisplacement experience, wage and unemployment regressions for each of the two years *prior to the base year* are provided. The coefficients on the dummy identifying displaced workers reveal that their wages (unemployment) are significantly lower (higher) than those of the nondisplaced. Interestingly, the coefficients on the dummy identifying the yet-to-be displaced also tend to be significantly different from those of job stayers in the two years prior to the base period observation, suggesting that they possess unobserved characteristics associated with reduced wages and increased unemployment. Differences between the two sets of coefficients are statistically insignificant for the wage regression, which Ruhm interprets to mean that the unobserved characteristics of the displaced and yet-to-be displaced are fairly similar. Finally, there are signs that unemployment increases prior to displacement.

Ruhm next charts the impact of base period displacements and subsequent permanent layoffs to unemployment duration in each of the two years prior to the displacement, the year of displacement, and for each of the four follow-up intervals. Differences between those displaced and the yet-to-be displaced are significant in all seven regressions. The pattern is for unemployment to rise somewhat prior to the point of layoff, to peak at the year of displacement, and then to fall off fairly rapidly. In nearly all years, the yet-to-be displaced have significantly higher unemployment than the nondisplaced, amounting to between two and four days for the first five years but rising to 1.4 and 2.8 weeks in the last two years of the observation period, which is of course the two year interval preceding their own displacement. This suggests that the observed differences between the displaced and the yet-to-be displaced controls over the two years prior to the displacement of the former are not the result of unobserved heterogeneity but rather the effect of impending base year displacement. On the assumption that the coefficients on the yet-to-be displaced worker dummy for the earlier interval provide a good measure of the impact of unobserved heterogeneity, the true effect of displacement on unemployment is 8.1 weeks in the year of displacement but only 3.4 weeks in the year after displacement. Indeed, by the end of the observation period, the effect of a base year displacement is approximately 1 week. *In short, the elevated joblessness produced by displacement is a transitory, albeit nontrivial, phenomenon.*

24

Ruhm provides additional information on the persistence of unemployment for the base period job losers, comparing the sum of their joblessness in the year of displacement and the following year with their probability of being unemployed over various duration intervals in the third and fourth years of the observation period. It is reported that 22% of displaced workers moved into new jobs without experiencing any unemployment in either the displacement year or the following year. Moreover, such individuals were out of work substantially less some three or four years later than were their counterparts who had experienced some initial joblessness. That said, among the latter groups there is no relationship between the length of their early joblessness and their subsequent unemployment duration. In general, irrespective of the initial spell of joblessness, unemployment spells some three and four years after displacement were brief. Thus, for example, even for those workers with jobless spells exceeding six months over the displacement and immediate postdisplacement year, somewhat in excess of one-half experienced no joblessness in the final two years of the observation period and less than one-quarter were jobless for more than three months. Finally, a regression of subsequent unemployment duration on initial joblessness indicated very limited persistence: an additional week out of work in the first two years of displacement was associated with less than one-seventh of a day's increase in duration during the final two years of the observation period.

Very different findings with respect to persistence, however, are obtained for earnings development in the wake of displacement. Ruhm runs separate wage change regressions for each of the five years of the observation period (both with and without correction for selectivity bias attendant upon the selection of workers into reemployment status). Vis-à-vis the nondisplaced, the displaced not only have significantly higher (two-year) wage losses in the year of the displacement but also for each of the following four follow-up years. Broadly speaking, the relative wage reduction is stable and enduring over the observation period at approximately 13% to 14% per year. Part of this retardation in wage growth is explained by unobserved heterogeneity since the wages of the control group also declined relative to job stayers over the same period. *Netting out the coefficients on the dummy variable for this group of yet-to-be displaced worker dummy variable produces a "true" displacement effect on earnings of around −10% in each of the four follow up years of the observation period.*

Ruhm also provides a battery of additional information on the variance and persistence of wage changes. He reports, first, that *all* groups, not just the displaced but also the yet-to-be displaced and nondisplaced, have significant variance in earnings growth over the observation period; second, that there is a high correlation between initial and subsequent earnings growth/retardation; and, third, that this persistence is not produced by observable characteristics that are associated either positively or negatively with earnings development. Ruhm calculates that 52.3% of the initial wage change lasts through the observation period.

On the basis of his analysis, Ruhm advances a number of conclusions for policy. Although his findings do not support the persistence of unemployment over a five-year period, he clearly feels that postlayoff unemployment during the first year is of sufficient magnitude to be a cause for social concern and hence a suitable case for policy treatment. *He recommends a lengthening of the UI waiting time from one week to one month (to minimize disincentive effects) while also advocating an extension of the benefit interval from twenty-six to thirty-nine weeks.* But rather more important than this are the conclusions he draws from the persistence of wage losses. Since workers initially holding low paying jobs do not appear to search successfully and obtain better jobs at a later date, he recommends that manpower policy should focus on the problems associated with initial reemployment in low-wage jobs. *Accordingly, he advocates an expansion of basic skills training in the form of a longer (than twenty-six weeks) training interval.* Note, however, that this recommendation applies to the minority of workers who obtain initial reemployment in low-wage jobs. Ruhm is thus not recommending an across-the-board ambitious retraining program. Moreover, he is at pains to urge cost sharing: workers should pay a proportion of the costs of providing them with program services (typically in the form of tuition fees). Relatedly, he proposes that the government extend loans to liquidity-constrained displaced workers on extended training programs.

Finally, Ruhm cautions that the slowdown in earnings growth that he observes in the run-up to displacement will typically lead to downwardly biased estimates of earnings loss in conventional "relative" wage studies. He also notes that, although low-wage workers tend to suffer relatively small reductions in earnings, the loss of the job may be much more important than the scale of the earnings reduction: it may prevent such workers from obtaining the employment stability essential to subsequent career development.

In chapter 7, Pedro Portugal discusses the distributional shape of unemployment duration. The material presented here has less to do with the impact of displacement on unemployment—although this question is addressed within his permanent separations sample—than with identifying the statistical procedure that best describes the process generating unemployment duration data. Although the content of this chapter may appear somewhat arcane, the issues raised are central to correct measurement of the effect of displacement on subsequent spells of joblessness and are at the forefront of modern unemployment duration analysis.

Using data on single spells of unemployment from the 1983 wave of the PSID and distinguishing between temporary and permanent separations, Portugal considers two dominant paradigms, namely the accelerated failure time and proportional hazards models. The former assumes that the natural logarithm of unemployment duration is linearly related to its determinants. The latter assumes that the natural logarithm of the hazard rate—depicting the escape rate from unemployment at a given time—is linearly related to its determinants. In the case of the proportional hazards model, the effect of a unit change in a particular regressor (or covariate) is to produce a constant proportionate change in the hazard rate, whereas for the accelerated failure time model the effect is to accelerate the escape rate (or time to failure). Each broad model nests a number of special cases or different continuous distributions. Portugal sets as his first task the selection of that special case that best fits the data. As a by-product of this exercise, predicted levels of unemployment duration—hazard rates for the proportional hazards model—and survival rates are reported for each parametric distribution. Major differences in predicted values are reported among the family of accelerated failure time models and minor differences among variants of the proportional hazards models. Portugal reports that the special case best approximating the most general distribution for the accelerated failure time model (the extended generalized gamma) is the lognormal distribution. Moreover, this result obtains not only for the sample of permanently separated workers but also for the temporarily laid-off group. For the proportional hazards models, the most general case examined, and hence that which best fits the duration data, is a three-parameter variant of the generalized Weibull. In both cases the results of this exercise reject, for this data set, a number of parametric distributions that have often been employed in the unemployment duration literature (principally the Weibull and exponential variants.)

Portugal then offers a test of the proportionality assumption for a form of the proportional hazards model that is distribution free with respect to the baseline hazard. This test rejects the assumption, at least for a linear form of the proportional hazards model. But since Portugal does not offer a similar test of the assumptions of the accelerated failure time model, the rejection of proportionality is perhaps best viewed as underlining the need for a more sophisticated specification that is capable of accommodating nonlinearities and the possibility of mixed hazard functions.

As a practical matter, there is little major difference in the magnitude and sign of coefficients obtained for the preferred cases of the general models. What *is* critical, however, is the distributional assumption made within each model. Choice of an inappropriate distribution produces major differences in the shape of the hazard function. But if, after all, we are to accept the accelerated failure time model, then monotonically declining hazard rates are contraindicated. The preferred lognormal distribution points to an inverse U-shaped hazard function, which implies that duration dependence only emerges after some nontrivial spell of unemployment. Portugal's finding also has relevance for the debate over duration dependence versus unobserved heterogeneity. As noted earlier in this section, it has often been argued that duration dependence is a chimera produced by those workers with better reemployment prospects, but similar observed characteristics, leaving unemployment before their less reemployable counterparts. As a result, the sample of unemployed workers will increasingly be made up of those whose unobservable characteristics produce longer duration. If, as Portugal discerns, hazard rates conform to an inverse U-shape *across very different samples* (namely, temporarily and permanently separated workers) then chance rather than choice may drive the unobservables.

Portugal's finding that duration dependence only begins to bite after some nontrivial spell length of unemployment calls into question the urgency of providing early relief to job losers *on grounds of stigmatization* but it does not deny that certain groups, such as the less well educated and blacks, confront major readjustment problems and that such observable characteristics indicate the need for targeting policy. This observation, of course, refers to permanently separated workers.

III. Policy

The final three chapters of the volume deal more directly with policy issues: Addison and Portugal (chapter 8) investigate the impact of prenotification of impending layoff on subsequent labor market performance; Leigh (chapter 9) evaluates federal displaced worker programs; and Kruse (chapter 10) takes up the vexed question of whether disadvantage rather than displacement should be the focus of federal (and state) manpower programs.

We preface this policy oriented material with some introductory remarks on the evolution of public policy toward displaced workers, which has undergone some major changes in emphasis over the last three decades. The first *major* postwar federal program for retraining displaced workers was the Manpower Development Training Act (MDTA) of 1962. This legislation was prompted by rising aggregate unemployment and a growing concern over the effects of technological change on the options of midcareer adult workers. Under MDTA, unemployed and underemployed workers could participate in training courses of up to one year's duration and draw income maintenance at ruling UI benefit levels. Although the basic thrust of MDTA was unequivocally to retrain adults, and in particular those displaced by new technology, within a period of just one year the emphasis of policy was to shift away from such workers, attendant on falling unemployment rates and reduced fears of structural unemployment. MDTA was initially modified so as to permit one-quarter of program funding to be allocated to young workers. After the passage of the Economic Opportunity Act in 1964, however, MDTA was gradually transformed into an instrument of the "war on poverty," geared to serving those who were perceived to suffer most from unemployment, namely, the economically disadvantaged. Amendments to the Economic Opportunity Act in 1966 and 1967 added small-scale job creation to the package of policy measures, and subsequently introduced a system of subsidies to private sector employers who hired disadvantaged workers. A change of administration produced a number of other changes and hence an increasingly fragmented manpower program with considerable duplication and overlap.

Under the next major manpower policy initiative, the Comprehensive Employment and Training Act (CETA) of 1973, the plethora of existing programs (nine in all, including MDTA) were consolidated and the responsibility for running the programs transferred from the federal government to a large number of prime sponsors (local communities acting under the direction of mayors, county officials, and, in some cases, state governors). The sponsors were to choose which clients to serve, the services to be offered, and decide on the identity of the organization responsible for delivering those services. In addition, CETA added a new public employment component. As a result of rising unemployment in the mid-1970s, the latter component grew and came to dominate reemployment assistance such that by the end of the decade training accounted for just one-quarter of CETA outlays, which had mushroomed from $1.4 billion to $10.3 billion in 1979.

Disquiet over public service employment led Congress to amend

CETA in 1978 when the program came up for reauthorization. Against the backdrop of allegations of careless management and large-scale enrollment of ineligible applicants—for example, under the Carter administration public sector employment was expanded from 300,000 to 725,000 job slots in just nine months—Congress reduced the maximum salaries payable for public service employment workers, and also placed a limitation on enrollments. Congress also provided for a new title (Title VII), which directed the prime sponsors to create private industry councils directly involving business interests in an effort to secure private sector employment for the disadvantaged. Concurrently, a small program was introduced for displaced workers. But CETA was already approaching the end of its life.

Before turning to the next major federal initiative, we should note that although the focus of manpower programs was now firmly upon disadvantaged workers (those receiving public assistance or in low-income families), a variety of special programs continued to serve displaced workers. These included measures to assist workers displaced as a result of railroad consolidation, modifications to federal health care policy, and even the expansion of a national park. But of all such legislation applying to displaced workers that covering workers adversely affected by increased imports was by far the most important. Trade adjustment assistance was first established in 1962 to compensate and retrain workers who lost their jobs to foreign competition arising from lowered tariffs. Benefits were made available to those certified by the Secretary of Labor as having incurred damage from this source. Income maintenance benefits under trade adjustment assistance were considerably more generous than those provided under the regular UI scheme, reflecting the view that certain workers were bearing a disproportionate share of the costs of a federal policy that yielded significant benefits to society at large.

Despite the generosity of the scheme, relatively few workers were reached during the first twelve years of the program's life because of its stringent eligibility requirements; namely, the burden of proving that the job losses in question were directly attributable to import competition. But as a result of a new Trade Act in 1974, the benefits payable under existing legislation were considerably liberalized, enhancing access to the program and the speed with which the notification and payments processes were activated. Now it had only to be demonstrated that imports "contributed significantly" to unemployment rather than that they were the "major cause" of unemployment. Not surprisingly, therefore, the number of workers served increased rapidly. Weekly benefits payable under the 1974 legislation amounted to 70% of the dislocated worker's average weekly wage, with the maximum being set at the national average weekly manufacturing wage. This replacement rate took into account any UI benefits received by the worker and was also reduced by 50% of any wages received. Income maintenance benefits were payable for twenty-five weeks in a two-year period, or, in the case of workers engaged in training schemes and those aged over sixty, seventy-eight weeks in a three-year period. Relocation allowances (80% of moving expenses plus a maximum lump sum payment of $500), training allowances (including travel and subsistence expenses), and job search support (80% of transportation and living expenses up to a $500 cap while looking for work) were also available.

As a practical matter, the main thrust of trade adjustment assistance was income maintenance. In fiscal years 1976 through 1980, for example, only one-quarter of all applicants sought employment assistance. And of those who received assistance only 13% received counseling, less than 3% were referred to training, and much the same tiny percentage were placed in jobs. A little over 70% of those receiving assistance returned to their previous employer, indicating that much of the unemployment was cyclical and short term. (Indeed, between 40% and 75% of trade displaced workers were reemployed at the time they applied for benefits.) Overall, program participants had longer unemployment duration and reemployment wages that were no higher than those of comparable workers.

The increasing number of those receiving trade assistance and the burgeoning costs of the program—at its peak in fiscal year 1980, 532,000 workers were receiving assistance and program outlays stood at $1.62 billion—produced major revisions to the program in 1981. As a result of the Omnibus Budget Reconciliation Act, maintenance support levels were capped at ruling UI benefits and were to be received only as a continuation of UI and for only up to one year in total duration. The act also authorized the Secretary of Labor to require those receiving benefits for more than eight weeks in an area of high unemployment offering no suitable employment to chose between job training and job search outside the area. As a result of these measures to reduce the disincentive features of the program, outlays fell significantly. By 1984, for example, just 24,000 workers received income support payments and program outlays amounted to $35 million.

But we are running ahead of broader manpower program developments. Our earlier discussion of CETA took us up to the 1978 revisions of that program. Further changes occurred after 1980 with the accession of the Reagan administration pledged to reducing government spending. The fiscal 1980 CETA budget of $9.6 billion was reduced for fiscal year 1982 to $3.5 billion and in October of that year a new program, the Job Training Partnership Act (JTPA), was enacted. JTPA was a broad-based program intended to train and place unemployed workers in private sector jobs. Under Title III of the act, dislocated workers were for the first time since the reorientation of MDTA almost two decades earlier offered a specific albeit highly flexible program geared to helping them find new jobs, encompassing job search assistance, vocational training, on-the-job training, and remedial education. But Title III outlays accounted for only $223 million out of the $3.8 billion allocated for the entire JTPA program in operating year 1984. In other words, the bulk of the funding was applied to other titles covering disadvantaged workers (most notably Title II-A).

Unlike its predecessor, JTPA made the direction of training programs the responsibility of state governors who were required to issue performance standards for evaluating the success of programs in their states. In addition, JTPA defined an altogether more active role for the business community in program development (via private industry councils), and concentrated resources on retraining and job search while deemphasizing income maintenance.

Under JTPA the states either distributed funds to local organizations, such as community-based institutions, educational institutions, unions, employers, and the service delivery area/private industry councils, or they might alternatively provide assistance to displaced workers through existing state agencies. The majority of Title III projects were operated by private industry councils, who also coordinated employment training assistance, closely followed by educational institutions and public sector organizations. About 9% of projects were operated by individual unions and employers or union/employer consortia.

As noted earlier, training and related employment services were sufficiently broadly defined under the legislation to include many forms of reemployment assistance. The nature of the services provided, the manner of their provision, and their targeting was left in the hands of the states. But to receive benefits workers had either to have been terminated (or to have received notice of their impending displacement), be eligible for UI benefits, and unlikely to return to their present employer *or* to have been laid off by reason of plant closure. In addition, the long-term unemployed adjudged to have little chance of reemployment in the same or in a similar occupation in their area of residence were also eligible for assistance under Title III.

One-third tranches of the total funding provided to states under Title III were determined by the ratio of their number of unemployed, excess unemployed, and long-term unemployed to the relevant national totals. Altogether, some 75% of Title III funds were allocated to states using these formulae. The residual 25% of the funds were reserved for allocation to states at the discretion of the Secretary of Labor. Such discretionary funds were to be used to assist individuals affected by mass layoffs, natural disasters, federal government actions, or who resided in areas of high unemployment.

In order to receive nondiscretionary federal funding, states had to match all or part of their allocation according to the state relative unemployment rate. Equal matching was required for those states with average or below average unemployment. But for states with above average unemployment the matching contribution was reduced by 10% for each percentage point that its unemployment rate exceeded the national average.

It was noted earlier that JTPA deemphasized income maintenance. While not explicitly prohibiting income payments to trainees, the legislation specified that 70% of funding be allocated to training and related employment services. In other words, no more than 30% of Title III funding was available for administrative costs and support services.

This almost concludes our introductory statement of federal policy toward displaced workers. Although the JTPA apparatus remains intact for disadvantaged workers, a major new program has recently been introduced for the displaced. The blueprint for the current legislation was established as a result of the Secretary of Labor's Task Force on Economic Adjustment and Worker Dislocation, appointed in August 1985 to examine the specific adjustment problems confronted by experienced workers displaced from their jobs by reason of plant closings and mass layoffs. The task force recommended a new national program that would fuse the existing JTPA Title III programs and trade adjustment assistance. The task force emphasized that manpower policy was to be viewed as a cooperative effort between the public and private sectors, and the thrust of its message was that policy should aim at an early and rapid response to the onset of displacement. (Here, the task force clearly modeled its policy initiative on the Canadian Industrial Adjustment Service.) Support for workers displaced by plant closings and mass layoffs and for other dislocated workers with three years of recent covered UI employment was to be provided through an improved delivery of labor market services with the formation of displaced worker units at the state level. With respect to training services, the task force made three principal recommendations. First, noting that some 20% of the young adult population aged between twenty-one and twenty-five years could not read at the proficiency level of the typical eighth grader and that most training curricula required competency at the seventh or eighth grade level, it proposed that remedial educational opportunities should be made available to those identified as lacking basic skills. Second, on-the-job training (OJT) was favored over classroom training (CT) in transitioning displaced workers to new employment. Customized training to meet the needs of a specific employer was regarded as the optimal approach to retraining. Finally, that vocational training provided as part of a comprehensive menu of services should meet clear performance standards. CT providers, then, should not be paid unless a substantial percentage of the trainees—the task force mentioned 80%—obtained jobs meeting specified criteria.

More than a tripling of current expenditures on displaced workers was recommended. Specifically, assistance was to be offerred to around 535,000 workers, representing approximately 45% of eligible workers on the basis of the 1986 DWS. On the assumptions that per participant costs would average $1,300 in 1988, that funding of federal functions and state dislocated worker units would cost $120 million, and that supplementation of benefits for UI exhaustees in CT would require a further $80 million, the task force recommended a gross total of $900 million for 1988. Since the JTPA Title III funding for 1988 was $200 million and trade adjustment assistance was budgeted at $30 million, the task force recommended net new outlays of a little under $700 million.

Interestingly, while noting the benefits of providing workers with advance notification of their impending redundancy, and emphasizing the rapid response concept, the task force was unable to reach a consensus on the question of mandated notice.

The recommendations of the task force are largely enshrined in current legislation—The Omnibus Trade Bill of 1988—which authorized a $980 million annual appropriation for assistance to displaced workers. Some 80% of these funds are allocated to states that develop satisfactory worker adjustment projects that evince the ability to respond rapidly with on-site assistance for major closings and layoffs, provide assistance to labor-management cooperative efforts to deal with dislocation, and serve to coordinate economic development and trade adjustment assistance plans. The legislation provides for a wide range of adjustment services, including, in addition to basic readjustment services (counseling, job search, testing, supportive services, and relocation assistance), training options and needs-based payments for individuals in training.

The legislation calls for the creation of a system for the local delivery of services much on the pattern of the JTPA and requires that 60% of the state's allocation of federal monies go to those designated substate areas. Moreover, one-half of all funds allocated to these delivery areas must be expended on training services. State governors are permitted to retain up to 40% of their state's allocation for state-wide or industry-wide projects, rapid response teams, administration and coordination, and discretionary allocation to areas in need of additional assistance. The balance of the $980 million annual appropriation is again reserved to the Secretary of Labor for discretionary allocation to states in need and to fund exemplary and demonstration projects related to worker readjustment. Note that at the time of writing the current appropriation level for the amended Title III programs is far below the authorized level, although the Bush administration has requested that appropriations be substantially increased.

Finally, despite the task force's natural reticence to grasp the nettle on the issue of mandated notice, the Worker Adjustment and Retraining Notification (WARN) Act, providing workers displaced by reason of plant closings and mass layoffs with sixty days' notice of their impending displacement, was enacted into law on August 4, 1988. Full details on WARN, which became effective on February 4, 1989, and earlier attempts to introduce analogous legislation are provided in chapter 8.

These, then, are the bare bones of federal policy measures as applied to displaced workers. The remaining three essays in this volume tackle some of the more important issues raised by past and current policy initiatives. In the first of these essays, Addison and Portugal (chapter 8) consider the controversy surrounding advance notification. Having documented in some detail the evolution of plant closing legislation at the federal and state levels, the authors examine the cases for and against mandated notice. In particular, it is argued that the market may provide suboptimal notice in circumstances where reputation effects are lacking and where individual contracts fall foul of a time inconsistency problem. The authors caution, however, that it is one thing to argue that voluntary exchanges may be expected to yield inadequate warning of impending redundancy, quite another to formulate an appropriate public standard. Although the gateways of the present legislation allow some flexibility, the notion that there should be a common, sixty-day notice interval in respect of plant closings and mass layoffs remains problematic (on which more below).

The balance of Addison and Portugal's contribution is given over to a detailed review of the empirical evidence. Necessarily, this evidence

35

charts the effects of voluntary notice provisions and does not offer an events analysis in which outcomes under voluntary and mandated notice regimes can be directly compared. Nevertheless, Addison and Portugal present a *preliminary* analysis that suggests how one might go about inferring the effects of mandated notice from outcomes observed under a voluntary notice regime. Much more work and improved data are required, however, before firm conclusions may be reached on the likely effects of WARN.

The emerging consensus would seem to be that advance notification can have a powerful negative effect on the spell length of joblessness in the wake of displacement. It stimulates job search in the lead time offered by the notice interval and, although there is no reduction in search time per se, produces a saving in unemployment time. If it is not in doubt that advance notification lowers joblessness, rather more controversy surrounds the time horizon over which its beneficial effects are observed, and the issue of whether or not its benefits extend beyond these duration effects. Although the main effect of prenotification obtains during the first week of joblessness, it does not necessarily follow that the instrument fails to have a more continuous effect. Pending improved analysis of time-varying effects we should resist the notion that advance notification reduces unemployment solely by promoting job finding without any intervening spell of unemployment. As for the effect of prenotification on postdisplacement wages, the variable does not appear to have a direct influence. That being said, given the strong negative relation between unemployment duration and subsequent wages (in exercises that control for simultaneity between the two arguments) it seems likely that, by reducing duration, advance notification has a potentially important indirect effect on earnings development.

Estimating the effect of advance notification on unemployment duration is a complex undertaking because the main data set, the displaced worker survey, does not actually provide information on length of notice. Accordingly, both the length of notice and its effects have to be inferred from the observed unemployment of notified and nonnotified workers. Moreover, the unemployment duration data are truncated, adding to the problems of estimation. More specifically , for both notified and nonnotified workers the duration data are right-censored in the cases of ongoing spells of unemployment and top-coded intervals. And, for notified workers, total search time is also truncated in respect of those workers who locate a new job without any intervening spell of joblessness. Each source of censoring has to be accomodated in quantifying the effects of notice.

In a very real sense, the studies identified in this chapter employ considerably ingenuity in attempting to obtain concrete results from unobserved data. At the point of writing, the data situation has improved somewhat with the publication of the 1988 DWS, as a result of which we now have information on notice intervals at least for that part of the sample of "notified" workers who received explicit formal communication of their impending displacement. The new information raises a new set of estimation problems—for example, the likelihood of receiving written notice has now to be modeled—but may be expected to lead to improved estimates of both the notice interval (general and specific notice) and the effects of notice. One key issue here concerns the impact of notice on job turnover, which may turn out to be as important as its effect on the initial spell of joblessness in the wake of displacement.

In the interim, the estimates from Addison and Portugal's preferred model suggest notice intervals in the range 5.7 to 8 weeks for workers displaced by plant closings, and from 4.3 to 5.7 weeks in the case of slack work. The effect of these notice intervals in reducing joblessness is estimated at between 5.2 and 7.5 weeks for the former group and between 4.1 and 5.5 weeks for the latter. These values, which must be regarded as tentative, translate into savings of unemployment time of close to 40% for plant closings and around 20% in the case of slack work. The smaller effects on unemployment observed for those workers displaced via slack work reflect both a shorter notice interval and a waiting for recall phenomenon (see chapter 5).

Up to this point we have not considered the endogeneity of notice. The issue is important in two major respects. First, if notice is given to workers who would in the normal run of events experience lower unemployment in the wake of redundancy, one will attribute to notification what is (partly) due to personal characteristics, and hence overstate the impact of the instrument. Second, the endogeneity of notice is of great importance in seeking to chart the effects of mandatory notice. Regrettably, rather limited progress has been made in identifying the determinants of notice. But it does seem to be the chase that the benefits to workers observed in single equation estimates can be generalized and as not being a chimera produced by sample selection. More troubling is the fact that the costs to employers of giving notice have received scant attention in modeling the determinants of notice. Such costs are of potential importance once one moves to a regime of mandated notice. Subject to this caveat, there are some signs in the data of a tortoise and hare effect. That is to say, notified workers are those who in the absence of notification would experience higher unemployment while the nonnotified would in similar circumstances experience lower unemployment. This phenomenon, if replicated in the 1988 data, would suggest that single equation estimates, if anything, understate the beneficial effect of notice on unemployment duration. Moreover, Addison and Portugal indicate how this evidence (of positive and negative sample selection, respectively) can be used to construct estimates of the effect of mandated notice. Unfortunately, given the poor performance of the authors' probit equation(s), they are reluctant to use their selection coefficients to proceed in this manner. This reluctance is of course underwritten by the parameter shifts occasioned by mandated notice, reflecting inadequately modeled costs to employers.

Finally, Addison and Portugal return to the vexed question of a mandated standard. In particular, is a sixty-day notice interval excessive? Given that this standard only moderately exceeds that computed for voluntary arrangements (at least with respect to plant closings), the gateways offered by the existing legislation, and the apparently large random element in the determination of notification status, they incline to the view that the benefits of WARN could well exceed the costs. Yet Addison and Portugal emphasize the superiority of an alternative procedure, suggested by Deere and Wiggins (1988), that would allow the sixty-day notice interval to operate as a default value that would apply only if the parties failed to negotiate around it. Moreover, they urge careful monitoring of the current legislation.

Attention shifts in chapter 9 to an evaluation of national manpower training initiatives. In this contribution, Duane Leigh examines among other things whether some types of training have worked better than others or have had a differential impact by type of worker served. Much emphasis is placed on the problems attaching to program evaluation and the need for an appropriate control group against which the performance of program participants (the treatment group) can be compared.

Leigh prefaces his discussion with a brief review of CETA program evaluations. Although, as we have seen, this federal program was geared toward disadvantaged rather than displaced workers, the CETA evaluations not only provide benchmark values but also illustrate important measurement issues. The CETA studies reviewed by Leigh typically report that women gained more than men from exposure to classroom training and on-the-job training. For males, program impacts were often zero or negative in relation to the earnings of the control group. It also emerges that CT is less effective than OJT, which is not altogether unexpected because the most job ready of enrollees are those likely to be selected for subsidized OJT slots. But of all the findings, the most notable result is the sheer diversity of reported program impact across studies—despite the fact that the evaluations use the same data to estimate what is effectively the same treatment effect. This diversity is in part explained by the manner in which the studies control for differences between members of the treatment and comparison groups in the absence of a true experimental methodology in which sample members are randomly assigned to either the treatment group or a control group. In practice, the control group is in all cases a sample of workers drawn from the Current Population Survey. The problem is to obtain an appropriate match (minimize differences) between the two groups. If the match is appropriate, the earnings function estimated over the controls should allow one to predict the earnings of program participants had they not been enrolled. A comparison of the predicted and actual earnings of program participants provides an indication of program impact. Note, however, that the matching technique employed and the specification of the earnings function differ between studies. A second problem stems from the fact that participation in manpower programs among the treatment group is not universal: not only do workers select into enrollment but also program operators in turn select from the ranks of enrollees. In other words, the problem that the two samples are not drawn from the same population is again encountered. Ideally, this selection process should be modeled; otherwise one may be attributing to program exposure what is really due to the nonrepresentative nature (both observed and unobserved characteristics) of the participant group. The various studies investigated by Leigh differ as to whether or not they take account of potential selectivity bias and, in the event that they do, in the manner of its correction. This provides another reason for the disparity in findings. Leigh concludes on the basis of an attempted statistical reconciliation of two of the major studies that *net* impact effects of the CETA program were negative for men and positive for women.

Leigh next turns to displaced workers per se and reviews the findings of four major demonstration projects conducted under JTPA Title III authority. These are the Downriver program, the Buffalo Dislocated Worker Demonstration Project, the Texas Worker Adjustment Demonstration Project, and the New Jersey Unemployment Insurance Reemployment Demonstration Project. The Downriver displaced worker program, chronologically first in operation, proceeded in two phases. The first made services available to workers laid off from two auto supply plants (BASF and DANA). The second extended assistance to workers displaced at the Ford Motor Company's Michigan Casting Company. Displaced workers were, in each case, first enrolled in an orientation and testing program followed by a mandatory, four-day job seeking skills workshop. Thereafter, the majority of participants received retraining, which was predominantly classroom based. For analytical purposes, the treatment group was randomly selected from among the plants' displaced workers and their experience contrasted with that of a randomly selected nontreatment group of displaced workers from two other auto industry plants in the area. The latter "controls" differed in the case of the two phases.

Treatment groups from both the BASF and DANA plants were found to enjoy significantly higher placement rates, employment rates, and weekly earnings than the controls. But the magnitude of these positive net impact effects varied by comparison plant and, more noticeably, by company; BASF workers recording generally higher gains than their DANA counterparts.[1] In the case of the Ford program, however, participating workers recorded lower placement and employment rates and lower earnings development than their two auto plant controls.

Differences between the two phases are held to reflect unobserved differences in the treatment plants and their controls and differences in estimating equations. But clearly the Downriver results are difficult to interpret in the light of differences between the two phases of the project. This led the Department of Labor to fund a number of additional demonstration projects. Leigh summarizes the findings from the Buffalo demonstration, the only project for which an analytical impact statement is available. This offered program services to two groups of displaced workers; namely, steel and auto workers, displaced from nine plants in that area, and a more heterogeneous group of permanently laid off workers drawn from some three hundred area plants. The treatment groups comprised workers randomly selected from six of the nine steel and auto plants (termed the target plant sample) and all other workers who received services on a first-come, first-served basis as program slots became available (the non-target plant sample). For both groups, outcomes for participants were compared with those of a control group made up of recruited nonparticipants and comparison group members.

Unfortunately, the reality of low take-up rates among workers who were offered program services implies selection bias, which was dealt with in this case by adding a variable that simultaneously provides consistent estimates of the parameters of the wage equation and information on the direction of selection if present (namely, would program participants have earned more or less than the average in a regime in which all workers participated in the program). It is reported that the Buffalo program yielded significant positive net placement, hours, employment, and earnings effects, particularly for target plant participants. Interestingly, the Buffalo project also allows a comparison to be drawn between job search assistance (JSA) and CT and OJT. Focusing here only on the (more reliable) results for target plants, it was found that JSA and CT had large effects of much the same order of magnitude on employment rates and average weekly earnings. (No significant effects were observed in the case of OJT.) Additional effects of CT above JSA were only observed in the case of employment rates and these were clearly not large enough to compensate for the higher cost of the former ($3,282 versus $851). Employment effects were found to be greater for women than for men, for individuals aged less than forty-five than for older groups, and for workers with greater than ten years' tenure on the predisplacement job than with less tenure.

The Texas projects documented by Leigh are notable for their true experimental methodology. The program randomly assigned workers to either of two treatment groups or to a control group; the first treatment group (Tier 1) receiving JSA alone, the second (Tier II) receiving JSA plus CT or OJT. The control group received conventional (i.e., non-Title III) employment assistance. Unlike the Buffalo experiment there was no problem raised by low rates of program participation. It was found that program participants experienced positive earnings and weeks worked development as well as reduced UI benefits. As in the Buffalo case, larger effects were again obtained for women than for men. But for both sexes the pattern is one of decaying effects with respect to net earnings over time. Effectively, the main impact of the program was to enable workers to find work more quickly than otherwise.

Again consistent with results reported for the Buffalo project, exposure to Tier II had no positive incremental effect on earnings (or employment) over that for Tier I alone.

The final case study referred to by Leigh investigates the interesting New Jersey UI Reemployment Demonstration. This project is notable for its attempt to identify workers likely to face prolonged spells of unemployment. This identification does not proceed on the basis of personal characteristics but rather via the application of a number of screens in the fourth week of unemployment, the net effect of which is to define a displaced worker population as comprising those with at least three years of tenure on the lost job who are aged twenty-five years or more. The New Jersey program offers *three* treatments to those circumnavigating the screens: job search assistance; OJT or, more typically, CT; and a reemployment bonus. (Maximum bonus is collected if a job is accepted by the participant two weeks after the fourth week of

41

unemployment. The amount of the bonus is one-half of the remaining UI entitlement from the time of interview and has a maximum value of $1600. It decreases by 10% per week and reaches zero at the end of the eleventh week.) Although we do not know whether the screens employed in the New Jersey project accurately identified those who would otherwise go on to experience reemployment difficulty, and although problems of low participation arise in the case of the second treatment group, there are signs that significant reductions in weeks of unemployment and UI benefits are realized vis-à-vis the controls. Not surprisingly perhaps, the reemployment bonus, which is only paid if the worker is subsequently in full-time unemployment that lasts for at least four weeks, is the most "productive" treatment. Consistent with almost all the other evidence, it is again found that retraining programs do *not* yield an incremental effect on either weeks of unemployment or the magnitude of UI benefits received.

Leigh's broad conclusions are as follows. First, job search assistance delivers positive labor market outcomes at relatively low cost, and is seen as the core service to be provided in the ideal system. Moreover, given the difficulty of identifying dislocated workers, Leigh notes that the degree of waste involved in offering job search assistance to those who will have little difficulty in obtaining reemployment is minimized. Second, classroom training does not appear to have a sufficiently high added value to compensate for its higher cost. Third, on-the-job training does not appear to have had a consistently positive effect on earnings or much effect on employment rates, which Leigh views as particularly inauspicious given the heavy emphasis placed on this instrument under current policy. Fourth, differential program effects by type of worker are most noticeable in the case of females. Finally, although he does not discuss the topic elsewhere in his paper, Leigh sees considerable scope for remedial or basic skills training given the apparent importance of educational deficits in prolonging unemployment duration.

As a postscript, very brief mention should be made of state-funded retraining initiatives, which are generally to be distinguished from federal programs in that they are usually tailored to the needs of employers. Table 1 provides details on innovative programs in three states, drawing on Leigh (1989). Although these initiatives have not been the subject of analytical "audit" on the lines discussed above the following observations might usefully be made. California's Employment Training Panel (ETP) program points to a "creaming" phenomenon, namely, the selection into training of those least in need of skills enhancement. Moreover, by subsidizing the training by firms of their existing employees at the expense of unemployed workers, the Californian program must to some degree be substituting public for private funds. Finally, and rather more positively, Minnesota's wage subsidy program does *not* appear to have been associated with any stigmatization by the market of enrollees despite the target groups being made up of disadvantaged workers. We will return to this theme below. Information on substitution and displacement effects is lacking.

We now arrive at the last chapter in this volume, in which Douglas Kruse considers the controversial question of whether manpower policy initiatives are better directed toward disadvantaged rather than displaced workers. Arguably, we are witnessing a shift in policy in favor of the latter. Is this apparent reorientation of policy justified? Or are displacement and disadvantage so inextricably linked such that policy may address both issues simultaneously? These are the types of questions considered by Kruse, and their formulation allows us to integrate within the discussion some of the lessons learned in the preceding chapters.

Kruse begins by distinguishing between two broad views on the relationship between disadvantage and displacement. He argues that the basic competitive labor model would admit of no association between the two variables on the grounds that wages will reflect the likelihood of displacement. And to the extent that risk aversion is greater among (disadvantaged) low-skill workers, their representation among the displaced should be further reduced. Kruse's other paradigm is the segmented labor market model, according to which (secondary sector) displacement and disadvantage go hand in hand. (There is some ambiguity here, however, to the extent that the source of secondary sector unemployment is turnover rather than displacement per se.) Moreover, if primary sector workers who became displaced are stigmatized or suffer depreciation of their human capital endowments (presumably reinforced by job rationing in this model) then displacement translates into disadvantage.

If there is a conventional view in this area, it is perhaps that the disadvantaged are more deserving of assistance than the displaced. This interpretation has a basis in the higher educational deficits of the disadvantaged, their lower resources and family incomes, and their higher minority representation. Unfortunately, as Kruse points out, definitional issues bedevil such comparisons, which in the limit may prove tautological. More importantly, he concludes that the failure of adherents to the conventional view to consider the causal links between displacement and disadvantage vitiates the conclusion that one group is necessarily more deserving than another. The balance of his discussion is thus given over to an examination of these links.

Table 1   **Selected State-Funded Retraining Initiatives**

State/Program	Clientele	Program description
California Employment Training Panel (ETP)	UI recipients, exhaustees, and those in danger of being laid off. More than half projects directed toward potentially displaced workers.	Retraining. Employer driven. Projects proposed by employers and if approved, employer selects trainees, sets standards for program completion, and approves curriculum if outside training provider is selected.
Minnesota Minnesota Employment and Economic Development (MEED) wage subsidy program	Unemployed workers who are ineligible for or who have exhausted UI benefits. Priority given to applicants eligible for general assistance and AFDC cases.	Wage subsidy. Job creation that in practice offers some retraining. Historically emphasized public sector job creation but today 75% of jobs created must be in private sector
Illinois Prairie State Authority (i) Employer Training Assistance Program (ETAP)	UI recipients and employed workers at risk of layoff.	Loans and grants to cover the direct cost of supplying training.
(ii) Individual Training Assistance (ITAP)	Unemployed with minimum of three years out of past ten in UI-covered employment. Employed applicants must be in need of additional skills to retain present jobs.	Retraining vouchers that may be redeemed at approved training institutions.

Table 1 (Continued)

Reimbursement	Impact	Funding	Average cost per trainee
Fixed-fee basis. Performance based. No payment until completion of training, workers placed in training related jobs at wages stipulated in contract, and workers retrained for at least ninety days.	Average posttraining earnings 76% and 27% higher than pretraining earnings for unemployed and employed trainees respectively. But no control group.	$55 million per year. Diversion of regular UI tax revenues: ETP funded by 0.1% payroll tax on firms with positive reserves in their UI accounts, regular UI taxes reduced by 0.1%.	$2,515 but higher for unemployed than employed trainees.
Subsidy of up to $4 per hour in wages and up to $1 per hour in fringes for a period not to exceed six months (twelve months if workers undergoing training).	85% of private sector participants employed in unsubsidized jobs at the time of a sixty-day follow-up survey at completion of subsidy interval.	$27 million via general tax revenues.	$4,680. Most individuals employed under MEED qualify for full subsidy over twenty-six weeks.
Loan option covers 100% of direct training costs; 25% of principal written off if employee retained for one year. Grant option covers 50% of costs, with half the grant paid in advance of training and balance after trainees retained for ninety days following completion of training.		$3 million via general tax revenues.	Average ETAP award of $16,207. Cost per trainee and hours of training per trainee average $136 and thirty-eight hours, respectively.
Vouchers of up to $2,000 for eligible unemployed and of up to $1,000 for eligible employed workers.	Reported placement rate and earnings gains for both categories of workers. But no controls.	General tax revenues.	

Beginning with the line of causation running from displacement to disadvantage, Kruse looks at two pieces of evidence: the relation between the escape rate from unemployment and the length of the ongoing unemployment spell, and that between current unemployment and future unemployment/earnings. In examining the shape of the hazard function (see chapters 5 and 7), Kruse notes that evidence of negative duration dependence points to the existence of a direct link between displacement and disadvantage. He qualifies this result by noting the complication introduced by unobserved worker heterogeneity, and conjectures that sample composition (in particular, the inclusion of those on temporary layoff within the displaced worker sample) may spuriously introduce negative duration dependence. It seems we can discount the notion that differently shaped hazard functions for temporarily versus permanently displaced workers are responsible for negative duration dependence and instead conclude that, after some nontrivial unemployment spell, there is evidence of negative duration dependence (see chapter 7). That said, there remains the problem of identifying ex ante those likely to experience greater unemployment. But given that certain observed worker characteristics are associated with longer spells of unemployment and that these are in a rough and ready way correlated with indices of disadvantage it seems clear that it is in principle possible to target these groups for program assistance. Unobserved heterogeneity limits what can be done in an ex ante sense but given inverse U-shaped hazard functions the problem may not be so acute; that is, a targeted policy might be applied or increased in intensity after that number of weeks of joblessness that define the turning point in the hazard functions for a typical worker.

In looking at the effects of unemployment spells on future labor market experience, Kruse reports a broad unanimity across a variety of studies as to the persistence of unemployment. Specifically, there is little association between current and future unemployment spells, so that displacement has only transitory unemployment effects (chapter 6). On the other hand, the effects of displacement on future earnings seem altogether more severe. As Christopher Ruhm's contribution to this volume makes clear, a significant proportion of the initial wage change observed following redundancy persists over a five-year observation period. Kruse takes this and other evidence as suggestive of an important causal link running from displacement to disadvantage. Consistent with the story told by Ruhm, he argues that workers do not job shop in such a way as to sequentially improve their labor market position in the wake of displacement. However, the mechanics of this process are not self-evident at the level of the causal link that motivates this part of Kruse's analysis.

Kruse next investigates the reverse line of causation running from disadvantage to displacement. He first questions whether the disadvantaged comprise a high proportion of those displaced. (If they did, of course, a policy geared toward the displaced could *in principle* simultaneously address the disadvantaged, and would have added benefits to the extent that stigmatization attends more narrowly targeted programs.) Kruse observes that there is virtually no difference in the representation of blacks in the labor force and in the displaced worker population, while women are underrepresented in the latter. Since he identifies both groups with secondary sector workers, he contends on this piece of evidence that it is unlikely that the disadvantaged constitute a high proportion of the displaced worker population. By the same token, he observes that the earnings of the displaced do not differ markedly from those of the nondisplaced, with and without correction for differences in education, experience, and other observed characteristics. He reports that the displaced are evenly split between those with higher and lower wages vis-à-vis predicted wages from an equation estimated over all workers. Other pieces of information assembled by Kruse include the family income composition of displaced workers and the presence of segmentation effects in the earnings of displaced workers. Neither piece of evidence points to disadvantage as being an indicator of the displaced.

Kruse's argument is that policy-relevant research should focus on the two sets of causal links, although he emphasizes that information on both processes is extremely sparse. His conclusions thus have more to do with a research agenda than with concrete policy recommendations. He is predisposed toward the provision of governmental assistance to displaced workers as a means of avoiding "scarring" effects but he is evidently rather more concerned about the difficulty of identifying the point at which this process begins to operate and more preoccupied with the issue of unobserved heterogeneity than others might consider warranted.

While recognizing that displaced workers are not primarily disadvantaged, Kruse nevertheless sees virtue in policies targeted toward the displaced for two reasons that have to do with disadvantage. First, he argues that the more advantaged of the displaced worker population may be expected to opt out of displaced worker programs by virtue of their relatively rapid reemployment. Second, to the extent that programs specifically targeted toward the disadvantaged may convey adverse signals to employers, a program ostensibly designed for the displaced might avoid this stigmatizing process. Here, Kruse is mindful of the results of the federally funded Dayton, Ohio program, which assigned welfare recipients to one of three groups: one entitling their new employer to a tax credit equal to one-half of earnings during the first year of employment and one-quarter of the next year's earnings; another providing vouchers redeemable for cash equal to the same percentages of first- and second-year earnings; and a control group. Members of each group were given two weeks' job search training followed by a further six weeks of structured job search. The results of this exercise were that only 13.0% of the first group and 12.7% of the second group found employment over the eight-week time frame as compared with no less than 20.6% of the controls. The role of vouchers was to give an unfavorable labor market signal to Dayton employers who apparently statistically discriminated accordingly. Against this, however, we should note the success of Minnesota's MEED wage subsidy program (see table 1) and more generally the success of workfare experimentation in its various guises. We should also note that in advocating the use of a nonstigmatizing criterion, Kruse is well aware of the costs stemming from the bluntness of the instrument.

But the emphasis of Kruse's treatment is a plea for more information on the relationship between displacement and disadvantage and in structuring a research agenda. To the latter we would add the requirement that more formal analysis be undertaken of the process generating the arrival rate of job offers, the wage offer distribution, and search costs, with especial attention being paid *at this level of analysis* to model specifications that are robust in the presence of unobserved heterogeneity (see chapter 7).

As a practical matter, one should note that the "disadvantaged" and the "displaced" have been served by very different programs. It is perhaps ironic that the less advantaged in each category have, for a variety of reasons, not been accommodated. Thus, for example, Title II programs under the JTPA, though ostensibly geared toward the disadvantaged, provide clear evidence of creaming in the provision of services to enrollees. As Levitan and Gallo (1988) note, the use of performance standards appears most responsible for this outcome. The existence of cost and job performance standards have apparently put pressure on the service delivery areas to select the most employable enrollees. Moreover, the practice among many service delivery areas of serving as many individuals as possible at the lowest per unit cost has militated against providing assistance to those requiring greater assistance. The role of business and recent emphasis on the needs of business has also promoted creaming. And yet, if workfare experimentation is any guide, the biggest societal payoffs may accrue from serving the truly disadvantaged. Nevertheless, the poorest individuals requiring income and other support services to initiate and complete a job training program will tend to be excluded from JTPA because of the limitations placed on support services.

On-the-job training offered under Title II programs goes disproportionately to adults, high school graduates, individuals *not* seeking public assistance, and those unemployed for less than six months. There is also evidence to suggest that on-the-job training more closely resembles a wage subsidy than reimbursement for the additional training time required for a "typical" disadvantaged worker.

Now it is of course very much easier to criticize JTPA program implementation than to design an appropriate policy, presumably one that steers a careful path between performance standards and flexibility, income maintenance and disincentives, and the needs of business and those of the enrollee. But frankly the efficacy of policy for each group *is* in question. Duane Leigh's material (chapter 9) has shown all too clearly the problems of (ambitious) displaced worker retraining programs. And to a greater or lesser extent most of the other contributions have pointed to the need to target services toward problem groups in a manner that policy has manifestly not succeeded in doing. Although our essays have not provided an exact blueprint for policy, they have set down what has been learned about the consequences of displacement, inter alia, and what questions still remain unanswered. Although the questions outnumber the answers, progress has been made, and the time is surely ripe to apply some of the more obvious implications to policy formulation.

NOTES

I am greatly indebted to John Owen for his perceptive remarks on the initial draft of this chapter.

1. For a sophisticated evaluation of "phase one" on unemployment duration using techniques similar to those employed in chapters 5 and 7 but with the addition of time-varying regressors, see Steinberg and Monforte, 1987.

REFERENCES

Addison, John T., and Pedro Portugal (1989a). "Job Displacement, Relative Wage Changes, and Duration of Unemployment." *Journal of Labor Economics* 7 (July): 281–302.

————— (1989b). "On the Costs of Worker Displacement: The Case of Dissipated Firm-Specific Training Investments." *Southern Economic Journal* 55 (July): 166–82.

Deere, Donald R., and Steven W. Wiggins (1988). "Plant Closings, Advance Notice, and Private Contractual Failure." Working Paper 88-39. College Station, Tex.: Texas A & M University.

Leigh, Duane E. (1989). *Assisting Displaced Workers: Do the States Have a Better Idea?* Kalamazoo, Mich.: Upjohn Institute.

Levitan, Sar A., and Frank Gallo (1988). *A Second Chance—Training for Jobs.* Kalamazoo, Mich.: Upjohn Institute.

Madden, Janice F. (1988). "The Distribution of Economic Losses Among Displaced Workers: Measurement Methods Matter." *Journal of Human Resources* 23 (Winter): 93–107.

Steinberg, Danny, and Frank A. Monforte (1987). "Estimating the Effects of Job Search Assistance and Training Programs on the Unemployment Duration of Displaced Workers." In *Unemployment and the Structure of Labor Markets,* edited by Kevin Lang and Jonathan S. Leonard. New York and Oxford: Basil Blackwell.

CHAPTER TWO

Who Are Displaced Workers?

ADAM SEITCHIK

I. Introduction

In January of 1984, the Bureau of Labor Statistics commissioned the Census Bureau to conduct a Displaced Worker Survey (DWS) as a supplement to the monthly Current Population Survey (CPS). For the first time in the United States, researchers and policy makers would be able to estimate the size and scope of the displacement problem directly, using a large-scale nationally representative data base. With minor modifications, the DWS was repeated in January 1986 and January 1988. It is the primary data set used by three of the authors in this volume.

This chapter is in large part an introduction to the population of displaced workers, as seen through the lens of the 1984 and 1986 DWS. (Although not available in time for use by most of the authors in this volume, the results from the 1988 survey reflect recent gains in manufacturing employment and reductions in the overall unemployment rate.) Also, the survey is compared to other data sources used in displacement research. This comparison highlights the possibilities and limitations inherent in the DWS.

Since the DWS has quickly become the "industry standard" in research on economic dislocation, it is tempting to use the survey's identification criteria when defining the population of displaced workers. In doing so, any civilian twenty years of age or older who loses or leaves a job because of a "plant closing, an employer going out of business, a layoff without recall, or some similar reason" becomes a displaced worker. Based on the inaugural DWS, for example, there were almost fourteen million workers displaced between 1979 and January 1984, which is equal to approximately 13% of the labor force aged twenty or older in 1984.

Useful as the DWS is, its broadest definition of the displacement population is problematic both at the conceptual level and for the purpose of determining eligibility for federal adjustment assistance. Thus it is worth considering the definitional question *Who are Displaced Workers?* before launching into results from the DWS using the survey's selection criteria.

II. Definitional Issues

The recent spurt of research interest in worker displacement was preceded by the establishment of assistance programs at the federal level. For example, Title III of the Job Training Partnership Act of 1982, as amended by the Economic Dislocation and Worker Adjustment Assistance Act of 1988, defines "eligible [for assistance] workers" as individuals who

> (A) have been terminated or laid off or who have received a notice of termination of layoff from employment, are eligible for or have exhausted their entitlement to unemployment compensation, and are unlikely to return to their previous industry or occupation;
> (B) have been terminated or received notice of termination of employment, as a result of any permanent closure of or any substantial layoff at a plant, facility, or enterprise;
> (C) are long-term unemployed and have limited opportunities for employment or reemployment in the same or a similar occupation in the area in which such individuals reside, including older individuals who may have substantial barriers to employment by reason of age; or
> (D) were self-employed (including farmers and ranchers) and are unemployed as a result of general economic conditions in the community in which they reside or because of national disasters, subject to regulations prescribed by the Secretary [of Labor].

These eligibility criteria are broadly consistent with definitions of displacement (or, synonymously, dislocation) being used by researchers. Browne (1985), for example, defines dislocated workers as "individuals with established work histories who have lost their jobs through no fault of their own and who are likely to encounter considerable difficulty finding comparable employment."

There are selection criteria in the legislation that seem somewhat arbitrary, and therefore have rarely been used in research. These include the eligibility for or exhaustion of unemployment insurance in (A), the requirement that a layoff be "substantial" in (B), and the focus on the long-term unemployed in (C).

An obvious operational problem affecting both program eligibility and empirical research is determining, at the time of job loss, the (future) difficulty of finding comparable employment. A likely indicator of future adjustment problems would be aggregate employment decline in the layoff industry and occupation. Accordingly, Jacobson (1984) assumes displaced workers to originate solely within locally declining industries. Others identify displaced workers as the long-term unemployed from declining industries, occupations, and regions (Bendick and Devine 1982). Browne (1985) notes the difficulty of distinguishing between industries experiencing enduring cyclical versus secular declines, since cyclical employment recovery in manufacturing has historically lagged behind that in other sectors.

More recent research using data sets that identify involuntary job losers directly does not define the displacement population based on sectoral or geographic growth rates. As D'Amico and Golon (1986) point out, analysis of only these subgroups of involuntary job losers may exaggerate the consequences of displacement. More importantly, they add that "defining displacement in terms of the likely consequences of displacement begs the central question of our inquiry, What are its consequences?"

Increasingly, then, displaced workers are simply job losers across all industries, occupations, and regions. Negative outcomes such as unemployment or earnings losses are specified as dependent variables, which in turn are affected by factors such as lagging industry growth rates and local labor market conditions (Howland and Peterson 1988) or high levels of industry import penetration (Kruse 1988). These conditions, however, do not define the displacement population itself.

A. Tenure Restrictions

Beginning with the initial analysis of the 1984 DWS (Flaim and Sehgal 1985), government researchers have restricted their sample of displaced workers to those with at least three years of accrued tenure on the lost job. Presumably, the motivation for tenure restrictions is to focus on those with established work histories who have developed on-the-job skills that may or may not be transferable on reemployment. Practically speaking, the crosstabular findings reported in government research limit the number of ways the data can be "cut"; presenting descriptive statistics for longer-tenure workers means restricting the analysis sample. While a more useful measure of specific skill accretion might be years in the industry or occupation, rather than with a particular employer, such data are not available within the DWS.

Some econometric research using longitudinal data has limited the sample of workers to those with a minimum number of years on the predisplacement job (Parnes and King 1977; D'Amico and Golon 1986). Such restrictions may significantly reduce the size of the estimated population. For example, the restriction to workers with at least three years of tenure within the 1984 DWS shrunk the government researchers' analysis population from an estimated 11.5 million workers to 5.1 million workers.

Ruhm (1987a) cautions that "defining displacement in terms of previous seniority is dangerously restrictive, given that displaced workers may have recently left a job of longer duration, and recent evidence calls into question the extent to which adjustment problems increase with tenure." Essentially, Ruhm is concerned about sample selection bias caused by the nonrandom exclusion of a large group of displaced workers.

B. Other Restrictions

Other common restrictions are to exclude industries where job attachments are presumed to be less important, such as construction (9% of displaced workers in the January 1986 DWS) and agriculture, forestry, and fisheries (3%); to set an upper age limit (usually sixty-one) in order to distinguish between displacement and retirement effects (exclusion of 4% of the sample); to exclude layoffs within government (5%) and unincorporated self-employment (2%); to exclude part-time workers (11%); to limit the sample to plant closings, layoffs without recall, and abolishment of position or shift, and thereby exclude seasonal displacements (4%), self-operated business closures (3%), and the mysterious, large, and unexplored "other" category (11%), which may for the most part be a residual of workers dismissed with cause (fired) or who left voluntarily (quit).

The distinction between firings, layoffs, and quits can be fuzzy both conceptually and empirically. Although federal assistance programs are designed to help workers who have lost jobs through "no fault of their own," in practice it is not always clear from worker responses whether a layoff was with cause (firing) or for some other reason. Voluntary job leavers (quits) who experience long-term unemployment seem to be eligible under category (C) of the economic dislocation legislation above, but recent research on displaced workers has in large part focused exclusively on involuntary layoffs and plant closings. As a further complication, when turnover is modeled as a sorting process wherein workers and firms strive for optimal matches, then the distinction between quits and layoffs is not meaningful (Borjas 1984). Even so, few researchers or policy makers would include voluntary job leavers as a category of displaced workers.

A more common distinction in displacement research is between plant closings and other involuntary separations (layoffs). Both groups of job losers are usually referred to as displaced workers; however, the underlying separation process may well be quite different in the two cases. At least some employers may have discretionary power in selecting workers for layoff. In contrast, a plant closing affects all workers in the plant with no employer discretion (although employers might choose *between* plants, or offer interplant transfers to selected employees).

The recognition of this fundamental difference is leading to the separate analysis of layoffs and plant closings. Hamermesh (chapter 3 of this volume), for example, develops a contract model for plant closings (which he calls "displacements"), and explicitly cautions against using the model to analyze layoffs. Portugal (chapter 7) distinguishes between "demand driven" separations (temporary layoffs because of slack work) and permanent separations influenced by both supply and demand conditions. The permanent category includes plant closings as well as individual displacements without the possibility of recall.

III. Data on Displaced Workers

During the "automation scare" in the late 1950s and early 1960s, concern over structural unemployment led to a number of case studies of plant closings and large-scale layoffs, exemplified by Shultz and Weber's classic research on the Armour meat-packing workers (1966). Like any set of case studies, this body of research is limited in its generalizability. Unionized, male manufacturing workers dominate the cases. Also, there may be a bias within the studies toward the kinds of employers, like Armour, who are most innovative and cooperative in their approach to worker adjustment programs. These may be the employers most likely to allow researchers access to their list of laid-off workers and other materials necessary to conduct a firm-specific or plant-specific study. There have been some case studies conducted in the 1980s, mostly as part of federally and state-funded displaced worker program evaluations.[1]

A. Longitudinal Data

The bulk of recent empirical research has been based on large, nationally representative household and individual surveys. Of these, the two most frequently used longitudinal data sets have been the Panel Study of Income Dynamics (PSID), administered by the University of Michigan's Survey Research Center, and the National Longitudinal Surveys (NLS) conducted by the Center for Human Resource Research at Ohio State University. The aforementioned Displaced Worker Survey (DWS) is a widely used cross-sectional database, which contains a retrospective component only for those identified as displaced workers.

The primary advantage of the longitudinal data bases is that they allow for the construction of a predisplacement control group. For example, it is possible to track the earnings and labor market behavior of a random sample of individuals over a number of years $t - n$ to $t - 1$, identify workers displaced in year t, and then follow both the job losers and the control group in years $t + 1$ to $t + k$. If predisplacement differences (i.e., worker heterogeneity) are properly controlled for, then residual variance in subsequent outcomes can be attributed to displacement (see, for example, Addison and Portugal 1989; Ruhm 1987b). Since the DWS does not contain information on the control group in the $t - n$ to $t - 1$ period, no such correction for worker heterogeneity is possible. What is called a displacement effect may in part be the result of unobserved individual characteristics.

A limitation of both the PSID and the NLS is relatively small sample sizes. Neither precise estimates of the national displaced worker population nor detailed breakdowns by categories such as industries or occupations can be calculated using the surveys. PSID data is usually analyzed only for household heads, which include most married men in the sample, a few married women, and unmarried family heads. The NLS is better suited for the tracking of individuals regardless of household status, but its generalizability is limited outside the surveyed age/sex cohorts (e.g., young men fourteen to twenty-four in 1966, women thirty to forty-four in 1967, etc.).

Both the NLS and the PSID can be used to track respondents' job changing and recall status for a number of years following job loss, thereby distinguishing between true displacements and temporary layoffs. A limitation is in the lumping together of various types of job loss. In the NLS "lay-off, plant closing or end of temporary job [this presumably includes seasonal employment]" is a single category, which can be differentiated only from quits and firings. The PSID isolates plant closings and relocations, but layoffs are lumped together with firings. Quits are identified separately, as are the previously self-employed.

B. The Displaced Worker Survey

One advantage that the Displaced Worker Survey (DWS) has over the longitudinal surveys is its sample size. As a supplement to the Current Population Survey (CPS), wherein the number of interviewed households is about 58,000, it is without question the largest nationally representative database on displaced workers. For example, the January 1986 CPS contained over 8,000 respondents who were included in the supplemental DWS. Even when restricting the sample to those with at least three years of job tenure who were between the ages of twenty and sixty-one at the time of the survey and displaced because of a plant closing, layoff without recall, or the abolishment of the worker's position or shift over a five-year period, the sample size is over 2,800 (about 560 per year). In comparison, a recent NLS study using the young men's cohort identified only 46 displacements per year over eight survey years between 1968 and 1978 (D'Amico and Golon 1986). Ruhm (1987b), analyzing household heads within the PSID between 1970 and 1976, samples about 180 displaced men and 25 displaced women per year.

Once an individual is identified as a displaced worker within the CPS household, the interviewer asks the supplemental questions about the lost job and the subsequent labor market experience. A household member is categorized as a displaced worker if he or she is twenty years of age or older and has lost a job in the past five years because of a plant closing, an employer going out of business, a layoff without recall at the time of the survey, or some similar reason. A follow-up question allows for differentiation between a plant closing, slack work, abolishment of position or shift, seasonal job completion, and self-employed business failure.

Comparisons can be made between current and former weekly wages, occupation, industry, full- or part-time status, and receipt of health benefits. Information is also available on advance employer notification of layoff, year of displacement, movement out of the city or county to look for or accept a new job, receipt of and subsequent exhaustion of unemployment benefits, weeks of unemployment, number of jobs held since displacement, and current weekly wages. The regular CPS includes standard demographic variables and information on labor market status at the time of the survey.

Displaced workers report their years of tenure on the lost job, although what constitutes a "job" may be ambiguous. For example, a

worker who has been with the same *employer* for ten years but promoted within the past year, may report *job* tenure as ten years or one
year. Most researchers have assumed that this question refers to years of
continuous employment within a single firm. Total years of labor market
experience across employers can only be approximated as the sum of all
years not in school since the age of six. No data is available on accrued
years of occupational or industry experience.

Several aspects of the structure of the DWS limit comparison between the former jobs and the reemployment jobs at the time of the
survey. Former earnings are reported weekly, not hourly, and precise
hours worked per week are not known. Also, while the DWS identifies
individuals moving to a different city or county to look for work or to
take a different job, we do not know where the movers resided when job
loss occurred. This is a serious constraint on any analysis of geographic
adjustments to displacement.

The retrospective nature of the DWS has two important implications. The first is that no control group is available for the predisplacement period. If layoffs and plant closings are nonrandom in some way
not controlled for by observable survey date characteristics, then the
DWS will allow only for biased estimates of displacement impacts. The
bias is likely to be less problematic where employers have little discretion in who they dismiss, such as with blue-collar seniority layoffs or
broad-based plant closings.

A more general concern pertaining to all retrospective data is the
accuracy of the response. Comparisons of labor force survey data from
the monthly CPS and its March Work Experience Supplement reveal
that workers tend to underreport spells of unemployment over time
(Horvath 1982). The further away from the unemployment spell, the
less likely that it will be reported. If this "retrospective bias" affects the
reporting of displacement, then results from the years farthest away
from the survey will underestimate the true incidence of job loss. Workers may simply forget that they have lost a job in the past five years.
Alternatively, the displaced worker may be identified accurately, while
the time since displacement is reported with error.

Overall, retrospective bias is likely to underreport the size of the
displaced worker population. In other ways the survey may overestimate
the displacement problem. This bias within the DWS, and especially in
comparison to the longitudinal data sets, occurs when some workers
identified as displaced are, in fact, on temporary layoff. Using the PSID
or NLS, short-term layoffs can be distinguished from permanent layoffs
by tracking job losers over the postdisplacement period. With the DWS,

the survey date is fixed, and therefore the time since layoff varies. Within the January 1986 DWS, for example, those losing jobs in 1981, 1982, or 1983 have been laid off at least two years and presumably have little chance of recall. Workers with a reported reason for job loss of "slack work" in 1984 or 1985 are included in the DWS, but clearly had a higher probability of recall in 1986 or 1987 than those losing jobs earlier. When the reason for job loss is a plant closing, relocation, or the abolishment of a position or shift, then post-survey recall into the prior job is less likely.

Although designed as a cross-sectional database with retrospective supplements, the CPS does have a quasi-longitudinal capability. Each month a new "rotation group" of approximately 7,300 households is selected. Each rotation group is interviewed for four consecutive months, rotated out of the sample for eight months, returned for four more monthly interviews, and then dropped from the sample. Four rotation groups, equalling 50% of addresses, are common between the January and March surveys. This allows for the matching of respondent data from the DWS with that from the annual work experience and family income supplement (Seitchik 1987, 1989). A 50% January-to-January match generates postdisplacement labor market data for individuals at the time of the initial DWS survey and one year later (Devens 1986). Using longitudinal data that are a byproduct of the sampling design has its pitfalls, the most important of which is the loss of individuals who have changed addresses between surveys.

IV. Size and Characteristics of the Displacement Population

Based upon the DWS, between 1.2 and 3.1 million wage and salary workers aged twenty or over lost jobs each year between 1979 and 1985 because of a plant closing or relocation, slack work without recall at the time of the survey, or abolishment of a position or shift. As shown in table 1, this translates into an annual displacement rate (as a fraction of the civilian labor force age twenty or over) of 1–3%. The displacement population each year is about one-tenth as large as the number of individuals experiencing unemployment.

Year-to-year comparisons of displacement rates are suspect with the DWS, because of the previously discussed retrospective bias in the DWS data and the inclusion of some job losers who will eventually be recalled by their former employers. For example, the January 1984 survey esti-

59

Table 1 **Size of the Displaced Worker Population**

Survey/year	Annual displacement rate[a]	Displaced/ unemp.[b]	Estimated number of displaced workers (in thousands)			
			Total	Plant closing	Slack work	Job abolished
Est. from the Jan. 1986 Displaced Worker Survey						
Jan. 1986	—	—	262	82	151	29
1985	.028	.143	2,991	1,086	1,482	423
1984	.019	.095	2,047	1,047	714	286
1983	.018	.078	1,859	994	609	256
1982	.020	.077	2,030	1,042	730	259
1981	.015	.065	1,531	902	452	178
1981–Jan. 1986[c]	.020	.091	10,784	5,178	4,174	1,431
Est. from the Jan. 1984 Displaced Worker Survey						
Jan. 1984	—	—	141	24	96	20
1983	.030	.131	3,115	1,116	1,599	400
1982	.030	.113	3,002	1,221	1,450	331
1981	.023	.097	2,274	963	1,020	291
1980	.017	.076	1,622	828	628	166
1979	.013	.067	1,237	717	387	133
1979–Jan. 1984[c]	.023	.097	11,467	4,904	5,216	1,347

Notes: Sample includes civilians 20 years or older at the time of the survey. Numbers may not sum due to rounding error.

An additional 2.3 million workers in January 1986 and 2.4 million workers in January 1984 had lost or left jobs in the past five years because a seasonal job was completed, a self-operated business failed, or for some other related reason. These workers have been excluded from the analysis in this chapter.

[a]Annual displacement rate is displaced workers as a fraction of the civilian labor force age twenty or over in that year.

[b]Displaced workers as a fraction of all individuals experiencing unemployment in that year. Unemployment data from BLS Bulletin 2307, *Labor Force Statistics 1948–87.*

[c]Totals include displaced workers with missing data on year of job loss.

mates that 3 million workers were displaced in recessionary 1982, including 1.4 million laid off because of "slack work." Two years later, the January 1986 survey finds 2 million workers displaced in 1982, only 730 thousand of whom reported their reason for job loss as "slack work." While some of this difference is likely due to the systematic under-reporting of 1982 displacements in 1986, it is also quite possible that some of the "displaced" identified in January 1984 were recalled to their old jobs in the two years between surveys.

Recall into lost jobs is less likely in the case of plant closings, making year-to-year comparisons more accurate. Using the retrospective data from the survey closest in time to the year of job loss (to minimize forgetfulness and the effect of multiple displacement), layoffs through plant closings and relocations rose from 717 thousand in 1979 to 963 thousand in 1981, peaking at 1.2 million in 1982. Despite three years of economic expansion, plant closings affected at least 1 million workers per year from 1982 through 1985.

A. Personal Characteristics

Based on comparisons from the January 1986 DWS as shown in table 2, displaced workers are highly representative of the U.S. labor force in terms of age, race, and marital and family status. The majority of job losers are under the age of thirty-four; however, one-fourth are forty-five years of age or older. These older workers may be subject to age discrimination in reemployment. Discrimination in reemployment may also be a factor affecting the labor market outcomes of the 14% of nonwhite displaced workers. Reflecting recent trends in family structure and female labor force participation, almost two-fifths of displaced workers are not married, 38% are women, and one out of every six of these women is maintaining a family with no husband present.

There are some important differences between displaced workers and the work force from which they come. Job losers are more likely to have been full-time workers (90% versus 84% of the employed in January 1986), and, significantly, are less educated than the labor force as a whole. On average, those in the labor force aged twenty and over had completed 13.0 years of school in January 1986. For displaced workers, the average was only 12.4 years. Compared to the labor force, relatively large fractions of job losers had either less than 12 years of education (20% versus 15%, respectively), or had graduated from high school and gone no further (46% versus 41%).

V. Characteristics of the Lost Jobs

The DWS contains selected questions relevant to the lost job, including one pertaining to employer notification of impending layoff. Recent federal legislation has mandated a minimum sixty-day worker notifica-

Table 2 **Characteristics of Displaced Workers**

Characteristic	Displaced workers, 1981–January 1986	Labor force aged 20+, January 1986
Age, in years		
20–24	14.4	14.8
25–34	37.4	32.1 ˙
35–44	23.1	24.4
45–61	21.1	24.4
62+	4.0	4.3
(Mean age)	(37.0)	(38.0)
Yrs. of schooling completed		
<12	20.5	15.4
12	45.7	41.0
13–15	20.3	21.2
16+	13.5	22.5
(Mean yrs. of schooling)	(12.4)	(13.0)
White	86.5	86.0
Black	11.2	11.2
Other	2.3	2.8
Marital and family status[a]		
Married women	20.1	23.6
Female family heads	6.4	5.5
Other women	11.5	15.1
Married men	41.9	33.7
Male family heads	2.3	1.6
Other men	17.9	20.5
Lost Job:		
Job tenure, in years		
<3	52.6	—
3–9	31.6	—
10–19	11.1	—
20+	4.7	—
		(1/86)[b]
Full-time	90.0	84.3
Part-time	10.0	16.7
Received advance notice of layoff	50.6	—

Notes: [a]Data from matched January and March 1986 CPS files (displaced workers) and from *Employment and Earnings* (labor force 16+) for 1986. All other data from the January 1986 CPS and Displaced Worker Survey.

[b]Excludes workers unemployed in January 1986.

tion period prior to some plant closings and large-scale layoffs. Although no such requirement was in place during the five-year period leading up to the January 1986 DWS, 51% of all workers surveyed report receiving some advance notification. One out of every seven displaced workers was able to quit his or her job before being officially laid off.

The 1986 DWS provides no information on the length of time between notification and layoff. Beginning with the 1988 survey, data is available on whether the notice was formally given, and the approximate number of weeks of advance warning. In an establishment-based survey of plant closings and large-scale layoffs in 1983 and 1984, the U.S. Government Accounting Office (1987) found that most firms provide advance notice, but only 19% give more than thirty days notice. Thus the new law will increase both the incidence of advance notice and the average length of notice. Results on advance notice from the GAO survey and the DWS are discussed in detail in chapter 8 of this volume.

Researchers and policy makers have placed much emphasis on long-tenure displaced workers, fearing that these workers will be unable to transfer their firm-specific skills learned on the job into productive, comparable reemployment. Research on displacement effects across tenure groups is now preliminary. If, in time, we conclude that readjustment difficulties are largely confined to those with many years of accrued job seniority (as distinguished from industry tenure, occupational tenure, or broad labor market experience), then the scope of the displacement problem will be greatly narrowed. According to results from the 1986 DWS as presented in table 2, 53% of the displaced had less than three years of accrued tenure on the lost job; 84% had less than ten years of tenure. While over one million workers with ten or more years of job seniority lost jobs between 1981 and January 1986, this represents only 16% of the population of workers usually classified as displaced.

The average job tenure among the displaced of almost 5 years, and their average age of thirty-six, obscure important differences by reason for job loss. Those laid off due to "slack work" may be subject to implicit or explicit seniority provisions that will systematically affect the low-tenure worker. Average tenure for the "slack work" group was only 3.3 years, a scant 9% had accrued 10 or more years of seniority with their employer, and only 19% were aged forty-five or older in January 1986. Plant closings and relocations reach an older and more tenured work force. The average tenure for workers affected by shut downs and relocations was 6.0 years, 22% had accrued at least 10 years of seniority, and 29% were aged forty-five or older.

Table 3   **Sectoral Incidence of Displacement**

Industry	Labor force 20+, 1/86	Lost jobs 1981–Jan 1986	Average annual industry displacement rate 1981–85[a]	Average annual employment growth 1980–86
Total	100%	100%	.020	1.5
Mining	1.0	3.7	.079	−4.4
Construction	6.3	8.8	.028	2.0
Manufacturing	22.2	43.3	.044	−1.1
Transportation & public utilities	7.4	7.5	.022	0.3
Wholesale trade	4.1	5.3	.027	1.4
Retail trade	14.6	9.6	.012	2.9
Finance, insurance and real estate	6.8	2.5	.008	3.4
Services	30.8	15.5	.010	4.3
Government	5.2	1.1	.005	0.5
Agriculture, forestry, and fisheries	1.6	2.7	.017	−0.8

Note: [a]Industry displacement rate for each year is displaced workers as a fraction of total industry employment. Industry employment data from *Employment and Earnings,* various issues.

Source: Data in the first two columns from the January 1986 CPS and the Displaced Worker Survey. Data in the last column from U.S. Department of Commerce, *Statistical Abstract of the United States,* 1988, Table 631.

A. Sectoral and Occupational Displacement Rates

Table 3 compares the industrial distribution of the experienced labor force aged twenty and over in January 1986 to the distribution for displaced workers on their old jobs. These are used to calculate annual industry displacement rates, defined as the ratio of the displaced to the experienced labor force in each industry. Average annual employment growth for 1980–86 is also shown for each major industry, using the census industrial classification system.

While the results clearly indicate that job loss touches workers from every major industry grouping, it is disproportionately affecting those in the nonagricultural goods-producing industries of mining, construction, and manufacturing. These three industrial sectors account for only 30% of the experienced labor force, but make up 56% of the displaced

64

worker population. The highest average annual industrial displacement rates were in mining (.079) and manufacturing (.044). These sectors also experienced declining employment during the 1980–86 period.

The direct association between displacement rates and sectoral growth is virtually tautological, since employment reductions can only be accomplished through voluntary attrition or forced layoff. The converse of this relationship is that high-growth industries have relatively low displacement rates. The high-growth leader is the service sector, with 4.3% annual employment growth for 1980–86. By January 1986, service industry workers accounted for 31 percent of the experienced labor force, but only 16% of displaced workers. The average annual displacement rate out of services (.010) was lower than that in all other sectors except government (.005) and finance, insurance, and real estate (.008).

Using an identical methodology as that for industries, occupational displacement rates were calculated and are shown in table 4. Average annual occupational growth rates for the 1980–86 period are measured with error, due to widespread changes in the census classification scheme implemented in 1983. Table 4 thus reports growth rates for the 1980–82 and 1983–86 periods separately.

The occupational distribution of displaced workers is skewed toward industrial blue-collar jobs, which can be broadly classified as skilled (precision production, craft, and repair), and semi-skilled (operators, fabricators, and laborers). Skilled and semiskilled blue-collar workers constitute the majority of the displacement population, with shares of 19% and 34%, respectively. Less than one-third of the experienced labor force is blue-collar, with skilled and semiskilled shares of 12% and 17%, respectively. Annual displacement rates for skilled blue-collar (.032) and semiskilled blue-collar workers (.046) exceed those from all other occupations, and the rate for semiskilled workers is more than double the rate for the work force as a whole (.022).

In the white-collar and service occupations, the largest contributors to the displacement population are administrative support workers, including clericals (10.2%); professional specialty, technical, and related support workers (9.8%); and salespersons (9.6%). In each case, however, occupational displacement rates are much lower than for blue-collar workers and are below 2% per year.

B. Regional Incidence of Displacement

There are several policy-relevant characteristics of the jobs lost by displaced workers that are not part of the DWS, including the geographic

Table 4   Occupational Incidence of Displacement

Occupation	Labor force 20+ Jan. 1986	Lost jobs 1981– Jan. 1986	Average annual occupation displacement rate 1983–85[a]	Average annual employment growth[b]		
				1980–82	1983–86	1980–86
Total	100%	100%	.022	1.8	3.0	2.5
Exec., admin., and managerial	11.6	8.8	.017	2.6	5.5	4.3
Prof. specialty, tech., and related support	16.4	9.8	.014	4.4	2.8	3.5
Sales occupations	10.5	9.6	.018	4.0	3.8	3.9
Admin. support	17.2	10.2	.014	1.7	2.7	2.3
Service	13.1	7.2	.013	4.2	2.5	3.2
Precision prod., craft, and repair	12.3	19.1	.032	−0.4	2.9	1.6
Other blue collar	17.3	33.8	.046	−1.6	2.3	0.7
Farming, forestry, and fisheries	1.6	1.5	.011	0.4	−1.6	−0.8

Notes: [a]Occupation displacement rate for each year is displaced workers as a fraction of total occupation employment. Occupation displacement rates were not calculated for 1981 and 1982 due to changes in the occupational classification system beginning in 1983. Occupation employment data from *Employment and Earnings,* various issues.

[b]Growth rates for 1980–82 and 1983–86 not strictly comparable due to changes in occupational classifications.

Source: Data in the first two columns from the January 1986 CPS and the Displaced Worker Survey. Growth rates in last three columns calculated from data in *Employment and Earnings.*

location of the plant closings and layoffs, and the union status of the workers affected. With the help of other sources it is possible to estimate both of these variables.

Although the DWS is a household survey, information on region of residence is provided only at the survey date, not at the time of layoff. In the intervening time between layoff and the January 1986 survey, 17% of respondents had moved to a new city or county to look for or accept a new job. The distance of the move and whether it was within or across states and regions is not known.

Using establishment survey data from 1983 and 1984, the Government Accounting Office (GAO) has estimated the extent of plant closings and large-scale layoffs across the nine geographic census divisions (U.S. GAO 1987). Unlike the DWS, the GAO survey locates

Table 5   **Regional Incidence of Displacement**

Region	Labor force 1983–84	Displaced Workers DWS 1/1981–1/1986	DWS 1983–84	GAO 1983–84	Total emp. growth, 1980–1986
Total	100%	100%	100%	100%	12.0%
New England	5.7	4.2	4.3	9	11.1
Middle Atlantic	15.4	12.6	12.3	15	7.4
East North Central	17.8	19.7	18.4	19	4.6
West North Central	7.7	7.6	7.0	7	4.5
South Atlantic	16.5	14.4	15.3	8	23.1
East South Central	6.0	7.0	7.8	5	9.8
West South Central	10.9	13.4	13.5	17	17.9
Mountain	5.4	6.2	6.3	5	22.1
Pacific	14.7	15.1	15.1	15	7.5
Est. number of displaced workers (in millions)	—	(10.7)	(3.9)	(1.3)	—

Note: The GAO survey focused on closures and permanent layoffs at business establishments with fifty or more employees. The establishment employment reduction must have reduced the work force by at least 20% or two hundred workers. Seasonal and temporary layoffs were excluded. Respondents were private sector establishment representatives.

The DWS data refer to region of residence at the time of the survey (January 1986), not at the time of displacement.

Source: Data on the regional labor force from Bureau of the Census, *State and Metropolitan Area Data Book,* 1986. Employment data from the *Statistical Abstract of the U.S.,* 1988 and 1981.

the workplace of the displaced worker, not his or her postlayoff household. The GAO survey also has a more restrictive sampling frame, including only layoffs and plant closings at establishments with fifty or more employees, which experienced employment reductions of at least 20% or two-hundred workers, excluding temporary and seasonal layoffs.

In table 5, the distribution of displaced workers across the nine census divisions is shown, based on both the January 1986 DWS and the GAO establishment survey. For comparative purposes, the DWS results are presented both in total and for 1983–84 displacements. The distribution of the labor force across census divisions, and the employment growth rate within each division, are shown as a guide to the relative rate of job loss out of the regions.

The results indicate that five of the census divisions are displacing

67

workers at a rate consistent with their share of the national labor force. These are the East North Central, the West North Centural, the East South Central, the Mountain, and the Pacific divisions. Each have shares of the U.S. population of displaced workers for 1983–84 (based on the average between the DWS and GAO surveys), which are within one percentage point of the regional fraction of the labor force.

The popular perception of displacement as a "rust belt" phenomenon confined to the Midwest is somewhat misleading. The heart of the industrial Midwest is comprised of the East North Central states of Ohio, Indiana, Illinois, Michigan, and Wisconsin. While it is true that this area has a higher percentage of all displaced workers for 1983–84 (18.4% DWS, 19% GAO) than any other in the country, it contains an almost equally large fraction of the labor force (17.8%). While there may be a higher rate of displacement in the East North Central region than in the nation as a whole, the difference is not substantial.

The "Oil Patch" states of Texas, Oklahoma, and Louisiana (along with Arkansas) comprise the West South Central division, and account for a disproportionate share of displaced workers. While containing only 10.9% of the national labor force during 1983–84, the GAO estimates the West South Central states to include 17% of all workers displaced through plant closings and large-scale layoffs during the two-year period. Even allowing for geographic mobility between the time of displacement and January 1986, the DWS found 13.5% of all displaced workers in 1983–84 to reside in the West South Central. The high rate of displacement occurred despite overall regional employment growth during 1980–1986 of 18% (well above the national average of 12%), and despite positive employment growth in each of the four states between 1983 and 1984.

The booming South Atlantic division (Delaware, Maryland, Virginia, West Virginia, North and South Carolina, Georgia, Florida, and the District of Columbia) contained a small share of displaced workers relative to its share of the labor force in 1983–84 (8% versus 16.5%). New England, on the other hand, experienced near-average employment growth during 1980–86 and led the nation in per capita personal income growth. Meanwhile, 9.3% of all the New England establishments surveyed by the GAO experienced a plant closing or large-scale layoff, the second-highest rate among the nine census divisions.

C. Estimates of Union Affiliation

The DWS provides no data on the union affiliation of displaced workers. Data are available on the union status of workers by industry

Table 6   **Union Status of Work Force and Estimates**
for Displaced Workers

Worker sample	Percent members of unions	Percent represented by unions
Total work force 1983–85 weighted averages	18.8	21.8
Estimates for displaced workers		
By industry:	19.9	22.2
By occupation:	22.9	25.4

Note: Estimates for displaced workers based on weighted average unionization rates in 1983–85 in eleven major industry groupings and nine major occupational groupings. For example, the percent of displaced workers who were members of unions, based on their major industry, was estimated as $\sum_{i=1}^{11} U_i D_i$, where U_i is the weighted average rate of union membership in industry i for 1983–85, and D_i is the fraction of displaced workers in 1981–January 1986 from industry i.

Source: Data on union affiliation of the work force from *Employment and Earnings.*

and occupation, and these can be used to construct estimates of union status for displaced workers. The key assumption in such an estimation is that union workers and other workers are losing jobs within each industry and occupation at the same rate. However, this assumption is suspect: union membership declined as a fraction of total employment during 1983–85 in each and every of the eleven major industry groupings and nine major occupational groupings between 1983 and 1985. Although we have no direct data, it seems likely that union workers have a greater probability of being displaced than their nonunion counterparts. As such, estimates based solely on industry and occupational affiliation may understate the extent of displacement among union members.

Using published census data, the weighted average percentage of workers who were members of unions during 1983–85, and who were represented by unions (members plus nonmembers covered by union contracts) was calculated for each major industry and occupational grouping. These were then used as weights applied to the industry and occupational distribution of displaced workers, in order to calculate the percentage of workers losing union jobs. Results are presented in table 6. Again, the key assumption is that the rate of unionization in each industry (or, alternatively, occupation) is the same for the displaced as it is for all workers.

Union membership had declined to 18.8% of all U.S. workers by 1983–85. An additional 3% of workers were not union members but

69

were covered by union contracts. Industries with relatively high concentrations of union members were transportation and public utilities (39.4%), government (36.1%), durable goods manufacturing (27.5%), and nondurable goods manufacturing (24.4%). Other than government, these are sectors with relatively high concentrations of displaced workers (cf., table 3). Based on the industry distribution of the displaced, it is estimated that 19.9% were union members and 22.2% were represented by unions. This is only a slightly higher rate of unionization than for the overall work force.

When the estimates of union affiliation are based on the occupational distribution of displaced workers, the unionization rates are slightly larger: 22.9% members of unions and 25.4% represented by unions. These estimates reflect the high rate of unionization among skilled (30.5%) and semiskilled (33.5%) industrial blue-collar workers, who comprise over half of all displaced workers, but only 30% of the work force as a whole.

These results, based solely on the industry and occupational distribution of displaced workers, do not imply unusually high rates of unionization among job losers. More precise estimates require direct survey information on the union status of displaced workers.

VI. Labor Market Adjustment

Most of the recent empirical studies of displaced workers, including the majority of the contributions to this volume, estimate the size and incidence of the economic losses following job loss, typically expressed in terms of unemployment and earnings.[2] Among the most important findings is the variety in outcomes across job losers, with some workers enjoying rapid reemployment at comparable (or improved) pay, while others experience prolonged periods of unemployment and/or reemployment at reduced wages. Basic descriptive statistics from the DWS ignore important statistical and theoretical issues necessary for both understanding the underlying displacement process and explaining subsequent outcomes. But the results do serve as a introduction to the heterogeneity in postdisplacement experience.

A. Reemployment and Unemployment

In January 1986, the employment rate among workers displaced since 1981 was 66.9%, while 19.5% were unemployed and the remaining

Table 7   **Reemployment Rates of Displaced Workers**

Reason displaced/year of job loss	Displaced 1/1981–1/1986, reemployed 1/1986	Displaced 1/1979–1/1984, reemployed 1/1984
All displaced	66.9%	61.6%
Lost job in:		
1985	49.8	—
1984	71.7	—
1983	75.1	45.9
1982	77.2	64.3
1981	75.2	67.6
1980	—	73.7
1979	—	68.9
Plant closing	70.1%	65.1%
Lost job in:		
1985	56.7	—
1984	72.4	—
1983	76.2	53.1
1982	74.4	65.6
1981	74.7	68.4
1980	—	75.3
1979	—	66.1
Slack work	62.2%	57.1
Lost job in:		
1985	43.0	—
1984	69.5	—
1983	74.5	37.2
1982	79.5	61.4
1981	77.6	67.4
1980	—	73.4
1979	—	72.2

Source: Data from the 1984 and 1986 Displaced Worker Surveys.

13.6% had left the work force (i.e., stopped looking for work for whatever reason). This translates into an unemployment rate of 22.6% of the active labor force [19.5/(19.5 + 66.9) · 100], as compared to an unemployment rate of 6.7% for the labor force as a whole aged twenty or over in January 1986. The distinction between unemployment (active job search) and nonemployment (joblessness with or without search) is increasingly blurry as the period between jobs is extended, and therefore many researchers, including Swaim and Podgursky in chapter 5 of this volume, focus on joblessness as opposed to unemployment.

Table 7 reports the reemployment rates in January 1984 and January

1986 for all workers displaced in the previous five years, as well as for the subset of workers losing jobs because of a plant closing or relocation. Consistent with increases in employment nationwide, reemployment rates among the displaced improved between the 1984 and 1986 surveys, from 61.6% to 66.9%.

Within each survey, reemployment rates improve rapidly one year after job loss, and then stabilize at a level below that for the labor force as a whole. In the January 1986 DWS, for example, only 49.8% of those displaced in 1985 had found new jobs, and their unemployment rate was 44.0%. For those losing jobs in 1981–84, the reemployment rate ranged between 72% and 77%, and the unemployment rate was 10.5%.

Workers displaced through plant closings or dislocations are reemployed more rapidly than those with hope of recall. As shown in table 7, the plant closing group from 1985 had a reemployment rate of 57% in January 1986, as compared to 43% for workers displaced through "slack work" (and therefore potentially awaiting recall). Low reemployment rates persist for workers laid off due to "slack work" in 1983 and 1984, none of whom have been recalled as of January 1986. Such workers are classified as unemployed (and displaced), although they may not be actively looking for work while awaiting recall. For 1981 and 1982 displacements, reemployment rates among workers losing jobs because of "slack work" are comparable to those for other displaced workers, indicating a movement away from "wait" joblessness over time.

Unemployment experience is reported in two ways within the January 1986 CPS and its displaced worker supplement: duration of the current, ongoing unemployment spell for workers unemployed at the time of the survey, and the total weeks of unemployment since displacement. The latter "total weeks" variable is top-coded within the survey at ninety-nine weeks, and therefore subject to censoring bias. Table 8 includes both sets of outcomes, with the total weeks of unemployment analyzed separately for the reemployed, the unemployed, and those who have left the labor force.

Among those unemployed at the time of the survey, the average duration of the current spell was 17.5 weeks. This is almost 3 weeks longer than the average for all unemployed workers aged twenty and over, displaced and otherwise. The mean total weeks of unemployment between displacement and the time of the survey was 27.1 weeks for the unemployed, 21.1 weeks for the reemployed, and 51.8 weeks for those out of the labor force. Across all displaced workers regardless of current employment status, 31.4% are found to have less than 5 weeks of unem-

72

Table 8   **Unemployment Durations of Workers Displaced**
January 1981–January 1986

Weeks of unemp.	Duration of current unemployment spell, workers unemp. 1/1986	Total weeks of unemployment since displacement, by 1/1986 employment status		
		Reemployed	Unemployed	Out of the labor force
0–4 weeks	31.0	37.0	22.0	17.0
5–14	33.5	21.9	26.8	11.2
15–26 weeks	18.1	15.7	19.9	10.4
27+ weeks	17.4	25.4	31.3	61.4
(Mean weeks)	(17.5)	(21.1)	(27.1)	(51.8)
Estimated number of displaced workers, in thousands		7,218	2,102	1,463

Source: Data from the January 1986 Displaced Worker Survey.

ployment since job loss. As if to highlight the variety in postlayoff experience, an identical 31.4% report over six months of unemployment.

B. Reemployment Earnings and Family Income

The first column of table 9 compares the weekly earnings on the layoff job to January 1986 weekly earnings, for the two-thirds of displaced workers who were reemployed at the time of the survey (prior earnings are adjusted to January 1986 equivalents using the CPI). The second column shows the results from the January 1984 DWS. Part-time workers are included, since 18% of those reemployed in January 1986 are part-time, and over half of these workers would prefer full-time jobs. Weekly earnings differences between jobs could be a function of changes in hourly earnings, changes in hours worked, or both.

In both the 1984 and 1986 surveys, the majority of the reemployed are found to be earning less in real terms on the new job than on the layoff job. However, the ratio of current to former earnings shows substantial variation. A full 43% of the reemployed in January 1986 had higher real earnings than on the layoff job, as did 39% of those reemployed in 1984. On the other hand, over 30% of the displaced in each survey were earning less than three-fourths of their former wages. Podgursky and Swaim (1987a, 1987b), Seitchik and Zornitsky (1989), and Kletzer in chapter 4 of this volume, among others, have documented variations in postdisplace-

73

Table 9   Weekly Earnings on the Layoff and Reemployment Jobs

Earnings ratio	January 1986	January 1984
Ratio of weekly reemployment earnings (1/1986 $) to predisplacement earnings (1/1986 $)		
<.5	13.6%	15.6%
.5–.74	17.3	16.5
.75–.99	26.1	28.8
1.00+	43.0	38.6
(Mean ratio)	(1.04)	(.995)
Layoff job, mean weekly earnings (1/1986 $)	$347	$343
Reemployment job, mean weekly earnings (1/1986 $)	$323	$307

Note: Data refer to displaced workers reemployed at survey date. Nominal earnings adjusted to January 1986 equivalents using the CPI.
Source: Data from the 1984 and 1986 Displaced Worker Surveys.

ment outcomes related to educational attainment, occupation, and gender. Possibly the most important finding from this research is the vulnerability of less-skilled and less-educated workers in general, and semiskilled blue-collar workers in particular, to prolonged joblessness as well as earnings reductions following reemployment.

In the 1986 survey, average weekly earnings on the reemployment job were $323, as compared to $347 on the layoff job (January 1986 dollars). Average earnings on the reemployment job were slightly above the average 1986 weekly earnings for all private sector workers in 1986 ($305), but below the average 1986 earnings in the industrial goods-producing industries ($414), where the majority of displacement occurs.

Most studies of postdisplacement outcomes have focused on weekly or hourly earnings for individuals. Analyzing annual earnings and family income provides a richer gauge of the economic impact of displacement upon the individual and the family. Percentage earnings losses of equal size for individuals will have varying effects on family income. The overall economic impact on the family will depend upon the availability of alternative income sources, and the family's ability to make economic adjustments to job loss.

While predisplacement family income data is not available from the DWS, it is possible to merge data on displaced individuals within the approximately 29,000 households common to both the January and March 1986 CPS sampling frames. The combined data include the 1985 annual earnings and family income of displaced workers, which are

Table 10   1985 Earnings and Income, Workers Displaced from Full-Time Jobs January 1981–December 1984

Earnings/income ratio	Married men	Married women	Female family heads
Ratio of 1985 earnings to 1985 family income			
0 (Nonearner)	9.7	22.1	23.0
<.1	2.6	12.8	6.6
.1–0.29	7.5	32.7	6.6
.3–0.49	16.3	21.5	14.8
.5–0.89	45.6	8.4	32.8
.90+	18.4	2.5	16.4
(Median ratio)	.618	.199	.475
Ratio of estimated predisplacement yearly earnings (1985 $) to family income			
<.1	0.1	1.3	0.0
.1–0.29	2.6	34.1	4.3
.3–0.49	16.9	43.2	15.4
.5–0.89	59.3	18.8	61.5
.90+	21.1	2.6	18.8
(Median ratio)	.692	.358	.725
Median 1985 earnings	$15,500	$ 6,000	$ 4,900
Est. median predisplacement yearly earnings (1985 $)	$21,527	$12,730	$11,230
Median 1985 family income	$26,426	$31,500	$10,072

Note: Predisplacement earnings adjusted to 1985 equivalents using the CPI.
Source: Data from matched January and March 1986 CPS files.

collected as part of the annual work experience supplement to the March CPS. Multiplying the former weekly earnings by fifty-two weeks allows for estimation of the worker's contribution to family income prior to job loss. By limiting the analysis to worker's displaced between 1981 and 1984, and by assuming no adjustment to family income following job loss, it is possible to estimate the impact of earnings losses on family income in 1985.

Table 10 shows the ratio of pre- and postdisplacement annual earnings (1985 dollars) to 1985 family income, for married men, married women, and female family heads losing full-time jobs between 1981 and 1984. Together married persons living with their spouses, and female family heads, comprise over two-thirds of the population of displaced workers.

Median annual earnings were reduced by over $6,000 for all three groups of workers, but in percentage terms the loss was much larger for married women and female family heads that it was for married men. Over one-fifth of the women from each group had no earnings in 1985, while only 10% of the married men had no earnings. During the postdisplacement year 1985, almost two-thirds of the married men and one-half of the female family heads earned at least 50% of their family's income (which includes all earned and unearned cash sources as well as food stamps). In contrast, less than one-third of the displaced married women earned at least 30% of the family income in 1985.

Table 10 also presents the ratio of estimated predisplacement annual earnings to 1985 annual income (which is adjusted only for the change in earnings). Such a comparison suggests that displacement is followed by significant reductions in the earnings contribution of women. Among married women, the estimated median earnings contribution to family income is reduced from 36% to 20%. For female family heads, the reduction is from 72% to 48%, accompanied by a likely increase in transfer payments (Seitchik 1987). For married men, the percentage contribution of their earnings to family income is reduced by displacement only 7 percentage points, from 69% to 62%. While these results indicate that women's contribution to the family income is greatly affected by displacement in percentage terms, confidence in the results is weakened by lack of data on predisplacement incomes.

C. Adjustment Difficulties and Job Tenure

Subsequent chapters of this volume carefully assess, within multivariate models, the characteristics of workers associated with postdisplacement adjustment problems in the labor market. Here we simply set the stage for that analysis by describing the cross section of workers who are experiencing difficulty. The minority of workers who have long spells of unemployment or who are reemployed at substantially reduced wages have naturally become the focus of policy.

Table 11 compares the characteristics of workers with postlayoff adjustment difficulties to the general population of displaced workers. Three partially overlapping groups are defined: the long-term unemployed, who have had at least twenty-seven weeks of unemployment since being laid off from their jobs; the earnings loss group, which has been reemployed as of January 1986, but at real wages that are less than 75% of their prior earnings; and the currently unemployed, those actively seeking work at the time of the survey.

Table 11   **Characteristics of Workers with Postdisplacement Adjustment Difficulties**

Characteristic	All displaced	Postdisplacement outcome		
		Long-term unemployment[a]	Large earnings losses[b]	Unemployed 1/1986
Est. no. of workers (in thousands)	10,784	3,222	1,863	2,102
Male	62.4	56.3	62.5	68.8
Female	37.6	43.7	37.5	31.2
Mean age	37.0	40.2	37.3	36.1
Mean years of schooling completed	12.4	12.0	12.3	11.7
White	86.5	81.2	87.9	79.9
Black	11.2	16.6	10.0	17.3
Other	2.3	2.2	2.1	2.7
Lost job:				
Rec'd adv. notice of layoff	50.6	50.8	49.4	46.1
Manufacturing	43.3	51.1	45.9	45.6
Mining and constr.	12.5	11.3	14.8	14.8
Precision prod., craft, and repair	19.1	19.1	20.6	20.5
Other blue collar	33.8	42.0	36.3	43.3
Mean yrs. of seniority	4.8	6.3	5.5	4.5
Region of residence, 1/1986				
New England	4.2	3.2	3.2	2.6
Middle Atlantic	12.6	15.1	9.5	14.8
East North Central	19.7	26.4	19.5	22.2
West North Central	7.6	6.8	9.0	6.0
South Atlantic	14.4	12.6	13.9	12.2
East South Central	7.0	8.4	9.0	8.2
West South Central	13.4	11.2	16.5	12.3
Mountain	6.2	4.7	8.0	6.1
Pacific	15.1	11.6	11.1	15.6

Notes: [a]Unemployed more than twenty-seven weeks since job loss, regardless of employment status at the time of the survey.
[b]Real reemployment earnings (1/1986) less than 75% of prior earnings.
Source: Data from the January 1986 Displaced Worker Survey.

Within the population of displaced workers, the long-term unemployed are disproportionately women, older workers, the less educated, manufacturing and semiskilled blue-collar workers, high-tenure workers, and those from the Middle Atlantic and East North Central states.

Table 12   **Comparison of Low-Tenure and High-Tenure**
Displaced Workers

Worker Characteristic/Outcome	Tenure on the lost job		
	<3 Years	3–9 Years	10+ Years
Estimated number of workers, in thousands	3,429	2,059	1,029
Male	60.3	62.5	69.0
Female	39.7	37.5	31.0
Mean age	33	38	49
Mean years of schooling	12.5	12.5	11.6
White	86.5	85.6	88.9
Black	11.0	12.2	9.7
Other	2.5	2.2	1.4
Lost job:			
Manufacturing	36.3	46.1	59.6
Mining and Construction	14.3	12.1	7.3
Precision production, craft, and repair	18.1	20.0	19.9
Other blue collar	31.1	34.0	42.0
Plant closing	42.1	49.2	65.4
Reemployed, Jan. 1986	67.1	71.4	58.1
Ratio of reemployment earnings (1/1986) to layoff earnings (1/1986 $)			
<0.5	11.1	14.4	21.9
0.5–0.74	15.6	17.9	22.4
0.75–0.99	24.8	26.6	30.6
1.00+	48.5	41.1	25.2
(Mean ratio)	(1.10)	(1.11)	(1.01)

Source: Data from the January 1986 Displaced Worker Survey.

High-tenure and semiskilled blue-collar workers are also most likely to experience large percentage earnings losses following reemployment. Men are more likely than women to be both reemployed and unemployed at the time of the survey. The converse of this result is that women are much more likely than men to be out of the labor force.

Displaced workers were divided into groups based on job tenure, in order to assess the effect of tenure restrictions upon the displacement sample. In table 12, selected personal and job characteristics are reported for workers with less than three years of tenure on the layoff job, three to nine years, and ten or more years of job tenure.

The results indicate that the high-tenure workers who are often analyzed within displacement research are disproportionately male, older, less educated, and from manufacturing and blue-collar jobs. They are more likely to lose jobs because of a plant closing. The highest tenure group also has the lowest reemployment rate, and the lowest ratio of reemployment earnings to former earnings. On the other hand, the similarities between the three groups probably exceed their differences, when compared to the labor force as a whole. Even those with two or fewer years of job tenure are disproportionately male, less educated, from the industrial goods-producing sectors, and blue-collar.

While some personal and job characteristics seem to be associated with postdisplacement difficulties, these results should be interpreted with caution. A simple inverse association between education and unemployment incidence, for example, does nothing to explain why less educated workers are not finding jobs as rapidly as other workers. And of equal importance, cross-sectional findings may not hold when controlling for a range of characteristics within an explicit model of the displacement process.

VII. Conclusion

Despite definitional problems and the various limitations of available information, recent empirical research using the DWS and other nationally representative data sets provides an improved view of the population of displaced workers. The one to three million workers displaced each year during the 1980s are more varied in their personal and job characteristics than would be implied by case studies of unionized, mostly male manufacturing workers in the Midwest. When defined broadly, the job losers include many women and low-tenure workers. Although disproportionately a phenomenon involving blue-collar workers and those from the goods-producing sectors, displacement affects large numbers of well-educated workers, white-collar workers, and service sector workers, from all regions of the country.

If displaced workers were to be defined as those who have difficulty making economic adjustments to layoff, then incorporating all job losers into the displacement population vastly overstates the problem. The majority of job losers seem to find reemployment without experiencing long-term unemployment. Most displaced workers endure real earnings losses, but over 40% have higher earnings on the new job than on the layoff job, and seven out of ten who find new jobs recapture at least 75% of their former earnings. There is also quite a bit of variation in the impact that earnings losses have within the context of family income. These findings reveal displacement as a varied, subtle process that is sometimes associated with severe labor market adjustment difficulties. Some workers move rapidly between seemingly comparable jobs, while others take large reductions in pay, or have prolonged spells of unemployment, or both.

The variation in the types of job losers and in their postlayoff experience justifies the long-standing emphasis within research upon identifying the individual, family, and job characteristics associated with unemployment and earnings losses. These findings also highlight the need for more research on the root causes of displacement, and for a better understanding of the essential processes through which unemployment and earnings losses are created. Only by comprehending these fundamental mechanisms can we both determine why so many workers are able to make smooth adjustments, and design appropriate policies for those workers having difficulty in the labor market.

Researchers and policy makers should be wary of excluding low-tenure workers, older workers, those from government and agriculture, or other workers from the population of the displaced until there is an improved understanding of job loss and the adjustments to it. Finally, research itself would progress more rapidly with some modifications in the data sets described herein. The DWS in particular would be a richer data set if retrospective earnings and family income information were available for both displaced workers and other individuals, if geographic and union affiliation variables were available retrospectively and at the time of the survey, if fired workers were isolated from other job losers, and if total years of industry and occupational work experience were known for each worker.

NOTES

Reiko Feaver provided excellent research assistance, supported by a Dana Fellowship at Wellesley College.

1. An example using randomly assigned "treatment" and control groups is Kulik and Bloom (1986). Leigh (chapter 9 of this volume) surveys the evaluation research.

2. Hamermesh (1989) briefly surveys this work. Podgursky and Swaim (1987c) document group health insurance coverage for displaced worker before and after job loss. For reemployed workers, coverage rates were identical. Overall coverage rates were reduced through joblessness.

REFERENCES

Addison, John T., and Pedro Portugal (1989). "Job Displacement, Relative Wage Changes, and the Duration of Unemployment." *Journal of Labor Economics* 7 (July):281–302.

Bendick, Marc, and Judith R. Devine (1982). "Workers Dislocated by Economic Change: Do They Need Federal Employment and Training?" In *National Commission for Employment Policy, Seventh Annual Report*. Washington, D.C.: U.S. Government Printing Office.

Borjas, George J. (1984). "Race, Turnover, and Male Earnings." *Industrial Relations* 23 (Winter): 73–89.

Browne, Lynn E. (1985). "Structural Change and Dislocated Workers." *New England Economic Review* (January/February): 15–30.

D'Amico, Ronald J., and Jeff Golon (1986). "The Displaced Worker: Consequences of Career Interruption among Young Men." In *The Changing Labor Market*, edited by Stephen M. Hills. Lexington, Mass.: Lexington Books.

Devens, Richard M. Jr. (1986). "Displaced Workers: One Year Later." *Monthly Labor Review* (July): 40–44.

Flaim, Paul O., and Ellen Sehgal (1985). "Displaced Workers of 1979–83: How Well Have They Fared?" *Monthly Labor Review* (June): 3–16.

Jacobson, Louis S. (1984). "A Tale of Employment Decline in Two Cities: How Bad Was The Worst Of Times?" *Industrial and Labor Relations Review* 37 (July): 557–69.

Hamermesh, Daniel (1989). "What Do We Know About Worker Displacement in the United States?" *Industrial Relations* 28 (Winter): 51–59.

Horvath, Francis W. (1982). "Forgotten Unemployment: Recall Bias in Retrospective Data." *Monthly Labor Review* (March): 40–43.

Howland, Marie, and George E. Peterson (1988). "Labor Market Conditions and the Reemployment of Displaced Workers." *Industrial and Labor Relations Review* 42 (October): 109–22.

Kruse, Douglas (1988). "International Trade and the Labor Market Experience of Displaced Workers." *Industrial and Labor Relations Review* 41 (April):402–17.

Kulik, Jane, and Howard Bloom (1986). "Evaluation of the Texas Worker Adjustment Demonstration." Cambridge, Mass.: Abt Associates.

Parnes, Herbert, and Randall King (1977). "Middle-Aged Job Losers." *Industrial Gerontology* 4 (Spring): 77–95.

Podgursky, Michael, and Paul Swaim (1987a). "Job Displacement and Earnings Loss: Evidence from the Displaced Worker Survey." *Industrial and Labor Relations Review* 41 (October): 17–29.

—— (1987b). "Duration of Joblessness Following Displacement." *Industrial Relations* 26 (Fall): 213–26.

—— (1987c). "Health Insurance Loss: the Case of the Displaced Worker." *Monthly Labor Review* 110 (April): 30–33.

Ruhm, Christopher J. (1987a). "Job Loss and Job Change: Discussion." *Industrial and Labor Relations Review* 41 (October):47–49.

—— (1987b). "The Economic Consequences of Labor Mobility." *Industrial and Labor Relations Review* 41 (October):30–42.

Seitchik, Adam (1987). "Displaced Workers, Income, and Family Structure." Report to the U.S. Employment and Training Administration, Office of Strategic Planning and Policy Development.

——— (1989). "Labor Displacement Within the New Family Economy." Ph.D. Thesis. Boston: Boston University.

Seitchik, Adam, and Jeffrey Zornitsky (1989). *From One Job to the Next: Worker Adjustment in a Changing Labor Market*. Kalamazoo, Mich.: Upjohn Institute for Employment Research.

Shultz, George P., and Arnold R. Weber (1966). *Strategies for the Displaced Worker*. New York: Harper and Row.

U.S. General Accounting Office (1987). *Plant Closings: Information on Advance Notice and Assistance to Dislocated Workers*. GAO/HRD-87-86BR. Washington, D.C.

CHAPTER THREE

Wage Concessions, Plant Shutdowns, and the Demand for Labor

DANIEL S. HAMERMESH

More Workers Resist Employers' Demands for Pay Concessions. Unions Say Past Givebacks Haven't Saved Any Jobs, See a Ploy to Trim Wages; but Firms Do Close Plants[1]

I. Introduction

The burgeoning literature on worker displacement has generated a substantial number of studies of workers' postdisplacement wages and unemployment. (See Ruhm 1987; Podgursky and Swaim 1987; Kruse 1988; Addison and Portugal 1989; Kletzer 1989; Hamermesh 1989.) Some attention has also been paid to the wage-tenure profiles of displaced workers prior to their displacement (Hamermesh 1987). No one, however, has examined how the wages of displaced workers vary compared to workers who are not displaced, and how that wage variation affects the likelihood of the plant closing. This study seeks to fill that gap by examining a model in which workers contract over wages and employment probabilities with the firm.

With the introduction of the notion of implicit contracts between workers and employers by Azariadis (1975) and Baily (1974) there has come a host of variants on the basic theme of long-term employment relationships. (See Rosen 1985, for a survey of many of these.) This burgeoning of theoretical work has not been matched, however, by a growth in the use of the basic concept to study empirical aspects of labor-market behavior in new ways. Other than a few studies (e.g., Lazear 1979; Raisian 1983) that have used the theory to motivate specific empirical results, its main application has been to make economists more aware of the importance of long-term employment relations in labor markets.

83

In this study workers are viewed as contracting with their employers for a package that includes a probability that the job will exist and an increment in wages above the entry-level wage. They are considered tied to the employer by a wedge between their wage in the firm and the wage they could obtain elsewhere. Using standard assumptions about workers' risk aversion, and a somewhat novel way of specifying employers' profit functions, I analyze the nature of the equilibrium combinations of observed risks (of the job disappearing) and changes in returns to these tenured workers.

The estimates allow one to infer the size of wage concessions that workers must offer to keep plants from closing. The study is thus the first to link analytically and explicitly the issues of plant closings and worker displacement, issues that have received increasing attention in the United States and elsewhere in the past decade.[2] As a very important by-product, the estimates provide a way of inferring parameters describing employment relations that could not otherwise be measured, or could not be measured so appropriately. There is a plethora of estimates of labor-demand elasticities, but very few are based on microeconomic data. As Hamermesh (1986) shows, the use of aggregated data on both the price and quantity of labor induces an inherent simultaneity in these estimates. By inferring elasticities from microeconomic data, this study may provide more precise estimates of this parameter than have heretofore been produced.

II. Contracting and the Risk of Displacement

In this section, I derive the equilibrium relationship between the wage rate received by homogeneous workers and the probability that their jobs will disappear because their employer closes the business. When workers sort themselves among firms, one of the risks they consider is that the job will disappear due to exogenous negative shocks. As with any other such risk, we may assume that the combination of workers' risk aversion and employers' production technologies results in a positive relationship between the observed probability that a plant will close and the wage rate.[3] Workers thus enter firms at a reservation wage W^r that makes them indifferent between choosing between that firm and at least one other. The market produces a compensating differential in the reservation wage at different firms that is positively related to the ex ante expected probability that the firm will close. This reservation wage, including the compensating differential for the firm-specific expected risk of closing, is the basis against which workers compare the wages they receive once they have joined the firm.

Workers who enter employment acquire firm-specific human capital that raises their wage rates above what they could obtain elsewhere, other things, including the expected risk of displacement, being equal. Assume, for the moment, that such training is instantaneous, so that all workers who have joined the firm are identical. I assume that the firm employing these workers faces a known distribution of random prices P, $h(P,S)$, where $P \geq 0$ and S is an index of demand. The index S may be viewed as an exogenous demand shock to markets in which the firm sells, with a higher S shifting the distribution of prices to the right (so that S can be viewed as a positive shock to the market in which the firm sells). I assume the capital stock is fixed at K^* and write the firm's profits as

$$\pi = PX - WL - rK^*,$$

where production is characterized by $X = F(L,K^*)$, W is the wage rate, and r is the cost of capital services.

I assume that wages are set by the firm and its workers at the start of each time period in full knowledge of the state of product-market shocks, as indexed by a particular value of S, say S^*. The firm then draws from the distribution $h(P,S^*)$ and decides whether or not to shut down. Let π^* be the critical level of profits that determines the firm's continued existence. Above this level the firm will stay in business. Below it the firm will close down. Then at this level of profits the product price must be

$$P^* = \frac{\pi^* + WL + rK^*}{X}. \tag{1}$$

This means that the probability the firm will close, p, is

$$p = \int_0^{P^*} h(P,S)\,dP. \tag{2}$$

Equation (2) implicitly defines a relationship between p and W for a given set of exogenous conditions indexed by S. This relationship can be viewed as the set of probabilities that the firm remains in business consistent with each particular wage rate at a given S^*. The probability depends on the distribution of stochastic prices, which is shifted by changes in S. The slope of the relationship is

$$\left(\frac{dp}{dW} \right)_{S=S^*} = h(P^*, S^*)\frac{dP^*}{dW}, \tag{3}$$

85

where

$$\frac{dP^*}{dW} = \frac{[W - P^*F_L]\frac{\partial L}{\partial W} + L}{X}.$$

Now $\frac{dP^*}{dW}$ can be rewritten as

$$\frac{dP^*}{dW} = \frac{L}{X}\left[1 + \eta - \frac{\eta F_L P^*}{W}\right], \tag{4}$$

where η is the total demand elasticity for labor. So long as workers are not paid in excess of their marginal revenue products, we can be sure from equation (3) that $\frac{dP^*}{dW} > 0$, and thus that $\left(\frac{dp}{dW}\right)_{s=s^*} > 0$. The *probabilistic shut-down frontier* for $S = S^*$ is shown in figure 1. It depicts the set of all points along which probabilistic profits are at the competitive minimum given values of W and the state of the market S. Viewed differently, it shows the probability of plant closing at each wage. Favorable shocks shift the frontier to the right, unfavorable ones shift it to the left. (In order to present both sides of the internal labor market, the frontier is drawn with W^r as the origin.)

The typical person attached to the firm is assumed to choose between a higher wage and a reduced risk that the firm will close. Hours of

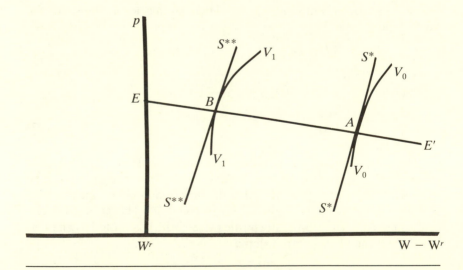

Figure 1   **Internal Labor-Market Equilibria with Random Prices**

86

work are assumed constant; workers simply choose among varying combinations of a wage and an uncertain probability of the job disappearing because the plant closes. I define workers' expected utility after they have taken a job with a particular firm (and acquired firm-specific training) in terms of $W - W^r$, the excess of wages with the employer over what they could obtain outside the firm. The typical worker's expected utility increment from remaining in the firm is, thus,

$$V = [1 - p]U(W - W^r) + pU(0), \quad U' > 0, \quad U'' < 0. \tag{5}$$

Obviously, if W falls below what can be obtained elsewhere, the worker will leave the firm voluntarily. (In order to avoid specifying a quits function, I assume that workers have a knife-edge decision about voluntary turnover. Relaxing this assumption would complicate the model without changing its implications.) I am thus implicitly examining changes in W and p within some limited range. Beyond that range the worker will break the contract with the employer.

Scaling U so that $U(0) = 0$ and setting the total differential of equation (5) equal to zero yields.

$$\left(\frac{dp}{dW}\right)_{V=V^*} = [1 - p]\frac{U'}{U} > 0. \tag{6}$$

Because of the assumptions about U, the indifference map between p and W contains curves that are concave to the origin.[4] A pair of typical indifference curves V_0 and V_1 is shown in figure 1. Combinations of wage rates and risks of plant closing along V_0 are preferred to those along V_1, for at each wage rate along the former the risk of losing the job is lower.

Equilibrium in the internal labor market is defined by the tangency of the indifference curve to the probabilistic shut-down frontier for fixed S^*, that is, at the point where

$$\left(\frac{dp}{dW}\right)_{S=S^*} = \left(\frac{dp}{dW}\right)_{V=V^*}. \tag{7}$$

The presence of firm-specific investment to some extent insulates the average worker from random shocks to product demand. For that reason the equilibrium is drawn for the average set of exogenous conditions, S^*, at point A in the first quadrant of figure 1. A shock to this equilibrium, for example, a negative shock that lowers S to S^{**} such that the probability mass of h is shifted to the left, produces a new equilibrium on the new shut-down frontier $S^{**}S^{**}$ in figure 1. Without specific assumptions about the shape of the zero-profit frontier, one cannot determine the slope of EE', the locus of equilibrium combinations (p, W). However, as I show in section III, under very reasonable assumptions the locus has the negative slope shown in figure 1.

The discussion has dealt with the contractual relationship between a worker and an employer in a firm whose continued existence is uncertain. The event under consideration—the demise of a plant or firm—is distinctly nonmarginal. Using the mechanisms of a minimum required rate of profit and workers' attitudes toward risk, the analysis explains why some plants or firms shut down rather than make marginal changes that would allow them to continue in existence if technology were neoclassical and there were individualized wage-setting.

The analysis applies to the discussion of plant closings and not to permanent layoffs from continuing enterprises. While the employers' side could be applied *mutatis mutandis* to analyze layoffs, changing the worker's side appropriately would require specifying a utility map that includes both workers' beliefs about their own probabilities of being subject to layoff should S decrease and a mechanism for ordering layoffs. (See Wright 1986, for an analysis that embodies such a mechanism.) Without these changes the model as presented in this section is not likely to go far in explaining layoff behavior. It is a model of plant closings, not a model of layoffs.

III. Estimating Equations and Data

To move from the set of equilibrium points defined by equation (7) under various values of S to an equation that allows inferences to be drawn about the shape of the locus of equilibria, we need to specify the shapes of the utility and production functions. In the case of the former, let

$$U = \frac{[W - W^r]^{1-\delta}}{[1 - \delta]}, \qquad \delta < 1,$$

a standard form, where δ is a measure of relative risk aversion. Then from equation (6),

$$\left(\frac{dp}{dW}\right)_{V=V^*} = \frac{[1 - p][1 - \delta]}{[W - W^r]} . \tag{8}$$

On the firm's side, very little can be concluded about the convexity or concavity of the zero-profit frontier without making very restrictive assumptions about the density function $h(P,S)$. Being unwilling to make these assumptions about the distribution of prices, I instead assume a linear approximation to equation (3), and let

$$\left(\frac{dp}{dW}\right)_{S=S^*} = \gamma. \tag{9}$$

Throughout the discussion thus far I have assumed that labor is homogeneous in production when it enters the firm and is then instantaneously trained. This assumption ignores the likelihood that the shared investment in firm-specific human capital that generates a wedge between workers' productivity and their wage is made over a long period of time. Assume, therefore, that effective units of labor, L', are related to nominal units, L, by

$$L' = LG(TN), \qquad \text{where } G(0) = 1, \ G' > 0, \ G'' < 0,$$

following the evidence that the amount of firm-specific human capital embodied in workers increases at a decreasing rate with their tenure, TN, in the firm (e.g., Mincer and Jovanovic 1981). The training adds more to workers' productivity than it does to their wages, and the difference widens over much of the range of TN. Then the slope in equations (3) and (4) can be rewritten as

$$\left(\frac{dp}{dW}\right)_{S=S^*} = G(TN)h(P^*,S^*) \frac{L}{X} \left[1 + \eta - \frac{\eta F_L P^*}{W}\right].$$

Equation (9) then becomes

$$\left(\frac{dp}{dW}\right)_{S=S^*} = \gamma G(TN). \tag{9'}$$

The empirical counterpart to the equilibrium condition in equation (7) is, thus,

$$p = -\frac{\gamma[W - W^r]G(TN)}{1 - \delta} + 1. \tag{10}$$

The estimating equation linearizes equation (10), assumes that some of the variables Z that determine δ are indicators of the degree of workers' relative risk aversion, and writes wages in logarithms.[5] Because workers' initial choices among firms were based on the expected risk of displacement, the reservation wage too will be positively related to the probability of displacement and should be included in the equation. W^r is therefore added to equation (10') to reflect the compensating wage

89

differential that differences in the ex ante risks of plant closings should produce between entry-level wages in the firm and the returns to otherwise identical workers. The basic estimating equation is

$$p = a_0 - a_1[\ln W - \ln W^r] + a_2 \ln W^r - a_3G(TN) + a_4H(Z). \quad (10')$$

If the hypotheses put forth here are correct: (1) The term in $[\ln W - \ln W^r]$ will have an inverse relation to p. Shocks to the distribution of prices will cause the internal labor market to trace out a locus of temporary equilibria like that shown in figure 1. (2) A quadratic in tenure will have alternating negative and positive coefficients. This results from the extra value added to the firm's net worth by the firm-specific human capital that is indicated by greater worker tenure, an increment whose value diminishes with additional tenure. (3) Any variable in Z that indicates greater relative risk aversion by workers will have a negative effect on p.

The ideal set of data for estimating equation $(10')$ would be a longitudinal matched worker-employer sample that contained information on workers' characteristics, their wages and the level of employment in their workplace. (See Hamermesh 1991.) No such set of data exists, nor is there even a close approximation. Lacking this appropriate source, I base the analysis on a longitudinal set of household data. I assume that the individuals represent the universe of worker-firm matches that contains plants that close and others that continue in existence. The data come from the Panel Study of Income Dynamics. The file of household heads was searched to find all those who reported that they had left their previous jobs some time in 1977–81 because the plant shut down (displaced workers) or because they were laid off permanently (laid-off workers). The PSID is unique among major data sets in distinguishing between these two types of involuntary job-leavers, a distinction that is crucial in estimating the model derived above. The restriction that data on all the required variables be available left samples of 114 displaced workers and 203 permanent layoffs. Data on 2533 household heads who were not displaced or permanently laid off during this five-year period were also added to the working data file.

This file was selected to increase the number of households who experienced the uncommon event—job displacement—above the population percentage. The choice-based sampling procedure reduces the randomness associated with the sample statistics calculated on the displaced and laid-off subsamples separately; it also results in probit estimation of equation $(10')$ yielding a biased constant term and biased standard errors. Accordingly, I estimate equation $(10')$ using the weighted

90

exogenous sampling maximum likelihood (WESML) estimator of Manski and Lerman (1977). The weight on each observation is the ratio of its population percentage (based on data for *all* household heads in the PSID) to its frequency in the sample. Given the sampling scheme I have used, the WESML estimates of equation (10') weight the observations on displaced and laid-off workers less heavily than those on nonseparated workers.

For each involuntarily separated worker denote by T the year the person was reported as separated. Then p_T is a dichotomous variable indicating whether or not the worker was displaced (laid-off in some of the estimates) between years $T - 1$ and T. The data are available both for hourly-paid workers and for salaried workers. The wage rate immediately before involuntary separation, denoted by W_{T-1}, is used to represent the worker's wage. To represent W^r I note that even the random components of workers' wages on their most recent jobs affect their search behavior (Kiefer and Neumann 1979; Feldstein and Poterba 1984). That being the case, W^r is measured as the worker's wage at time $T - 2$, minus an adjustment equal to the wage effect of the worker's tenure with the firm.[6] Years of tenure with the employer measure TN. Because data on wages at $T - 1$ and $T - 2$ are required, the sample is restricted to workers who have been with the firm for at least one year at the time of displacement. Since the underlying theory is based on contracting, and since workers with less than one year of tenure are less likely to have established a contractual relationship with the employer, the necessity of restricting the sample in order to observe two years' wages causes no problems.

It is difficult to determine what variables to include in the vector Z, as there has been little empirical work establishing the correlates of risk aversion in the labor market. Partly following Thaler and Rosen (1975) I include years of education (EDUC), and dummy variables for union membership (UNION) and race (BLACK) in Z. Presumably, ignoring issues of selection, more schooling reduces risk aversion, while membership in a union or in a minority group increases it. Clearly, however, these are merely expectations based on casual observation and are not in any sense derivable.

Data on industry-specific output shocks are available, but do not belong in equation (10'). Such shocks are what move workers and firms along the equilibrium locus EE'; they do not shift the locus. These data were collected, though not included in the probits, to examine whether negative shocks are associated with leftward movements along the locus. The particular data used to measure lagged percentage changes in output between $T - 1$ and $T - 2$, and $T - 2$ and $T - 3$, ΔY_{T-1} and ΔY_{T-2}, are series on output in the two-digit industry in which the household head worked at time $T - 1$.

IV. Estimates of the Locus of Equilibria

Before examining the shape of the locus EE', let us compare the characteristics of displaced workers to those of other workers. Table 1 shows statistics describing the subsamples, with the data weighted to reflect the fractions of all household heads in each category during the

Table 1	**Means and Their Standard Errors**		
	(1) Displaced	(2) Not separated involuntarily	(3) Laid off
$\ln (W_{T-1}) - \ln (W^r_{T-2})$	.081 (.03)	.150 (.01)	.128 (.02)
WKS_{T-1}	42.37 (1.14)	46.87 (.25)	40.68 (1.16)
WKS_{T-2}	47.11 (.77)	47.12 (.24)	49.05 (.94)
HRS_{T-1}	43.98 (1.05)	42.75 (.27)	43.42 (.85)
HRS_{T-2}	43.72 (.92)	42.89 (.27)	44.49 (.47)
TN_{T-1}	7.84 (.82)	8.02 (.16)	4.59 (.29)
UNION	.291 (.04)	.331 (.01)	.332 (.03)
BLACK	.367 (.05)	.320 (.01)	.589 (.04)
EDUC	11.03 (.30)	11.96 (.08)	11.63 (.27)
ΔY_{T-1}	3.43 (.59)	4.34 (.11)	2.48 (.50)
ΔY_{T-2}	2.55 (.50)	3.78 (.13)	3.00 (.45)
$\ln W^r_{T-2}$	6.16 (.10)	6.23 (.03)	6.43 (.11)
Manufacturing	.418 (.05)	.349 (.01)	.375 (.03)
Number in sample	114	2,522	203

five years, 1977–1981. As table 1 clearly indicates, displaced workers on average received significantly smaller wage increases the year before their plants closed than did other workers. This simple difference in means suggests that the equilibrium locus has the expected negative slope.

Aside from these differences, however, the two groups differ in only three respects: (1) The displaced workers suffer a sharp decline in weeks worked during the calendar year before they report having been displaced. This decline is not accompanied by any measured drop in the intensity of work: Hours stay roughly constant for this group of workers. The decline may thus be an artifact of the timing of interviews, insofar as some workers were displaced well before the end of the previous year and reported reduced weeks at work during that year. In any case, it is noteworthy that their weeks worked were essentially the same as those of other workers two years before displacement. (2) The average educational attainment of displaced workers is significantly below that of other workers. (3) Output changes in the industries in which displaced workers were employed were below those in the industries where the sample of nonseparated workers held jobs, implying that shocks to output did move workers and firms leftward along an EE' locus. In all other respects, particularly in years of tenure with the employer, workers whose plants close are not significantly different from those who are not separated involuntarily.[7]

It is interesting to note that displaced workers as a group differ in several important respects from workers who are laid-off permanently (on whom data are shown in the third column of table 1). Unlike displaced workers, employees who were permanently laid off received wage increases during the year before layoff that did not differ significantly from those received by other workers. Also, and not surprisingly, given the prevalence of seniority rules even in nonunion workplaces (see Abraham and Medoff 1984), the average tenure of permanent layoffs is significantly below that of other workers, including displaced workers.[8] Also, laid-off workers had significantly higher wage rates than nonseparated workers. These considerations corroborate our expectation in section II that the process that induces permanent layoffs is basically different from that which generates the wage-employment outcomes observed before and during plant closings.

Equation (10') is estimated over the 2636 displaced and nonseparated workers using weighted probit (WESML) analysis, with the results for the complete specification, and for selected modifications of (10'), presented for displaced workers in table 2. The standard errors that are

Table 2 **Probit Analysis of the Probability of Displacement**[a]
(N = 2636)

	(1)	(2)	(3)	(4)
Constant	−1.916	−1.833	−.528	−.744
	(−26.36)	(−15.02)	(−.69)	(−.97)
$\ln(W_{T-1}) - \ln(W_{T-2})$	−.587	−.579	−.701	−.629
	(−1.74)	(−3.85)	(−3.58)	(−5.56)
TN_{T-1}		−.0246	−.0230	−.0289
		(−1.04)	(−0.96)	(−1.20)
TN^2_{T-1}		.00088	.00088	.00094
		(1.11)	(1.08)	(1.17)
$\ln(W_{T-2})$			−.210	−.0834
			(−1.73)	(−1.19)
Black				−.0265
				(−.19)
Years of school				−.0437
				(−1.94)
Union				−.0768
				(−.58)
$\ln L$	−465.06	−463.52	−459.79	−456.77

[a]The effect of a unit increase in a particular variable on p is its coefficient estimate times .0539.

used to compute t-statistics were calculated using the matrices suggested by Manski and Lerman (1977). The simple bivariate probit of the probability of displacement on the previous period's percentage wage change shows that shocks that increase the probability of displacement also significantly reduce the wage increase. The slope of this relationship is fairly small, −.034: Each 1% drop in real wage growth is associated with an increase in the probability of the plant closing of .00034. Since the mean probability of plant closing is .023, a 1% wage decrease is associated with a 1.5% increase in the probability the plant closes. This suggests that, while the absolute effect on the probability of closing is small, so that most of the impact of a shock is taken up by reductions in wage growth, the relative effect is fairly substantial.

When quadratic terms in tenure are added to the basic bivariate probit, the results (in column [2]) provide some confirmation of the idea that the firm shares ownership in an asset that adds more to output than to costs. There is a U-shaped response of the probability that the worker will be displaced (that a plant closes) to increases in workers' tenure. Since the theory of investment in on-the-job training suggests that the stock of this type of training increases at a decreasing rate with tenure,

94

and since I viewed firm-specific training as augmenting the value of raw labor, I expected these effects on the probability of displacement. At the mean of tenure in the sample of 2636 displaced and nonseparated workers, the marginal effect of a year of tenure on the probability the plant closes is $-.00076$. Though its absolute effect is quite small, relative to the mean probability of displacement additional firm-specific experience substantially reduces the probability that the firm will close. The embodiment of additional firm-specific human capital in its work force partly insulates the firm from product-market shocks.

Although the results on tenure are not very significant, it is worth thinking about what they imply about the nature of relationships between firms and workers. It is impossible to infer from the wage-tenure relationships in standard earnings equations whether the results reflect firm-specific investment, learning without investment, or payment by seniority to provide incentives not to shirk. While the admittedly weak results on the effects of tenure in table 2 do not permit one to distinguish between the first two explanations, it is difficult to concoct an explanation for them based on incentives to avoid shirking. Indeed, since the difference between wages and productivity rises with tenure in models of shirking, the value of the firm will fall as average tenure increases, other things equal. This means that we would observe firms with a work force with greater tenure being more liable to close when faced with a negative demand shock. Obviously, one piece of empirical work hardly provides a definitive test of two hypotheses that have hitherto been observationally indistinguishable. However, the results do point the way toward further tests, and do indicate the tendency of some preliminary evidence.

The estimates in columns (3) and (4) of table 2 reflect the inclusion of ln W^r and of terms designed to capture proxies for workers' preferences toward risk. The results in column (4) contain the full specification in equation (10'). The derivation in section III indicated that characteristics that might be expected to proxy a higher degree of relative risk aversion will have a negative effect on the probability of displacement, other things equal. Only one of the three estimated parameters is significantly different from zero (and its sign is unexpected); but the other two, those on union status and race, have the expected negative signs. Perhaps the best conclusion from these disappointing results is that it is difficult to find readily available empirical proxies for attitudes toward risk. Unexplained heterogeneity is all one can identify as causing differences among workers in how they respond to shocks to product demand among otherwise identical firms.

Contrary to the derivation, there is a significant negative effect of a

Table 3   Probit Analysis of the Probability of Permanent Layoff[a]
(N = 2725)

	(1)	(2)	(3)	(4)
Constant	−1.706	−1.455	.424	−.642
	(−26.61)	(−15.31)	(.69)	(−1.49)
$\ln(W_{T-1}) - \ln(W_{T-2})$	−.265	−.215	−.340	−.213
	(−1.02)	(−.87)	(−1.30)	(−.77)
TN_{T-1}		−.0340	−.0306	−.0453
		(−1.95)	(−1.45)	(−1.85)
TN_{T-1}^2		−.00095	−.00102	−.00071
		(−1.86)	(−1.61)	(−.99)
$\ln(W_{T-2}^r)$			−.305	−.0562
			(−3.02)	(−.80)
Black				.320
				(2.95)
Years of school				−.0498
				(−2.88)
Union				.0656
				(.70)
$\ln L$	−721.24	−689.77	−678.24	−660.69

[a]The effect of a unit increase in a particular variable on p is its coefficient estimate times .0871.

worker's market wage rate on the probability that the plant will close. Apparently, as is common in the literature on compensating wage differentials (e.g., Brown 1980), the trade-off between security and the wage rate is more than offset by the income effect of higher earnings on the demand for security. From this point of view, it is not surprising that the negative effect of ln W^r becomes much smaller and less significant once the vector of three variables is added, since the variables I have modelled as reflecting tastes can also be viewed as reflecting market opportunities.[9]

Summarizing the results as a whole, a number of the factors discussed in section III do have the expected effects on the probability of a plant closing. None of the effects is very large in absolute terms. Relative to the underlying chance that a worker will be displaced, though, they are quite substantial.

An examination of the same weighted probits estimated for the probability of permanent layoff (shown in table 3) shows that the predictions of the derivations in section II apply only when one can assume that there is an identifiable locus of equilibria between workers' preferences and firms' probabilistic shut-down frontiers. The sample consists of the 203 laid-off workers and the same group of non-separated workers used in the estimates shown in table 2. As suggested by the means in table 1, the relationship between the probability of permanent layoff and wage change in the previous year is much weaker than in the sample of displaced and other workers. Indeed, while there is a negative relationship between $\ln W - \ln W^r$ and the probability of permanent layoff, it is never significant at conventional levels.

In Hamermesh (1987) I demonstrated a substantial flattening of wage-tenure profiles among workers who would later experience permanent layoff, but no flattening among those whose plants would later close. I interpreted this to mean that the probability of permanent layoff becomes clear to workers much earlier before the event occurs than does the probability of displacement. Here one can interpret the difference in the results between tables 2 and 3 as reflecting the unwillingness of workers in plants where wage structures exist to accept wage cuts that at best will reduce the probability of layoff for a few (junior) workers, but will surely reduce the wages received by all workers. On the other hand, workers seeing a shock that increases the probability that the entire plant will close are willing to accept a general reduction in wage growth that reduces in part the increased risk that they will all lose their jobs.

The supporting evidence provided by the coefficients on the terms in *TN* in the probits for displacement is not observed in these probits. Increased tenure does reduce the probability of permanent layoff; but there is no quadratic effect of opposite sign.[10] As in the weighted probits describing displacement, the union status variable is insignificant; the dummy variable for race, and the measure of schooling attainment too, have coefficients that are significantly different from zero. However, these variables affect the probability of permanent layoff in directions that differ in all three cases from what we predicted, but that support what evidence from other sets of data leads one to expect: There is a higher probability of permanent layoff with union status, among blacks and with lower educational attainment.[11]

V. Applications of the Estimates

The probit coefficients in table 2 can be used in conjunction with the derivation of equation (10') to examine two aspects of labor-market behavior. The general idea is to note that each point along the estimated probit represents an equilibrium of an indifference curve and a probabilistic shut-down frontier, and to infer something more about their shapes and locations under specific assumptions about the nature of these maps. The inferences rest on approximations that hold only locally around the locus of equilibria; but in that region the assumptions, together with the notion of a probabilistic shut-down frontier, enable us to analyze labor-market behavior in ways not heretofore possible. Although the major focus is on the relationship between wage concessions and displacement, I deal first with inferring labor-demand elasticities, as that discussion provides a useful introduction to measuring the relationship of major interest.

A. Labor-Demand Elasticities

Throughout I assume that workers' indifference maps are homothetic around the point of equilibrium. I assume that the map of probabilistic shut-down frontiers is homothetic too, though I relax that assumption in some of the calculations. The approach can be used to infer the typical firm's "demand elasticity" for an individual worker. With both maps homothetic the slope of the shut-down frontier at a point on the equilibrium locus is the inverse of the slope of that locus. The resulting measure is not a standard total labor-demand elasticity, since it does not relate employment levels to wage levels. Rather, it is an analogue that can be made comparable to standard estimates if we assume that the rate of change in the individual worker's probability of employment induced by higher wages equals the expected percentage decline in the typical firm's demand for workers.

At the mean values of all the variables a fraction p of all workers will be displaced in each time period if demand conditions in the typical firm are indexed along the particular shut-down frontier S^*S^*. An increase in ln W will raise this fraction, so that in percentage terms the effect of a 1% increase in wages is

$$p\left(\frac{\partial p}{\partial \ln W}\right)_{S=S^*}.$$

Since the change in ln W is just the change along the horizontal axis in a version of figure 1 that has $w = \ln W - \ln W^r$ on the horizontal axis, we can measure the slope of S^*S^* as the inverse of the slope of the EE' locus.

If the probabilistic shut-down frontiers do not exhibit parallel shifts as demand shocks occur, the linear approximation to their slopes at the locus of equilibria will be incorrect. Consider figure 2, which shows $\overline{CD'}/\overline{AC}$, the slope of the equilibrium locus EE' at a particular point A.

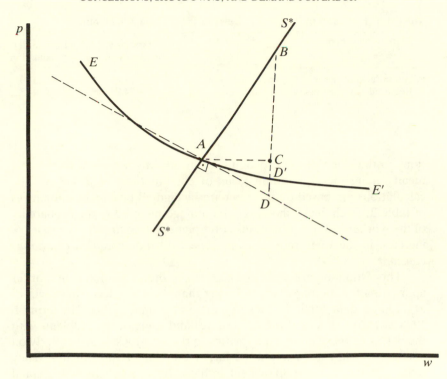

Figure 2   **Calculating the Slope of S***

The frontier tangent to the indifference curve at A is S^*S^*. As the particular example is drawn, the inverse of the slope of EE' at A over-states the slope of S^*S^*, for EE' is becoming flatter as w increases. Thus the slope of S^*S^*, $\overline{BC}/\overline{AC}$, should be calculated as $\overline{AC/CD}$ rather than as $\overline{AC/CD'}$. To accomplish this I use a second-order approximation to EE' and infer that

$$\frac{\overline{BC}}{\overline{AC}} = \left[\frac{\partial p}{\partial W}\right]^{-1} \left[1 - \frac{\partial^2 p/\partial W^2}{\partial p/\partial W}\right].$$

This modification corrects the estimate of the slope of S^* for the chang-ing slope of EE', a change that in turn is assumed to be produced by the possible nonhomotheticity of the family of probabilistic shut-down frontiers.[12]

The first row of table 4 shows the first- and second-order approxima-

99

Table 4   Estimates of Parameters Derived from Table 2, Column (4)

	First-order approximation	Second-order approximation
a. Labor-demand elasticity	−.86	−.37
b. Required wage concession, in percent	−34.93	−34.97

tions to the slope of the probabilistic shut-down frontier at the sample means along the equilibrium locus of combinations of p and w. The calculations are based on the estimated weighted probits in column (4) of table 2. Each figure shows the percentage increase in the probability of the worker losing a job because of a plant closing in response to a 1% increase in the wage rate, *holding expected product-market conditions constant.*

The estimates are well in line, or, in the case of the first-order approximation, perhaps slightly higher than those produced in studies of aggregated data for industries or entire economies. (See Hamermesh 1986, for a discussion of these estimates and some of the problems with them.) Since the estimated elasticities in this study are based entirely on micro data, they are likely to be larger than standard estimates. They reflect all changes in employment induced by wage changes in a small unit, instead of netting out employment increases in other firms and among other demographic groups that occur in an industry or economy when a particular wage increases. That they are not much larger than commonly-cited estimates indicates that the gross-net distinction is not particularly vital. This suggests that using aggregate estimates to infer the likely impacts of proposed changes in taxes on or subsidies to wages may not create very large errors.

B. The Response to Product-Market Shocks

The estimates of section IV can also be used to infer the size of the wage concession required to keep a plant's probability of closing constant when a negative demand shock occurs. In light of the recent interest in wage concessions (e.g., Mitchell 1982, 1985), these estimates should indicate both the extent of the concessions needed to prevent employment declines when product demand drops, and the willingness of workers to offer these concessions. Examining a few collective bargaining situations (e.g., Gerhart 1987) that describe responses to threat-

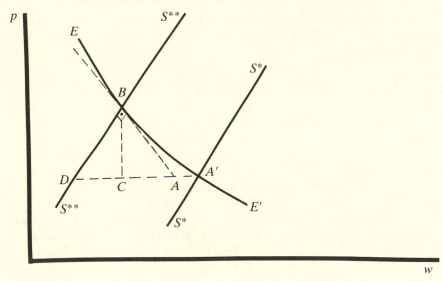

Figure 3   **Calculating Required Wage Concessions**

ened plant closings can be very useful. The calculations here, though, provide a more general set of evidence on the issue. They explicitly link wage concessions to employment protection, which is, after all, the concessions' ostensible purpose.

Consider the schematic in figure 3, in which I assume a negative demand shock has shifted the probabilistic shut-down frontier from S^*S^* to $S^{**}S^{**}$. A wage concession of $\overline{A'D}$ will be required if the probability of plant closing is not to rise above what it was at A'. It will not be optimal for workers to offer this large a concession, as D is not on the locus of equilibria. The firm and the typical worker are better off accepting a higher risk of plant closing than keeping the risk constant by agreeing to a larger wage decline. I calculate it in order to indicate what is needed, not what will occur. Assume one knows the size of the increase in the probability of closing, $\overline{BC}$, that accompanies a move from A' to B. If both the equilibrium locus EE' and the new zero-profit frontier $S^{**}S^{**}$ were linear, I could calculate the required wage decrease $\overline{A'D} = \overline{A'C} + \overline{CD}$ as $\{[\partial p/\partial W]^{-1} + \partial p/\partial W\}$ times the change in the probability of displacement, $\overline{BC}$, that would have otherwise occurred. While I cannot adjust for the possible nonlinearity of $S^{**}S^{**}$ I can obtain a better measure of the true distance $\overline{CD}$ by making the same

101

second-order approximation used before. In particular, the corrected decrease required to keep the probability of displacement from rising by an amount $\overline{BC}$ is

$$\overline{A'D} = \overline{A'C} + \overline{CD} = \left\{ \left[\frac{\partial p}{\partial W} \right]^{-1} + \frac{\partial p}{\partial W} \left[1 - \frac{\partial^2 p / \partial W^2}{\partial p / \partial W} \right] \right\} \overline{BC}.$$

Assuming that p would rise by .01 in response to a particular shock ($\overline{BC}$ = .01), the estimates of the percentage change in wages required to return the probability of displacement to its preshock level are shown in the second row of table 4. The flatness of the equilibrium locus guarantees that the required wage cuts are quite large. Decreases of over 30% are needed to prevent the probability of plant closing from rising by one percentage point when a negative shock occurs. (Of course, a one percentage-point rise in this probability represents a 41.8% increase in the risk that the plant closes.) The behavior implicit in the estimated equilibrium locus perhaps explains why workers are loath to make wage concessions to "save jobs": The required concessions are so large relative to their effect on the probability of retaining employment that even risk-averse workers would take the increased probability of the plant closing rather than accept the certainty of a substantial cut in pay. Given the shapes of utility functions and probabilistic shut-down frontiers, it is socially optimal for workers to bear this increased risk rather than take larger pay cuts.[13]

Pay cuts of the magnitude needed to hold constant the probability of plant closing are not accepted because uncertainty about this probability makes their acceptance an inferior solution from the worker's point of view. However, the estimates in table 2 clearly show that some wage cuts are accepted in response to negative product-market shocks. This stands in sharp contrast to the suggestion of Lawrence and Lawrence (1985) that, as part of bargaining in the face of declining demand, unions and firms will agree to above-average wage increases. It may be true that such increases are observed in isolated cases of declining product demand; our results show, though, that they do not describe the responses of most firms and their employees.

VI. Conclusions

In this study I have developed a contracting approach to examining plant closings. These are viewed as probabilistic events whose likelihood is exogenously changed by variations in product demand, and is also affected by workers' attitudes toward risk and by firms' technology. The exogenous shocks interact with the taste and technology parameters to produce a locus of equilibrium combinations of wage changes and probabilities of plant closings. Because workers' tenure represents an asset that produces quasi-rents for the firm (as well as quasi-rents for workers in the form of higher wages), changes in workers' tenure affect the relation between wage changes and the probability of plant closing when a shock occurs.

This approach is examined using data from the Panel Study of Income Dynamics, the only available longitudinal data set that distinguishes people who have lost their jobs due to plant closings from those separated involuntarily for other reasons. The estimates based on these data show the expected negative relation between wage changes and the probability of plant closing. Additional years of worker tenure are shown to reduce the probability of plant closing at a fixed rate of wage changes; and the marginal reduction diminishes as tenure rises, implying the same quadratic shape to the relationship between the quantity of firm-specific human capital and its empirical proxy, tenure with the firm, as is implied by estimated wage-tenure relations.

The results on the determinants of the probability of plant closing allow one to infer that negative demand shocks have to be met with wage increases far below average if increases in the probability of shutdown are to be avoided. Workers who accept small cuts in wages as a way of staving off the closing of their plant are unlikely to be successful. This suggests one reason for workers' resistance to wage concessions in the face of what often seems like a riskier labor market: Why accept the certainty of a substantial wage cut in return for only a small reduction in the risk that the plant will close?

If nothing else, the estimates demonstrate clearly the simple empirical fact that average wages grow less rapidly in plants that will soon close. I use these results to support an underlying model of internal labor markets in which firms and the workers tied to them respond to exogenous shocks by accepting wage changes and a new probability of plant shut-down. To refine the approach and link the estimates still more closely to the underlying model, one needs data that allow the inference of specific forms of the underlying utility functions and probabilistic shut-down frontiers, thus obviating the need to make the assumptions required here.

Data linking firms and workers are needed to permit better estimates to be drawn. The estimates provided here are generally significant; and the approach to the problem finds additional support from the conjunction of its good description of wage dynamics in plants that close and its failure to describe wage changes of workers who are laid off from plants that continue to operate. The estimates are not always significant, a failing that may result from the small sample of displaced workers in the total PSID. Longitudinal data on larger samples of displaced workers and their employers are clearly necessary if we are to understand the wage and employment dynamics that result from demand shocks.

NOTES

Work on this project was funded by the National Science Foundation, grant SES-8408206. Helpful comments were provided by Harry Holzer, Steven Matusz, participants in the NBER Summer Institute and in seminars at several universities, and especially by Jack Meyer. Francis Cheung provided excellent programming and research assistance. Some of the material in this article appeared previously in the *Review of Economics and Statistics,* November 1988.

1. *Wall Street Journal,* October 13, 1982, page 1.

2. See Congressional Budget Office (1982) for a discussion of the magnitude of the plant-closing problem; Hamermesh (1987) for an analysis of its social costs; and Mitchell (1982, 1985) for a discussion of the growth of wage concessions in union contracts.

3. While this relationship has not heretofore been tested, the argument is, of course, the same as that of Rosen (1974) and has been applied to estimating the relationships between wage rates and various job-related risks.

4. Differentiating in equation (6), one sees that under standard assumptions,

$$\frac{d^2p}{dW^2} = \frac{[1 - p][UU'' - U'^2]}{U^2} < 0.$$

5. This transformation is made to scale the wage measure to account for the heterogeneity of general training among workers as they enter the firm.

6. The size of the adjustment is based on standard wage equations estimated over the entire sample for year $T - 1$ and including the usual array of demographic variables, industry dummy variables, education, total experience and its square, and years of tenure and its square. Because the observations come from different years, wage rates are made comparable across calendar time by inflating using the growth in private nonfarm hourly earnings between the time each W is observed and 1980.

7. While 59% of displaced workers have five or fewer years' tenure at time $T - 1$, 25% had more than ten years' tenure with their employer at that time.

8. Only 8% have more than ten years' tenure with their employer.

9. The results on this measure, on $\ln W - \ln W^r$ and on the tenure variables differ only slightly when $\ln W^r$ is defined as $\ln W_{T-2}$, unadjusted for differences in tenure.

10. Though the individual terms in TN in the probits in columns (2)–(4) are not

highly significant, $\partial p/\partial TN$ is significantly negative, as the existence of rules requiring layoffs by inverse seniority suggests will be the case.

11. See Blau and Kahn (1981) for evidence on layoffs using data on young men and women from the NLS.

12. The correction is equivalent to a Maclaurin-series approximation to the equilibrium locus, as David Hamermesh has pointed out.

13. One union leader noted, "But, worker concessions won't save our jobs, revive our industries or help the economy" (Tony Mazzocchi, OCAW District 8, in Worker's Policy Project, *It's Time for Management Concessions.* New York, 1983).

REFERENCES

Abraham, Katharine G., and James L. Medoff (1984). "Length of Service and Layoffs in Union and Nonunion Work Groups." *Industrial and Labor Relations Review* 38 (October): 87–97.

Addison, John T., and Pedro Portugal (1989). "On the Costs of Worker Displacement: The Case of Dissipated Firm-Specific Training Investments." *Southern Economic Journal* 55 (July): 166–82.

Azariadis, Costas. (1975). "Implicit Contracts and Underemployment Equilibria." *Journal of Political Economy* 83 (December): 1183–1202.

Baily, Martin N. (1974). "Wages and Unemployment under Uncertain Demand." *Review of Economic Studies* 41 (January): 37–50.

Blau, Francine D., and Lawrence M. Kahn (1981). "Causes and Consequences of Layoffs." *Economic Inquiry* 19 (April): 270–96.

Brown, Charles (1980). "Equalizing Differences in the Labor Market." *Quarterly Journal of Economics* 94 (February): 113–34.

Congressional Budget Office (1982). *Dislocated Workers: Issues and Federal Options.* Washington, D.C.: Government Printing Office.

Feldstein, Martin S., and James M. Poterba (1984). "Unemployment Insurance and Reservation Wages." *Journal of Public Economics* 23 (February/March): 141–67.

Gerhart, Paul F. (1987). *Saving Plants and Jobs.* Kalamazoo, Mich.: W. E. Upjohn Institute. 1987.

Hamermesh, Daniel S. (1986). "The Demand for Labor in the Long Run." In *Handbook of Labor Economics,* edited by Orley Ashenfelter and Richard Layard. Amsterdam: North-Holland Press.

——— (1987). "The Costs of Worker Displacement." *Quarterly Journal of Economics* 102 (February): 51–75.

——— (1989). "What Do We Know About Worker Displacement in the United States?" *Industrial Relations* 28 (Winter): 51–59.

——— (1991). "Data Difficulties in Labor Economics." In *Fifty Years of Economic Measurement,* edited by Ernst R. Berndt and Jack E. Triplett. Chicago: University of Chicago Press.

Kiefer, Nicholas M., and George R. Neumann (1979). "An Empirical Job Search Model, with a Test of the Constant-Reservation-Wage Hypothesis." *Journal of Political Economy* 87 (February): 89–107.

Kletzer, Lori Gladstein (1989). "Returns to Seniority After Permanent Job Loss." *American Economic Review* 79 (July): 536–43.

Kruse, Douglas L. (1988). "International Trade and the Labor Market Experience of Displaced Workers." *Industrial and Labor Relations Review* 41 (April): 402–17.

Lawrence, Colin, and Robert Lawrence (1985). "Manufacturing Wage Dispersion: An End Game Interpretation." *Brookings Papers on Economic Activity* 1: 47–106.

Lazear, Edward P. (1979). "Why Is There Mandatory Retirement?" *Journal of Political Economy* 87 (December): 1261–84.

Manski, Charles F., and Steven R. Lerman (1977). "The Estimation of Choice Probabilities from Choice-Based Samples." *Econometrica* 45 (November): 1977–88.

Mincer, Jacob, and Boyan Jovanovic (1981). "Labor Mobility and Wages." In *Studies in Labor Markets,* edited by Sherwin Rosen. Chicago: University of Chicago Press.

Mitchell, Daniel J. B. (1982). "Recent Union Contract Concessions." *Brookings Papers on Economic Activity* 1: 165–201.

——— (1985). "Shifting Norms in Wage Determination." *Brookings Papers on Economic Activity* 2: 575–99.

Podgursky, Michael, and Paul Swaim (1987). "Job Displacement and Earnings Loss: Evidence from the Displaced Worker Survey." *Industrial and Labor Relations Review* 41 (October): 17–29.

Raisian, John (1983). "Contracts, Job Experience, and Cyclical Labor Market Adjustment." *Journal of Labor Economics* 1 (April): 131–51.

Rosen, Sherwin (1974). "Hedonic Prices and Implicit Markets." *Journal of Political Economy* 82 (January): 34–55.

——— (1985). "Implicit Contracts." *Journal of Economic Literature* 23 (September): 1144–75.

Ruhm, Christopher J. (1987). "The Economic Consequences of Labor Mobility." *Industrial and Labor Relations Review* 41 (October): 30–42.

Thaler, Richard H., and Sherwin Rosen (1975). "The Value of Saving a Life: Evidence from the Labor Market." In *Household Production and Consumption,* edited by Nestor Terleckyj. New York: Columbia University Press.

Wright, Randall (1986). "The Redistributive Roles of Unemployment Insurance and the Dynamics of Voting." *Journal of Public Economics* 31 (December): 377–99.

CHAPTER FOUR

Earnings after Job Displacement: Job Tenure, Industry, and Occupation

LORI GLADSTEIN KLETZER

I. Introduction

Since the late 1970s, increasing international competition, technological change, a deep recession, and changes in the composition of demand have lead to the displacement of millions of workers from their jobs because of plant closings or large-scale reductions in operations. The ability of these displaced workers to adjust to their permanent job loss is a subject of considerable interest to economists, policymakers, and the general public.

The relationship between losses of job seniority, firm- and industry-specific skills, and difficult labor market adjustments is a common theme in many policy discussions (see Lovell 1984; Browne 1985; Flaim and Seghal 1985). In a study of trade-displaced workers and Trade Adjustment Assistance, Neumann (1978) found demographic and individual labor-market characteristics to be important determinants of the outcomes of permanent job loss, in particular age at displacement, job tenure on the predisplacement job, and education. Since then, several papers have examined the relationship between the characteristics of displaced workers and their probability of reemployment, reemployment earnings, and durations of unemployment (see Kiefer and Neumann 1979; Gladstein 1986; Addison and Portugal 1987, 1989; Hamermesh 1987, 1989; Podgursky and Swaim 1987a,b; Ruhm 1987a,b; Howland and Peterson 1988; Kruse 1988; Kletzer 1989).

The notion implicit in discussions of the costs of permanent job loss is that the earnings power of an individual is tied to a specific job. Given the well-established evidence of rising wage-tenure profiles, an important consequence of permanent job loss is the potential reduction in the value of previous job tenure.[1] More generally, the consequences of displacement can be viewed as a function of what an individual stands to "lose" when a job is terminated. The human capital framework emphasizes specific skill investments as measured by job tenure. In this approach, permanent job loss causes a loss of specific skills.[2] From an institutional perspective where jobs, not individual characteristics, determine wages, it is the characteristics of predisplacement industry and occupation that determine the consequences of job displacement. If displacement occurs from jobs in internal labor markets, from unionized industries with economic rents, or from industries with efficiency wage differentials, rationing of these jobs implies that on average, postdisplacement earnings will be lower than earnings before displacement.

With these theories as a framework, this chapter examines the earnings consequences of permanent job loss for a large, nationally representative sample of workers displaced from jobs between January 1979 and January 1986. The goal is to identify the determinants of postdisplacement earnings. Particular attention will be paid to the roles of previous job tenure, predisplacement industry, industrial and occupational change, and unobserved individual heterogeneity. Section II presents a simple model of earnings determination and discusses the role of previous job tenure. The construction of the data set follows in section III. The empirical specification and results are discussed in section IV, and section V concludes.

II. A Model of Earnings Determination

Several research areas in labor economics provide a background for this paper. Research on displaced workers, analyses of tenure-earnings profiles (and heterogeneity bias in estimating these profiles), and job-search models provide a foundation for the analytical framework. Most empirical work in this area follows a human capital framework in estimating the loss associated with job displacement to be a loss of firm-specific skills (see Neumann 1978; Kiefer and Neumann 1979; Hamermesh 1987; Podgursky and Swaim 1987a). Rising wage-tenure profiles do not necessarily imply that permanent job loss results in a loss of human capital. Unobserved heterogeneity across individuals and job matches suggests that the relationship between job tenure and earnings is a statistical artifact. Recent papers by Topel (1986), Abraham and Farber (1987,

1988), Altonji and Shakotko (1987), and Marshall and Zarkin (1987) cast doubt on the importance of job seniority in wage growth.[3] These papers show that standard estimates of the return to seniority are biased upward by job/match and individual heterogeneity. Correcting for the upward bias reveals substantially smaller returns to job tenure than is estimated by standard cross-section earnings functions.

These insights can be incorporated into the analysis of the costs of permanent job loss through a simple model of earnings determination. Assume that the earnings of individual i on job j at time t (the predisplacement job) can be written:

$$\ln W_{ijt} = \beta_1^0 T_{ijt} + \beta_2 X_{ijt} + \epsilon_{ijt}, \tag{1}$$

where W_{ijt} is weekly earnings, T_{ijt} is the number of years on job j at time t, X_{ijt} is a vector of characteristics of the individual and job (it includes industry and occupation), ϵ_{ijt} is a disturbance term, and β_1^0 represents the return to an additional year of tenure.[4] The error term can be written as

$$\epsilon_{ijt} = A_i + \mu_{ij} + \nu_{ijt}, \tag{2}$$

where A_i is an individual fixed effect, μ_{ij} represents the job/match quality component, and ν_{ijt} is a person/job/time-specific component. Assume that A_i is fixed over an individual's lifetime. The job/match component is fixed over the length of a job.

Because job tenure is a function of past quit and layoff decisions, it may be positively correlated with characteristics of individuals and jobs that lead to lower quits and layoffs. Through these separation probabilities, tenure is likely to be correlated with the ability and job/match components of the error term.

The postdisplacement earnings of displaced workers will be less influenced by heterogeneity bias, providing some insights into the transferability of skills and the role of individual ability. For reemployed displaced workers, there is an earnings observation at time $t + 1$ (earnings on the new job k at the survey date):

$$\ln W_{ikt+1} = \beta_1^1 T_{ijt} + \beta_2 X_{ikt+1} + \epsilon_{ikt+1}, \tag{3}$$

where the variable definitions are the same as equation (1). The error term for this earnings function is

$$\epsilon_{ikt+1} = A_i + \mu_{ik} + \nu_{ikt+1}, \tag{4}$$

where we assume $E(\nu_{ijt}, \nu_{ikt+1}) = 0$.

It is expected that β_1^1 will be less than β_1^0 because of the loss of firm-specific human capital and the reduction of heterogeneity bias. The reduction of heterogeneity bias follows from some reasonable assumptions about the relationship between previous job tenure and the job/match components. If the job/match component on the old job (μ_{ij}) is uncorrelated with the job/match component on the new job (μ_{ik}), then previous job tenure (T_{ijt}) in equation (3) will be correlated only with ability, and not with the job/match component on the new job (μ_{ik}).[5]

This model shows how losses of firm-specific human capital will be overestimated if heterogeneity bias is ignored. The difference between β_1^0 and β_1^1 reflects the loss of job/match effects and specific skills; by ignoring heterogeneity bias, losses of firm-specific human capital will be overestimated. The composition of the bias in predisplacement earnings influences the determination of postdisplacement earnings: as the job/match component increases, the returns to tenure become increasingly job-specific (capturing both returns to skill investments and job/match effects). These returns will be lost on job displacement. If individual heterogeneity plays a major role in the bias, the returns to tenure are more individual-specific, and more likely to be transferable to the postdisplacement job. Using the Displaced Worker Survey, Kletzer (1989) finds that the composition of the bias varies by occupational group. For blue-collar workers, job/match effects are relatively more important than individual fixed effects in accounting for the relationship between tenure and earnings. For managerial, professional, and technical workers, individual heterogeneity appears to be relatively more important.

The model also generates the hypothesis that the returns to tenure on the postdisplacement job will be positive because of the effect of individual ability and partial transferability of some "specific" skills.[6] Addison and Portugal (1989) and Kletzer (1989) find that the returns to previous job tenure are not lost entirely with displacement; previous job tenure is positively related to postdisplacement earnings. This positive relationship reflects both individual heterogeneity, which is transferable across jobs, and skill transferability.

An institutional perspective suggests other characteristics of interest in postdisplacement earnings. An implication of a job characteristics approach is that outcomes depend on the postdisplacement industry and occupation. For example, losses of economic rents depend on the rationing of union or efficiency wage jobs. Workers who are able to retain these positions may not experience losses relative to other displaced workers. Changes in industry and/or occupation can result in a loss of rents as well as a loss of specific skills. Consistent with this framework, the empirical analysis in section IV includes a variable denoting changes in 2-digit SIC industry or occupation.[7]

III. Data

A large nationally representative microdata sample that identifies individuals who lose jobs because of plant shutdown or permanent reduction in the workforce is available from recent surveys conducted by the Bureau of Labor Statistics. These surveys, conducted in January of each of three years, 1984, 1986, and 1988, were supplements to the January Current Population Survey. For this paper, data were drawn from the first two surveys, January 1984 and January 1986. To identify displaced workers, CPS respondents were asked if they, or any member of their household, twenty years of age or older, had lost or left a job in the five years prior to the survey date because of a "plant closing, an employer going out of business, a layoff from which (the individual in question) was not recalled, or other similar reasons." For respondents answering yes, a series of questions followed to determine the precise reason for the job loss, the nature of the lost job, events during the time following displacement, and if reemployed, postdisplacement industry, occupation, and earnings. The 1984 survey covers displacements occurring between January 1979 and January 1984; the 1986 survey covers displacements occurring between January 1981 and January 1986. For this analysis, I identified as displaced those individuals whose job loss was due to plant closing or relocation, elimination of position or shift (the plant or company still operating), and slack work (the plant or company still operating). Sixty-one percent of individuals in this sample were displaced by a plant closing or relocation. The sample was confined to workers twenty to sixty years of age (at displacement) who were displaced from full-time nonagricultural jobs over the full five years preceding each survey date.[8] Certain industries were excluded where the notion of job displacement is not well defined: these industries are construction, forestry, national security, and the armed forces. These restrictions produced a sample of 6,042 workers, of whom 62.3% were reemployed at their respective survey dates. Individuals not employed at the survey date were either unemployed or out of the labor force. Information on labor force status refers to the survey date. No information was collected on completed spells of employment that occurred before the survey date, therefore individuals who had been employed following job loss but who were not employed at the survey date were not counted as employed. For the employed, postdisplacement earnings are measured at the survey date, not at the time the job offer was accepted. Descriptive data on the full sample and the subsample of reemployed are presented in table 1.

Descriptive statistics on the earnings of the reemployed are presented

Table 1   **Descriptive Statistics**

Variable	Full sample		Reemployed sample	
	Mean	Std. dev.	Mean	Std. dev.
Age	34.53	11.01	33.42	10.05
Education	12.49	2.49	12.83	2.41
Job tenure	5.42	6.91	4.86	5.93
ln old earnings	5.64	0.53	5.70	0.52
ln new earnings			5.53	0.61
State unemploy rate	3.21	4.29	3.21	4.29
Nonwhite	.124		.100	
Male	.605		.647	
Plant closing	.613		.625	
Position eliminated	.228		.215	
Advance notice	.523		.530	
Northeast	.197		.198	
North central	.257		.254	
West	.238		.233	
Blue collar	.532		.499	
White collar/service	.468		.501	
Part-time			.178	
Industry change			.720	
Occupation change			.670	
Mining	.053		.048	
Durable goods	.317		.314	
Nondurable goods	.190		.183	
Transportation and public utilities	.088		.085	
Wholesale and retail trade	.167		.177	
Services	.186		.194	
Displaced in:				
1979	.051		.052	
1980	.058		.067	
1981	.167		.184	
1982	.220		.237	
1983	.207		.202	
1984	.120		.130	
1985	.178		.128	
1984 Survey	.379		.373	
1986 Survey	.621		.627	
No. of observations	3,765		2,277	

in table 2. The earnings comparison uses the ratio of post-displacement weekly earnings to pre-displacement weekly earnings (all earnings are adjusted to 1982 dollars using the gross national product [GNP] deflator). There are sizeable differences in the amount of earnings loss associated with permanent displacement. As might be expected, earnings differ-

112

Table 2 **Ratio of Postdisplacement Weekly Earnings to Predisplacement Weekly Earnings**

Earnings Ratio	Blue-Collar				White-Collar			
	Men		Women		Men		Women	
< .5	16.3	(12.3)	15.3	(9.4)	10.0	(7.9)	14.0	(6.5)
.5–.74	20.4	(20.3)	21.5	(22.8)	15.8	(15.4)	16.2	(14.7)
.75–.99	31.1	(33.5)	30.4	(31.1)	29.1	(29.8)	29.0	(31.8)
1.00 +	32.3	(33.9)	32.8	(36.7)	45.1	(46.9)	40.8	(47.0)
Mean ratio	.933		.887		1.003		.985	
(Std. dev.)	(1.016)		(.427)		(.473)		(.670)	
Mean ratio by predisplacement industry (% reemployed)								
Mining	.71	(54.5)	.79	(33.3)	.81	(69.8)	1.01	(50.0)
Durable mfg.	.97	(62.3)	.80	(50.5)	.98	(75.6)	.91	(55.3)
Nondurable mfg.	.91	(68.3)	.92	(46.1)	1.00	(75.0)	1.01	(62.0)
Transport and public util.	.90	(57.0)	.88	(57.7)	.96	(71.5)	.91	(56.5)
Wholesale and retail trade	.99	(64.7)	.97	(69.9)	1.01	(73.1)	.96	(58.0)
Services	.97	(62.3)	1.11	(43.1)	1.07	(74.0)	1.03	(63.0)

Note: Earnings adjusted to 1982 dollars using GNP deflator.

ences (losses) are larger for blue-collar workers than they are for white-collar workers. There is also variation by gender, as reemployed women earn less, relative to their old jobs, than do men. Across all groups, there is considerable variation in the ratio of current to former earnings. For blue-collar workers, approximately 32% were earning more on the post-displacement job than they were on the old job, while approximately 15% were earning less than half of their predisplacement earnings. For white-collar workers, the distribution is skewed toward real earnings gains (at least 40% of white-collar workers were earning more on their current job than on their displacement job).

Although all workers in the full sample were displaced from full-time jobs, 17.8% of the employed were in part-time jobs after displacement. Differences in weekly earnings, pre- and postdisplacement, can be a combination of changes in hourly wages and changes in hours worked. The numbers in parentheses are for the full-time employed only (working at least 35 hours/week). As expected, real earnings reductions are smaller for this group, and white-collar workers report real earnings gains.

The bottom half of table 2 presents earnings ratios by predisplacement industry group. The numbers in parentheses are percentages of the full sample reemployed for each industrial group. While no firm conclusions can be drawn from cross-tabulations, the numbers are suggestive of some patterns. First, individuals displaced from trade and services are less likely to experience large earnings losses. In general, in these industrial groups, earnings reductions are either small or there are real earnings gains. This might be expected, given the relatively low-wage status of these industrial groups and their strong employment growth. Second, workers displaced from relatively "high-wage" industries do not necessarily experience large earnings reductions. Across mining and durable goods manufacturing, there is considerable variation in the earnings ratios (it is clear, however, that blue-workers displaced from mining experienced large real earnings reductions). For blue-collar men, some of the "smaller than expected" earnings reductions are likely due to the pattern of reemployment. The pattern of reemployment is described in appendix tables A-2–A-5. For all groups, there was substantial movement out of mining and manufacturing. For each gender/occupational group, the percentage employed in mining and manufacturing fell by at least 40%. Blue-collar workers exhibited the strongest tendency to stay in mining and manufacturing, particularly men. Forty-three percent of blue-collar men displaced from durable goods manufacturing were reemployed in durable goods manufacturing. For nondurable goods manufacturing, this "return" percentage was 38%, and for transportation and public utilities, the return percentage was 43%. The "return" percentages were slightly smaller for women. White-collar women were the most likely to move out of mining and manufacturing.

IV. Empirical Specification and Results

There are two earnings observations for individual i:

$$\ln W_{ijt} = \beta_1^0 T_{ijt} + \beta_2 X_{ijt} + \epsilon_{ijt}, \tag{5}$$
$$\ln W_{ikt+1} = \beta_1^1 T_{ijt} + \beta_2 X_{ikt+1} + \beta_3 T_{ikt+1} + \epsilon_{ikt+1}, \tag{6}$$

where T_{ikt+1} is tenure on the postdisplacement job. Direct measures of this variable are not available and dummy variables for year of displacement are used as a proxy. In equation (6), the key variables of interest are job tenure (β_1^1, capturing individual heterogeneity and transferable skill), predisplacement industry and occupation, and changes in industry and occupation. Equation (6) also includes a control for part-time status. The pre-displacement equation is specified similarly, omitting all variables that refer to time after displacement. Both equations contain information on race, skill level, education and experience.[9]

Using the subsample of employed, equations (5) and (6) were estimated first using OLS. The predisplacement earnings function estimates are reported in appendix table A-1 for four gender/occupational groups: blue-collar men, blue-collar women, white-collar men, and white-collar women. The coefficient estimates are of the expected signs. OLS estimates of postdisplacement earnings for blue-collar men, blue-collar women, white-collar men, and white-collar are reported in tables 3–6, respectively. The discussion will concentrate on blue-collar workers because this group is the focus of attention in displaced worker policy. Turning first to table 3 for blue-collar men, as expected from the discussion in section II, the coefficient on previous job tenure is positive (and statistically significant at a 5% level of significance). This coefficient captures transferable skills from the returns to tenure on the predisplacement job (skills not captured by age), and the individual ability component of the heterogeneity bias in predisplacement returns to tenure.

Comparing column one of table 3 to column one of appendix table A-1, we see that the returns to previous job tenure are, as expected, smaller in the postdisplacement job. The difference between the estimated coefficients represents the loss of job-specific factors (job-specific skills and job/match effects). The returns to job tenure pre- and postdisplacement can be compared by calculating the contribution to log earnings of an additional year of job tenure.[10] These calculations are reported in table 7 for the four gender/occupation groups.[11] Across groups, there is considerable variation in the reduction in estimated returns to previous job tenure. For a blue-collar male with mean predisplacement job tenure of 6.6 years, the return to an additional year of job tenure on the postdisplacement job is 28.6% of the return received on the predisplacement job. The return to an additional year of previous job tenure on the postdisplacement job is approximately one-half of the return on predisplacement jobs for white-collar workers. Blue-collar women have the smallest reductions in the value of job tenure; for them an additional year of previous job tenure on the postdisplacement job yields a return that is 74.5% of its return on the predisplacement job. Larger losses for blue-collar men, and at higher values of tenure for all workers, suggest an increasing role for job-specific factors. At higher values of tenure, there are likely to be sizeable investments in job-specific skills. If good job matches are less likely to be broken off, it is expected that the relative importance of job/match effects would increase with years of job tenure.

It is interesting to note that tenure losses for blue-collar women are smaller than the estimated losses for men. From a human capital

Table 3　　**Postdisplacement Earnings: Blue-Collar Men (N = 1,403)**
OLS and Sample Selection Corrected (SS)

Variable	(1) Mean	(2) OLS	(3) SS	(4) SS
Age	32.73	.01571	.00615	.00809
	(9.87)	(.01009)	(.01013)	(.00941)
Age squared	1168.9	−.00017	−.00008	−.00006
	(733.2)	(.00013)	(.00013)	(.00013)
Education	12.98	.05014*	.04216*	.04812*
	(2.09)	(.00652)	(.00666)	(.00615)
Job tenure	5.85	.01664*	.01673*	.01595*
	(6.65)	(.00562)	(.00551)	(.00502)
Tenure squared	78.61	−.00085*	−.00080*	−.00077*
	(173.4)	(.00021)	(.00020)	(.00018)
Nonwhite	.095	−.10972*	−.05705	−.07188**
	(.293)	(.04539)	(.04599)	(.04257)
Married	.748	.16773*	.11994*	.12954*
	(.434)	(.03145)	(.03326)	(.03071)
Craft	.405	.16125*	.14228*	.12552*
	(.491)	(.02767)	(.02771)	(.02556)
Part-time	.166	−.45253*	−.44775*	−.37385*
	(.372)	(.03534)	(.03472)	(.03183)
Mining	.081	.09507	.14505*	.12205*
	(.273)	(.06661)	(.06604)	(.06097)
Durable Mfg.	.435	.08212**	.07847**	.09108*
	(.496)	(.05260)	(.05184)	(.04707)
Nondurable Mfg.	.193	.03416	.00943	.01102
	(.395)	(.05738)	(.05740)	(.05234)
Transport and Utilities	.113	.26401*	.27894*	.21888*
	(.317)	(.06238)	(.06148)	(.05631)
Trade	.103	.01222	.00563	.01119
	(.303)	(.06287)	(.06221)	(.05665)
Industry change	.724			−.13736*
	(.447)			(.02829)
Occupation change	.667			−.16888*
	(.471)			(.02704)
Residual				.40393*
				(.02891)
Constant		4.3095*	4.7662*	4.8693*
		(.1894)	(.2095)	(.2079)
Lambda			−.27629*	−.15447*
			(.06710)	(.07211)
R^2		.2382	.2441	.3795

Standard errors in parentheses.

*statistically significant at 5% (two-tailed test).

**statistically significant at 10% (two-tailed test).

Note: Specifications include controls for year of displacement and region.

Table 4 Postdisplacement Earnings: Blue-Collar Women ($N = 477$)
OLS and Sample Selection Corrected (SS)

Variable	(1) Mean	(2) OLS	(3) SS	(4) SS
Age	35.30	.01649	−.01122	−.00466
	(10.64)	(.01391)	(.01616)	(.01546)
Age squared	1359.4	−.00026	.00010	.00002
	(811.9)	(.00018)	(.00021)	(.00020)
Education	12.72	.03797*	.02342*	.03791*
	(1.97)	(.01070)	(.01145)	(.01110)
Job Tenure	5.02	.03003*	.03275*	.02838*
	(5.74)	(.00895)	(.00867)	(.00836)
Tenure squared	58.14	−.00115*	−.00116*	−.00103*
	(138.5)	(.00035)	(.00034)	(.00033)
Nonwhite	.165	−.03849	−.02109	−.00022
	(.372)	(.05552)	(.05785)	(.05529)
Married	.559	.03788	.04896	.05263
	(.497)	(.04215)	(.04182)	(.03974)
Craft	.191	.03631	.08221	.07427
	(.393)	(.05247)	(.05266)	(.05029)
Part-time	.243	−.45546*	−.44691*	−.41979*
	(.429)	(.04713)	(.04615)	(.04403)
Mining	.008	.32244	.41065**	.39833
	(.091)	(.23410)	(.22530)	(.21530)
Durable Mfg.	.396	−.22325*	−.23344*	−.23771*
	(.489)	(.08501)	(.08389)	(.07907)
Nondurable Mfg.	.392	−.20916*	−.21132*	−.23413*
	(.489)	(.08621)	(.08509)	(.08109)
Transport and utilities	.031	−.28159*	−.32055*	−.29847*
	(.175)	(.13690)	(.13740)	(.13050)
Trade	.107	−.28934*	−.40997*	−.40436*
	(.309)	(.09928)	(.10400)	(.10050)
Industry change	.744			−.08039**
	(.436)			(.04731)
Occupation change	.708			−.07613**
	(.455)			(.04591)
Residual				.32744*
				(.10600)
Constant		4.4604*	5.4533*	5.3071*
		(.2952)	(.4083)	(.3949)
Lambda			−.34396*	−.27109*
			(.10890)	(.10600)
R^2		.2742	.2596	.3284

Standard errors in parentheses

*statistically significant at 5% (two-tailed test).

**statistically significant at 10% (two-tailed test).

Note: Specifications include controls for year of displacement and region.

117

Table 5 Postdisplacement Earnings: White-Collar Men ($N = 1033$)
OLS and Sample Selection Corrected (SS)

Variable	(1) Mean	(2) OLS	(3) SS	(4) SS
Age	33.95	.03208*	.01334	.02443*
	(9.74)	(.01183)	(.01203)	(.01090)
Age squared	1248.1	−.00037*	−.00009	−.00027*
	(733.8)	(.00016)	(.00016)	(.00014)
Education	15.15	.06001*	.05393*	.05282*
	(2.44)	(.00681)	(.00675)	(.00617)
Job tenure	4.56	.01901*	.01984*	.02018*
	(5.92)	(.00676)	(.00650)	(.00585)
Tenure squared	55.88	−.00075*	−.00069*	−.00075*
	(153.5)	(.00025)	(.00024)	(.00021)
Nonwhite	.067	−.16166*	−.09197	−.11294*
	(.249)	(.06095)	(.05878)	(.05418)
Married	.690	.17095*	.13704*	.14193*
	(.463)	(.03427)	(.03423)	(.03085)
Sales	.276	−.09291*	−.10922*	−.09283*
	(.447)	(.04274)	(.04224)	(.03731)
Clerical	.121	−.19953*	−.16217*	−.34683*
	(.326)	(.04973)	(.04844)	(.05211)
Service	.089	−.33504*	−.29238*	−.16988*
	(.285)	(.05876)	(.05718)	(.04384)
Part-time	.107	−.45236*	−.44869*	−.40924*
	(.308)	(.04950)	(.04781)	(.04282)
Mining	.042	.08786	.12290	.12251**
	(.202)	(.07970)	(.07703)	(.06934)
Durable Mfg.	.258	.09737*	.08871*	.09437*
	(.438)	(.04326)	(.04241)	(.03759)
Nondurable Mfg.	.107	.00255	−.01264	−.00174
	(.309)	(.00531)	(.05441)	(.04826)
Transport and utilities	.080	.04989	.05736	.04493
	(.272)	(.06089)	(.05949)	(.05300)
Trade	.266	−.00187	.01672	.00386
	(.442)	(.04706)	(.04586)	(.04084)
Industry change	.687			−.05292**
	(.464)			(.03046)
Occupation change	.632			−.11555*
	(.482)			(.02994)
Residual				.49905*
				(.03183)
Constant		4.0968*	4.6815*	4.5659*
		(.2200)	(.2412)	(.2235)
Lambda			−.39078*	−.17091*
			(.08384)	(.07971)
R^2		.3126	.3262	.4686

Standard errors in parentheses.

*statistically significant at 5% (two-tailed test).

**statistically significant at 10% (two-tailed test).

Note: Specifications include controls for year of displacement and region.

Table 6   Postdisplacement Earnings: White-Collar Women ($N = 852$)
OLS and Sample Selection Corrected (SS)

Variable	(1) Mean	(2) OLS	(3) SS	(4) SS
Age	32.808	.07004*	.03908*	.06662*
	(10.18)	(.01184)	(.01315)	(.01144)
Age squared	1179.9	−.00093*	−.00047*	−.00088*
	(752.19)	(.00016)	(.00018)	(.00016)
Education	13.272	.08249*	.06202*	.08031*
	(2.189)	(.00837)	(.00972)	(.00821)
Job tenure	3.493	.02300*	.02716*	.02155*
	(4.218)	(.00948)	(.00981)	(.00851)
Tenure squared	29.977	−.00106*	−.00086*	−.00098*
	(82.27)	(.00047)	(.00046)	(.00042)
Nonwhite	.110	−.07449	.03856	−.07197
	(.313)	(.05370)	(.05848)	(.05107)
Married	.481	−.00092	.16353*	.01079
	(.499)	(.03372)	(.04525)	(.03937)
Sales	.175	−.00087	−.04399	.00530
	(.380)	(.05100)	(.05555)	(.04628)
Clerical	.317	−.01251	.00404	−.01185
	(.465)	(.04133)	(.04482)	(.03723)
Service	.123	−.13053*	−.01857*	−.14087*
	(.329)	(.05801)	(.06450)	(.05664)
Part-time	.245	−.55593*	−.53779*	−.49047*
	(.430)	(.03866)	(.04181)	(.03486)
Mining	.021	.16472	.20314**	.07892
	(.144)	(.11640)	(.11930)	(.10800)
Durable mfg.	.134	−.03872	.04703	.02197
	(.341)	(.05233)	(.05760)	(.04920)
Nondurable mfg.	.142	.06158	.04496	.06278
	(.349)	(.05157)	(.05658)	(.04621)
Transport and utilities	.071	−.00700	.07155	.00954
	(.258)	(.06655)	(.07084)	(.06065)
Trade	.230	−.03123	−.02395	−.03786
	(.421)	(.04463)	(.04831)	(.04012)
Industry change	.739			−.05942**
	(.439)			(.03570)
Occupation change	.697			−.07591*
	(.459)			(.03370)
Residual				.44280*
				(.04149)
Constant		3.0102*	4.1312*	3.2553*
		(.2384)	(.3039)	(.2703)
Lambda			−.81495*	−.07513
			(.13150)	(.12380)
R^2		.3688	.4011	.4773

Standard errors in parentheses.

*statistically significant at 5% (two-tailed test).

**statistically significant at 10% (two-tailed test).

Note: Specifications include controls for year of displacement and region.

119

Table 7 **Comparison of Returns to Previous Job Tenure**
Ratio of Postdisplacement Return to Predisplacement Return

	Blue-Collar		White-Collar	
	Men	Women	Men	Women
Median	.4670	.8347	.6301	.5598
	($T = 3.0$)	($T = 3.0$)	($T = 2.0$)	($T = 2.0$)
Mean	.2860	.7452	.5589	.5292
	($T = 6.60$)	($T = 5.02$)	($T = 4.56$)	($T = 3.49$)
Top quantile	.1819	.6346	.5442	.4879
	($T = 8.0$)	($T = 7.0$)	($T = 5.0$)	($T = 5.0$)

Ratio is $[(\delta \ln W_{t+1}/\delta T_{ijt})/(\delta \ln W_t/\delta T_{ijt})]$ evaluated at values of previous job tenure. Number in parentheses is years of tenure.

perspective, women may make smaller investments in job-specific skills (on-the-job training) because they expect to spend less time on the job. Equivalent amounts of tenure for men and women may represent different degrees of skill specificity if women are, relative to men, undertaking more general skill investments. By choice, or as a result of employer discrimination, women may be in occupations that do not provide opportunities for specific skill acquisition. It may also be the case that individual heterogeneity is a relatively more important factor for women. It should be noted that blue-collar women have larger real earnings reductions than the other groups, despite smaller losses of the returns to job tenure. Appendix table A-3 shows that blue-collar women are more likely than men to leave mining and manufacturing industries, which suggests that larger earnings losses may be due to the loss of economic rents.[12]

The OLS estimates are likely to suffer from sample selection bias. Postdisplacement earnings are available only for the subsample of employed. This censoring of employment can create statistical problems if postdisplacement earnings are not independent of the process that determines their observability. If reemployment is a function of expected postdisplacement earnings, as is suggested by job-search models, then estimates of earnings that do not account for this relationship will be biased.

The probability of employment can be modeled within a simple job search framework. An individual becomes reemployed if she receives a wage offer greater than or equal to her reservation wage. Express the reservation wage function as

$$W^* = X_1'\beta_1 + u_1, \qquad u_1 \sim N(0, \sigma_1^2). \tag{7}$$

120

The wage offer function can be similarly expressed:

$$\bar{W} = X_2'\beta_2 + u_2, \qquad u_2 \sim N(0, \sigma_2^2). \tag{8}$$

The employment condition can be written as

$$\begin{aligned}\bar{W} - W^* &= X_2'\beta_2 - X_1'\beta_1 + u_2 - u_1 > 0 \\ &= X_3'\beta_3 + u_3 > 0,\end{aligned} \tag{9}$$

with $E(u_3) = 0$, $E(u_3)^2 = \sigma_2^2 + \sigma_1^2 - 2\sigma_2\sigma_1 = \sigma_3^2$. Define an indicator variable, r_i, where $r_i = 0$ if an individual is not employed, and $r_i = 1$ if an individual is employed and postdisplacement earnings are observed.[13] Using equation (9) and its distributional assumptions, the probabilities of employment and nonemployment are probit functions, given respectively by

$$\begin{aligned}Pr(r_i = 1) &= \Phi\,(X_3'\beta_3/\sigma_3) \\ Pr(r_i = 0) &= 1 - \Phi\,(X_3'\beta_3/\sigma_3),\end{aligned} \tag{10}$$

where Φ is the standard normal distribution function.

The two-step sample selection correction procedure suggested by Heckman (1979) can be used to estimate postdisplacement earnings, incorporating information from the employment probit estimation. The sample selection-corrected specification of postdisplacement earnings is

$$\ln W_{ikt+1} = \beta_1^1 T_{ijt} + \beta_2 X_{ikt+1} + \gamma_1\lambda_i + \epsilon_{ikt+1}, \tag{11}$$

where $\lambda_i = \phi(Z_i)/\Phi(-Z_i)$ and $Z_i = -\,[(X_3'\beta_3)/(\sigma_{33})^{1/2}]$. The probit estimates are reported in table 8.

For the four gender/occupation groups, the sample selection-corrected estimates are in columns 3 and 4 of tables 3–6. The selection correction procedure has little effect on the estimated tenure coefficients. Other variables unaffected by sample selection are education, race, marital status, and occupational skill levels (for white-collar workers), and they have the expected signs and are statistically significant. Among blue-collar men, highly skilled workers (craft workers) continue to earn more than their semiskilled and unskilled counterparts. It is interesting to note that this effect is not found for blue-collar women. Whereas craft women earned more than lesser-skilled women on the predisplacement job, their earnings differential is not statistically significant in the postdisplacement job.

Other work on displaced workers has not considered the effect of predisplacement industry. In the predisplacement earnings functions, these variables capture industry wage differentials caused by efficiency wages, monopoly rents shared by unions, or perhaps compensating wage differentials. In the postdisplacement earnings functions, these variables are likely to capture patterns of employment whereby individuals may continue to earn industry wage differentials by becoming reemployed in the predisplacement industry. For blue-collar men, there is evidence of continued predisplacement industry wage differentials in postdisplacement earnings. Workers displaced from mining, durable goods manufacturing, and transportation and public utilities continue to earn positive wage differentials relative to services (these are the same industry groups with positive wage differentials in predisplacement earnings). In sign, the predisplacement industry effect is the same for white-collar workers, however it is not estimated with precision. There is a curious result for blue-collar women, where workers displaced from manufacturing, transportation and public utilities, and wholesale and retail trade appear to earn less than workers displaced from services.

For blue-collar men, these results suggest patterns of employment that result in persistent wage differentials. Job rationing by seniority and industry experience may provide the mechanism for this pattern, one that suggests that the reemployed from these industries are those who are able to regain jobs in these industries. The probit estimates in table 8 reveal that blue-collar men displaced from mining, durable goods manufacturing, and transportation and public utilities are less likely to be employed (only the coefficient on mining is statistically significant at standard levels). These industry differences in the probability of employment suggest a loss of economic rents with displacement from these relatively high wage, unionized industries. With the increased rationing of jobs (employment shares declined in these industries over the period), and perhaps without the skills to earn a comparable wage in the growing trade and service sector, blue-collar men displaced from these industries faced a downward shift in their wage-offer distribution. The lower probabilities of employment suggest that, on average, these workers were more selective in their search for a new job and that they had high reservation wages. Because these industries were relatively high-wage, supplemental unemployment benefits, severance pay or other financial assets may have been available to support high reservation wages. High reservation wages are consistent with the finding that those who did become employed continue to earn positive wage differentials.[14]

While the ideal explanatory variable, in terms of job characteristics, is postdisplacement industry and occupation, the actual pattern of employment is endogenous to the model; postdisplacement industry/occupation is an outcome similar to postdisplacement earnings. To provide a rough indication of the losses of specific skills and/or rents associated with indus-

122

trial and occupational change, dummy variables denoting changes in 2-digit SIC industry and occupation are added in column 3 of tables 3–6. Consistent with the discussion above, industry changes lower postdisplacement earnings by approximately 14% for blue-collar men, approximately 7% to 9% for blue-collar women, and 5% to 7% for white-collar workers.[15] Changes in occupation also lower postdisplacement earnings by approximately 10% to 14% for white-collar workers, 7% to 8% for blue-collar women, and 20% for blue-collar men.

The standard earnings function specification used in the applied job-search literature includes previous earnings.[16] The usual justification for including this variable is that it serves as a proxy for unobserved individual characteristics. There are obvious problems with this specification. The explanatory variables are likely to be highly correlated with previous earnings, with the result that we will not have good measures of the effects of the explanatory variables of interest, because some of the effect of these variables will be captured in previous earnings.

Another approach is to use the residual from the estimated predisplacement earnings equation. The estimated residual is the unexplained variation in predisplacement earnings, and it can be used as a proxy of unobserved individual heterogeneity. The advantage of using the residual is that it is orthogonal by construction to the explanatory variables. If the residual is related to ability, we expect it to be positively related to postdisplacement earnings. The residual is added to the specification in column 4 and it is positive and statistically significant.

For all groups, the postdisplacement earnings equations exhibit negative selection. This effect of censoring means that the employed are predicted to have lower postdisplacement earnings than equivalent nonemployed workers. If postdisplacement earnings and wage offers are positively correlated, and wage offers and reservation wages are positively correlated, this suggests that the nonemployed have higher reservation wages than the employed.[17] The nonemployed receive high offers, but the offers do not exceed their reservation wages. These offers can exceed the offers accepted by the employed.

Turning briefly to the results for the probability of employment (table 8), previous job tenure is negatively related to employment probability (holding age constant). Workers displaced by plant closing or relocation are more likely to be employed than workers who lost jobs because of "slack work" (this effect is statistically insignificant for white-collar women). Advance notice increases the probability of employment for blue-collar workers. "Local" economic conditions, as measured by state unemployment rates, are important determinants of the probability of

123

Table 8　　　　　　　**Probability of Employment (Probit)**

	Blue-Collar		White-Collar	
	(1)	(2)	(3)	(4)
Variable	Men	Women	Men	Women
Age	.06286*	.11663*	.08924*	.04704*
	(.01966)	(.02777)	(.02781)	(.02336)
Age squared	−.00111*	−.00154*	−.00132*	−.00072*
	(.00025)	(.00036)	(.00035)	(.00031)
Education	.04763	.05574*	.02886**	.03528*
	(.01370)	(.02117)	(.01734)	(.01871)
Job tenure	−.01173*	.00959	−.01280**	.02189*
	(.00466)	(.00804)	(.00688)	(.00804)
Nonwhite	−.31684*	−.37079*	−.31350*	−.20978*
	(.08825)	(.10820)	(.13290)	(.10970)
Married	.33131*	−.14694*	.21144*	−.38725*
	(.06620)	(.08771)	(.08610)	(.07201)
Craft	.14354*	−.21647		
	(.06218)	(.10750)		
Sales			.09030	−.06797
			(.11520)	(.11020)
Clerical			−.20615**	.00012
			(.12020)	(.09124)
Service			−.14171	−.23651*
			(.13660)	(.11850)
Mining	−.52512*	−.23115	.23776**	−.44728*
	(.14440)	(.44000)	(.19060)	(.22270)
Durable mfg.	−.09063	.09531	.04047	−.20041**
	(.11580)	(.17530)	(.11410)	(.10940)
Nondurable mfg.	.16771	.01894	.09155	−.00674
	(.12740)	(.17570)	(.14650)	(.11230)
Transport and utilities	−.19299	.32365	−.05703	−.22777
	(.13540)	(.30430)	(.15760)	(.14030)
Trade	.08517	.54104	−.05939	−.03495
	(.13940)	(.22650)	(.12230)	(.09712)
ln (old earnings)	.14683*	.04996	.18959*	.30493*
	(.06895)	(.10880)	(.09049)	(.07910)
Advance notice	.14554*	.11665**	.01495	−.07809
	(.05778)	(.08530)	(.07908)	(.07172)
State UN rate	−.03039*	−.02940*	−.04958*	−.02763*
	(.00783)	(.01279)	(.01149)	(.01331)
Year of displacement:				
1979	.53916*	.54592*	1.0637*	.27476
	(.14740)	(.19420)	(.2086)	(.18340)
1980	.71865*	.82842*	1.5966*	.68744*
	(.13040)	(.19430)	(.2523)	(.19760)
1981	.82887*	.62955*	.99095*	.24760*
	(.08999)	(.13670)	(.14330)	(.12790)
1982	.75551*	.35089*	1.0366*	.43418*
	(.08240)	(.13050)	(.1317)	(.12350)
1983	.70407*	.62208*	.75690*	.29249*
	(.10760)	(.15660)	(.12840)	(.12000)

124

Table 8 (Continued)

Variable	Blue-Collar		White-Collar	
	(1) Men	(2) Women	(3) Men	(4) Women
1984	.63304*	.27999*	.81687*	.48078*
	(.10540)	(.15250)	(.13460)	(.13550)
Constant	−2.5221*	−3.2078*	−2.9275*	−2.2724*
	(.4906)	(.7570)	(.6195)	(.6026)
Log L	−1,299.5	−607.65	−698.50	−886.71
N	2,255	963	1,398	1,426

Standard errors in parentheses.

*statistically significant at 5% (two-tailed test).

**statistically significant at 10% (two-tailed test).

Note: Excluded year = year preceding each survey (1983 for 1984 survey, 1985 for 1986 survey).

employment. Individuals living in states with high average unemployment rates are less likely to be employed than individuals living in lower unemployment states.[18]

Combining the 1984 and 1986 surveys provides a wide variation in economic conditions, because the job losses took place over the period 1979–1985. For 1979, the civilian unemployment rate was 5.8%, for 1982 it was 9.7%, by 1985, the rate had fallen to 7.2%. Until recently, displaced worker studies have not examined the role of economic conditions.[19] In a recent paper, Howland and Peterson (1988) examine the impact of local labor market conditions on the financial losses of displaced manufacturing workers, using the 1984 Displaced Worker Survey. Although their emphasis is on local and industry variables, they find that workers displaced during a recession experience larger earnings losses than workers displaced during an upturn. Their sample contained a limited range of national economic conditions because they used only displacements from the years 1979–82.

To investigate the difference between expansions and recessions, the blue-collar male sample was divided into two periods, an expansionary period (1979, 1983–85) and a recessionary period (1980–82). Recessions were defined as years where the national civilian unemployment rate increased from the preceding year (expansions if it decreased).

Separate estimates for the expansion and recession periods are presented in table 9, both for post displacement earnings and the probabil-

Table 9   Postdisplacement Earnings and Probability of Employment
Blue-Collar Men

	Earnings		Employment[a]	
	(1)	(2)	(3)	(4)
Variable	Expansion	Recession	Expansion	Recession
Age	.02342**	−.00469	.01880	.10935*
	(.01265)	(.01516)	(.02769)	(.02854)
Age squared	−.00026	.00009	−.00055	−.00168*
	(.00017)	(.00021)	(.00036)	(.00037)
Education	.04505*	.04937**	.05794**	.03255
	(.00841)	(.00883)	(.01874)	(.02049)
Job tenure	−.01519*	.01728**	−.01333*	.01337*
	(.00659)	(.00757)	(.00653)	(.00682)
Tenure squared	−.00069*	−.00087*		
	(.00023)	(.00028)		
Nonwhite	−.15355*	.01429	−.19112	−.42413*
	(.05429)	(.06879)	(.12130)	(.13040)
Married	.06745**	.17694*	.27348*	.41083*
	(.03970)	(.05065)	(.09012)	(.09944)
Craft	.11191*	.13660*	.20076*	.06659
	(.03409)	(.03672)	(.08392)	(.09432)
Mining	.15699*	.09299	−.64500*	−.34803
	(.07957)	(.09113)	(.19230)	(.22150)
Durable mfg.	.10684**	.08886	−.11780	.00293
	(.05918)	(.07330)	(.15280)	(.17980)
Nondurable mfg.	−.02179	.06612	.23011	.16918
	(.06599)	(.08100)	(.16890)	(.19640)
Transport and utilities	.28221*	.16584*	−.35613**	.07996
	(.07410)	(.08533)	(.17780)	(.21310)
Trade	−.02703	.03656	−.01716	.31306
	(.07384)	(.08799)	(.18280)	(.22090)
ln (old earnings)			.22978*	.07687
			(.09527)	(.10350)
Residual	.48652*	.32726*		
	(.04083)	(.04047)		
Advance notice			.22273*	.05634
			(.07906)	(.08688)
State UN rate			.00021	−.05123*
			(.01204)	(.01052)
Part-time	−.39165*	−.35970*		
	(.04379)	(.04533)		
Industry change	−.13507*	−.14476*		
	(.03837)	(.04092)		
Occupation change	−.14554*	−.18473*		
	(.03650)	(.03898)		
Constant	4.6277*	5.0775*	−2.4381*	−1.9704*
	(.2561)	(.3503)	(.6669)	(.7450)
R^2	.4482	.3339		
Log L			−701.14	−579.15
N	647	756	1,183	1,072

Standard errors in parentheses.

*statistically significant at 5% (two-tailed test).

**statistically significant at 10% (two-tailed test).

[a]Earnings equations include controls for region, and probits include dummy variables for year of displacement.

126

ity of employment. For both equations, a null hypothesis of no structural differences between expansion and recession can be rejected.[20] Turning first to the probability of employment, the advantages of skill and education are statistically significant only during expansions. Higher state unemployment rates lower the probability of employment, but only during an expansion. High state unemployment rates during an expansion may encourage out-migration. Advance notice increases the probability of employment; the effect is statistically significant only during expansions. The advantage of advance notice is likely to be diminished when labor markets are slack (see the contribution by Addison and Portugal in this volume for an examination of advance notice).

For postdisplacement earnings, columns 1 and 2 of table 9 reveal that the ability to retain industry wage differentials depends on economic conditions. Workers displaced from mining, durable goods manufacturing, and transportation and public utilities continue to earn statistically significant positive wage differentials only if displaced during economic upturns.[21] A somewhat surprising result is that lower earnings for nonwhite men are found only during expansions.

This analysis has not examined the earnings effects of unemployment duration. Addison and Portugal (1989) analyze this relationship in a simultaneous model of unemployment duration and postdisplacement earnings. They find that longer durations are an important source of earnings loss: a 10% increase in duration lowers wages by approximately 1%.

V. Conclusion

One of the stylized facts of worker displacement is that many displaced workers experience difficult labor market adjustments because of losses of job tenure and firm-specific skills. This chapter has evaluated this assumption by examining the role of previous job tenure in determining earnings after permanent job loss. In comparison to earlier related work, the Bureau of Labor Statistics (BLS) Displaced Worker Surveys provide a more accurate identification of displaced workers and the econometric technique used here produces improved estimates of the effects of previous job tenure and predisplacement industry.

The analysis revealed that job tenure accumulated up to the time of displacement is positively related to postdisplacement earnings. The returns to tenure postdisplacement are smaller than predisplacement measures because of the loss of job/match effects and some specific skills. With permanent job loss, there is no job or match quality bias in the relationship between postdisplacement earnings and previous job tenure. With a built-in control of job/match heterogeneity, this outcome is likely to reflect the transferability of specific skills (skills not captured by labor market experience) and heterogeneity in worker ability. The positive relationship is stronger for displaced white-collar workers, where a greater degree of skill transferability is expected. Relative to blue-collar women, blue-collar men experience larger losses of the returns to job tenure. This difference suggests that blue-collar women acquire more general skills than men (for each year of job tenure). If women face discrimination in promotions, it may be the case that the ability component of the returns to job tenure is larger for women, and because the returns to ability are not lost at job displacement, the reduction in the yield to job tenure is smaller.

For blue-collar men, predisplacement industry is an important factor in postdisplacement earnings. Individuals displaced from high-wage industries are less likely to be employed, but those who are employed continue to earn positive wage differentials relative to similar workers displaced from other industries. An important (and unexamined) issue is whether these workers earn positive wage differentials because they return to the old job. Reported cross-tabulations are consistent with this outcome. The pattern of reemployment of displaced workers remains an open area of research, one that has implications for losses of specific skills.

Although much of the variation in outcomes can be linked to the characteristics of jobs lost, this analysis has identified factors appropriate for microeconomic manpower policy, such as education and skill training, that would ease the labor market adjustments of displaced workers. If the loss of jobs earning economic rents results in lower probabilities of employment, job counseling and retraining programs might address problems of reservation wages that do not adjust to the new distribution of wages as well as provide skills that alter that distribution. The large impact of unemployment rates on the probability of employment suggests that the labor market adjustments of individuals displaced by structural change has a cyclical component; an appropriate set of macroeconomic policies would make the adjustment easier.

There is substantial variation in who gets displaced and in postdisplacement earnings outcomes. These findings suggest that the appropriate focus for displaced worker policy is toward the individual and job characteristics associated with earnings losses, rather than categorical programs for all displaced workers. The results on job tenure point to a need for more research on the losses of specific skills.

APPENDIX

Table A-1   **Predisplacement Earnings (OLS)**

	Blue-Collar		White-Collar	
Variable	(1) Men	(2) Women	(3) Men	(4) Women
Age	.02634*	.01963	.06891*	.05484*
	(.00862)	(.01251)	(.01043)	(.01042)
Age squared	−.00026*	−.00027**	−.00076*	−.00070*
	(.00012)	(.00016)	(.00014)	(.00014)
Education	.05159*	.03621*	.05542*	.04659*
	(.00555)	(.00959)	(.00600)	(.00734)
Job tenure	.02951*	.03203*	.02825**	.03891*
	(.00479)	(.00789)	(.00596)	(.00831)
Tenure squared	−.00080*	−.00072*	−.00071*	−.00135*
	(.00018)	(.00031)	(.00022)	(.00042)
Nonwhite	−.12844*	−.05242	−.25724*	−.08077**
	(.03825)	(.04905)	(.05373)	(.04672)
Married	.06553*	.03389	.05462**	−.05194**
	(.02684)	(.03760)	(.02998)	(.02969)
Craft	.12337*	.08743**		
	(.02364)	(.04692)		
Sales			−.08432*	−.07502**
			(.03768)	(.04490)
Clerical			−.22763**	−.10568*
			(.04380)	(.03641)
Service			−.23934	−.31958*
			(.05159)	(.05099)
Mining	.44183*	.64845*	.36234*	.11877
	(.05671)	(.21060)	(.06950)	(.10200)
Durable mfg.	.09358*	.10065	.10818*	.08262**
	(.04483)	(.07620)	(.03809)	(.04648)
Nondurable mfg.	.01964	−.07976	.03658	.06700
	(.04896)	(.07773)	(.04847)	(.04512)
Transport and utilities	.29074*	−.00786	.13801*	.15169*
	(.05335)	(.12300)	(.05373)	(.05861)
Trade	−.05990	−.17958*	.04699	−.02850
	(.05384)	(.08917)	(.04152)	(.03930)
Constant	4.2016*	4.3251*	3.5583*	3.8643*
	(.1620)	(.2649)	(.1926)	(.2083)
R^2	.2515	.1795	.3381	.2082
N	1,403	477	1,033	852

Standard errors in parentheses.
*statistically significant at 5% (two-tailed test).
**statistically significant at 10% (two-tailed test).

Table A-2 Pattern of Postdisplacement Employment—
Blue-Collar Men

Old/New	Mining	Durable	Ndurable	TPU	WRT	Serv	Agr	Constrt	N
Mining	75.0	3.9	1.1	6.8	5.8	6.8	10.0	9.4	114
	34.2	12.3	1.7	8.8	11.4	15.8	1.7	14.0	
Durable	7.7	74.4	25.1	24.5	33.0	41.8	45.0	42.9	611
	0.6	42.7	7.2	5.9	12.1	18.0	1.5	11.9	
Ndurable	7.7	11.7	58.9	8.8	13.4	17.1	25.0	17.6	271
	1.5	15.1	38.0	4.8	11.1	16.6	1.8	11.1	
TPU	3.8	2.3	4.6	46.9	9.8	10.3	10.0	12.3	159
	1.3	5.0	5.0	43.4	13.8	16.9	1.3	13.2	
WRT	3.8	3.1	6.8	8.2	26.3	12.5	5.0	7.7	143
	1.4	7.7	8.4	8.4	41.3	23.1	0.7	9.1	
Services	1.9	4.6	3.4	4.8	11.6	11.4	5.0	10.0	104
	0.9	15.4	5.8	6.7	25.0	28.8	0.9	16.3	
N	52	351	175	147	224	263	20	70	1,402

Durable = durable goods manufacturing; Ndurable = nondurable goods manufacturing; TPU = transportation and public utilities; WRT = wholesale and retail trade; Agr = agriculture; Constrt = construction.

Note: The industry groups across the top are the postdisplacement industry; the industry groups listed on the left are predisplacement industry. In each cell, the top number is the percent of those employed in the postdisplacement industry who were displaced from the predisplacement industry; the bottom number is the percent of the predisplacement industry displaced who were employed in the postdisplacement industry.

Table A-3 Pattern of Postdisplacement Employment—
Blue-Collar Women

Old/New	Mining	Durable	Ndurable	TPU	WRT	Serv	Agr	Constrt	N
Mining	100.0	0	0	0	0	2.3	0	0	4
	25.0	0	0	0	0	75.0	0	0	
Durable	0	69.8	22.8	40	30.9	37.1	0	20.0	188
	0	39.4	12.7	3.2	18.1	26.1	0	0.5	
Ndurable	0	21.7	72.4	6.7	35.4	33.3	0	80.0	187
	0	12.3	40.6	0.5	20.9	23.5	0	2.1	
TPU	0	0	0	26.7	4.5	3.8	50.0	0	15
	0	0	0	26.7	33.3	33.3	6.7	0	
WRT	0	4.7	1.9	20.0	22.7	11.4	50.0	0	51
	0	9.8	3.9	5.8	49.0	29.4	1.9	0	
Services	0	3.7	2.8	6.7	6.4	12.1	0	0	31
	0	12.9	9.7	3.2	22.6	51.6	0	0	
N	1	106	105	15	110	132	2	5	476

Durable = durable goods manufacturing; Ndurable = nondurable goods manufacturing; TPU = transportation and public utilities; WRT = wholesale and retail trade; Agr = agriculture; Constrt = construction.

Note: The industry groups across the top are the postdisplacement industry; the industry groups listed on the left are predisplacement industry. In each cell, the top number is the percent of those employed in the postdisplacement industry who were displaced from the predisplacement industry; the bottom number is the percent of the predisplacement industry displaced who were employed in the postdisplacement industry.

130

Table A-4   **Pattern of Postdisplacement Employment— White-Collar Men**

Old/New	Mining	Durable	Ndurable	TPU	WRT	Serv	Agr	Constrt	N
Mining	69.2	1.8	0	5.7	3.1	3.6	0	7.6	44
	20.4	6.8	0	13.6	20.4	25.0	0	13.6	
Durable	0	65.4	19.4	15.2	18.4	18.3	0	27.8	267
	0	39.7	5.2	5.9	19.8	20.9	0	8.2	
Ndurable	7.7	3.7	41.7	5.7	9.4	9.5	37.5	11.4	111
	0.9	5.4	27.0	5.4	24.3	26.1	2.7	8.1	
TPU	7.7	3.1	2.8	37.1	3.8	6.2	0	7.6	83
	1.2	6.0	2.4	46.9	13.2	22.9	0	7.2	
WRT	7.7	17.3	16.7	19.0	49.6	16.4	12.5	25.3	275
	0.4	10.2	4.4	7.3	52.0	18.2	0.4	7.3	
Services	7.7	8.6	19.4	17.1	15.6	46.0	50.0	20.2	253
	0.4	5.5	5.5	7.1	17.8	55.7	1.6	6.3	
N	13	162	72	105	288	306	8	79	1,033

Durable = durable goods manufacturing; Ndurable = nondurable goods manufacturing; TPU = transportation and public utilities; WRT = wholesale and retail trade; Agr = agriculture; Constrt = construction.

Note: The industry groups across the top are the postdisplacement industry; the industry groups listed on the left are predisplacement industry. In each cell, the top number is the percent of those employed in the postdisplacement industry who were displaced from the predisplacement industry; the bottom number is the percent of the predisplacement industry displaced who were employed in the postdisplacement industry.

Table A-5   **Pattern of Postdisplacement Employment— White-Collar Women**

Old/New	Mining	Durable	Ndurable	TPU	WRT	Serv	Agr	Constrt	N
Mining	0	2.7	0	5.8	1.4	2.4	0	0	18
	0	11.1	0	16.7	16.7	55.6	0	0	
Durable	16.7	46.7	18.6	3.8	12.1	8.9	0	5.0	114
	0.8	30.7	9.6	1.7	22.8	33.3	0	0.8	
Ndurable	16.7	8.0	37.3	7.7	12.1	13.4	100	20.0	121
	0.8	4.9	18.2	3.3	21.5	47.1	0.8	3.3	
TPU	0	6.7	0	36.5	3.7	6.1	0	15.0	61
	0	8.2	0	31.1	13.1	42.6	0	4.9	
WRT	50.0	14.7	13.6	19.2	42.3	16.5	0	15.0	196
	1.5	5.6	4.1	5.1	46.4	35.7	0	1.5	
Services	16.7	21.3	30.5	26.9	28.4	52.6	0	4.5	342
	0.3	4.7	5.3	4.1	17.9	65.2	0	2.6	
N	6	75	59	52	215	424	1	20	852

Durable = durable goods manufacturing; Ndurable = nondurable goods manufacturing; TPU = transportation and public utilities; WRT = wholesale and retail trade; Agr = agriculture; Constrt = construction.

Note: The industry groups across the top are the postdisplacement industry; the industry groups listed on the left are predisplacement industry. In each cell, the top number is the percent of those employed in the postdisplacement industry who were displaced from the predisplacement industry; the bottom number is the percent of the predisplacement industry displaced who were employed in the postdisplacement industry.

131

NOTES

I am grateful to Anne MacEachern for valuable research assistance.

1. For empirical evidence of rising wage-tenure profiles, see Mincer and Jovanovic (1981) and Bartel and Borjas (1981).

2. Models of job/match and individual heterogeneity imply that the returns to human capital are overestimated in traditional earnings functions. These models are discussed in section II. Rising wage-tenure profiles have also been linked to agency models (see Lazear 1981).

3. Revising his earlier results, Topel (1988) concludes that the job/match part of the returns to seniority is small.

4. This model is discussed in detail in Kletzer (1989). No generality is lost by ignoring higher order terms in T; they will be introduced in the empirical analysis.

5. This assumption is reasonable if information acquired on the old job is specific to that job. Any correlation between the two job/match components is likely to be individual-specific, and captured by A_i, because the jobs differ across observations.

6. The assumption of complete specificity of "specific" skills (skills captured by job tenure, holding experience [general skills] constant) may be too strong. The transferability of occupational skills is discussed in Shaw (1987).

7. The role of changing industry or occupation in determining postdisplacement earnings has been suggested by other work in this area. Neumann (1978) found longer durations of unemployment and lower reemployment earnings for reemployed trade-displaced workers who changed 2-digit industry. Using the Displaced Worker Survey, Podgursky and Swaim (1987a) and Addison and Portugal (1989) report a similar result for earnings.

8. From the 1984 survey, the sample includes workers displaced in the years 1979–83, and from the 1986 survey, displacements occurred in the years 1981–85.

9. A direct measure of labor market experience at the time of displacement is not available from the Displaced Worker Survey. The usual constructed measure (age-education-6) is likely to overestimate labor-market experience for women, therefore age at displacement will be used as a proxy.

10. The marginal contribution of previous job tenure is obtained from the partial derivative of the (log) earnings function with respect to previous job tenure:

$$\ln W_t = \beta_1 T + \beta_2 T^2 + \beta_3 X + \epsilon$$
$$\delta \ln W_t / \delta T = \beta_1 + 2\beta_2 \bar{T}$$

The ratio of $[(\delta \ln W_{t+1}/\delta T)/(\delta \ln W_t/\delta T)]$ yields a measure of the reduction in the value of previous job tenure.

11. See Addison and Portugal (1989) for a similar discussion.

12. See Madden (1987) for a discussion of gender differences in the costs of displacement. Consistent with the results reported here, Madden finds greater wage losses for women than men using the January 1984 Displaced Worker Survey.

13. The model presented here is a model of "first job" reemployment, that is, the probability of reemployment directly following permanent job loss. The data, however, are censored by survey date employment, which is a function of either (1) continued employment (getting a job as in the model and keeping it) or (2) the probability of finding a second job. Modeling the probability of employment in this simple framework ignores the influence of the probability of continued employment.

132

14. It is also consistent with the limited reallocation of labor across sectors by employed blue-collar men.

15. Using a sample of men from the 1984 Displaced Worker Survey, Addison and Portugal (1989) estimate a larger effect of industry change.

16. See Neumann (1978), Kiefer and Neumann (1979), Podgursky and Swaim (1987a), and Addison and Portugal (1989). Addison and Portugal use a more flexible specification than the earlier papers.

17. On the correlation between reservation wages and wage offers, see Kiefer and Neumann (1979).

18. The average state unemployment rate over the appropriate five-year period was used to capture economic conditions that might have influenced both initial employment and continued employment. The coefficient estimate points to the importance of "local" labor market conditions, although because the variable refers to survey date residence, its coefficient reflects both mobility and the influence of a depressed labor market on the probability of employment.

19. The case study literature has documented the interaction between plant closings and local labor market conditions. See Gordus et al. (1980) for a review of this literature.

20. For the probit, $(2 \cdot \Delta LR) = 98.4$ and $\chi^2(12,.05) = 21.03$. For postdisplacement earnings, $F^* = 2.626$ and $F(21,1361) = 1.57$.

21. Results in Howland and Peterson (1988) are complementary. They find that the earnings outcomes for blue-collar workers are influenced by employment growth in the predisplacement industry. They find smaller earnings losses where industry demand is strong and they conclude that a high proportion of blue-collar skills are industry-specific and workers continue to earn returns to these skills only in labor markets where jobs are available.

REFERENCES

Abraham, Katharine G., and Henry S. Farber (1987). "Job Duration, Seniority, and Earnings." *American Economic Review* 77 (June): 278–97.

———(1988). "Returns to Seniority in Union and Nonunion Jobs: A New Look at the Evidence." *Industrial and Labor Relations Review* 42 (October): 3–19.

Addison, John, and Pedro Portugal (1987). "The Effect of Advance Notification of Plant Closings on Unemployment." *Industrial and Labor Relations Review* 41 (October): 3–16.

———(1989). "Job Displacement, Relative Wage Changes, and Duration of Unemployment." *Journal of Labor Economics* 7 (July):281–302.

Altonji, Joseph, and Robert Shakotko. (1987). "Do Wages Rise with Job Seniority?" *Review of Economic Studies* 54 (July): 437–59.

Bale, Malcolm D. (1973). "Adjustment to Freer Trade: An Analysis of the Adjustment Assistance Provisions of the Trade Expansion Act of 1962." Unpublished Ph.D. dissertation, University of Wisconsin.

Bartel, Ann P., and George J. Borjas (1981). "Wage Growth and Job Turnover: An Empirical Analysis." In *Studies in Labor Markets*, edited by Sherwin Rosen, pp.

65–90. National Bureau of Economic Research, Chicago: University of Chicago Press.

Browne, Lynn E. (1985). "Structural Change and Dislocated Workers." *New England Economic Review* (January–February): 15–30.

Corson, Walter, and Walter Nicholson (1981). "Trade Adjustment Assistance for Workers: Results of a Survey of Recipients under the Trade Act of 1974." In *Research in Labor Economics*, 4, edited by Ronald G. Ehrenberg, pp. 417–69. Greenwich, Conn.: JAI Press, Inc.

Flaim, Paul, and Ellen Seghal (1985). "Displaced Workers of 1979–83: How Well Have They Fared?" U.S. Department of Labor, Bureau of Labor Statistics, Bulletin 2240, Washington, D.C.

Gladstein, Lori Ann (1986). "Employment and Earnings Outcomes of Permanent Job Loss." Unpublished doctoral dissertation, University of California, Berkeley.

Gordus, Jeanne Prial, Paul Jarley, and Louis A. Ferman (1981). *Plant Closings and Economic Dislocation.* Kalamazoo, Mich.: W.E. Upjohn Institute for Employment Research.

Hamermesh, Daniel S. (1987). "The Costs of Worker Displacement." *Quarterly Journal of Economics* 102 (February): 51–75.

———(1989). "What Do We Know About Worker Displacement in the U.S.?" *Industrial Relations* 28 (Winter): 51–59.

Heckman, James J. (1979). "Sample Selection Bias As Specification Error." *Econometrica* 46 (July): 153–61.

Howland, Marie, and George E. Peterson (1988). "Labor Market Conditions and the Reemployment of Displaced Workers." *Industrial and Labor Relations Review* 42 (October): 109–22.

Jovanovic, Boyan (1979). "Job Matching and the Theory of Turnover." *Journal of Political Economy* 87 (October): 972–90.

Kiefer, Nicholas M., and George R. Neumann (1979). "An Empirical Job-Search Model, with a Test of the Constant Reservation Wage Hypothesis." *Journal of Political Economy* 87 (February): 89–107.

Kletzer, Lori G. (1989). "Returns to Seniority After Permanent Job Loss." *American Economic Review* 79 (June): 536–43.

Kruse, Douglas L. (1988). "International Trade and the Labor Market Experience of Displaced Workers." *Industrial and Labor Relations Review* 41 (April): 402–17.

Lazear, Edward (1981). "Agency, Earnings Profiles, Productivity, and Hours Restrictions." *American Economic Review* 71 (June): 606–20.

Lippman, Steven, and J. McCall (1976). "The Economics of Job Search: A Survey." *Economic Inquiry* 14 (June): 155–89.

Lovell, Malcolm R., Jr. (1984). "An Antidote for Protectionism." *The Brookings Review* 3 (Winter): 23–28.

Madden, Janice F. (1987). "Gender Differences in the Cost of Displacement: An Empirical Test of Discrimination in the Labor Market." *American Economic Review* 77 (May): 246–51.

Marshall, Robert C., and Gary A. Zarkin (1987). "The Effect of Job Tenure on Wage Offers." *Journal of Labor Economics* 5 (July): 301–24.

Maxwell, Nan L., and Ronald D'Amico (1986). "Employment and Wage Effects of Involuntary Job Separation: Male-Female Differences." *American Economic Review* 76 (May): 373–77.

Mincer, Jacob, and Boyan Jovanovic (1981). "Labor Mobility and Wages." In *Studies in*

Labor Markets, edited by Sherwin Rosen, pp. 21–63. National Bureau of Economic Research, Chicago: University of Chicago Press.

Neumann, George R. (1978). "The Labor Market Adjustments of Trade Displaced Workers: The Evidence from the Trade Adjustment Assistance Program." In *Research in Labor Economics,* 2, edited by Ronald G. Ehrenberg, pp. 353–81. Greenwich, Conn.: JAI Press.

Podgursky, Michael, and Paul Swaim (1987a). "Job Displacement and Earnings Loss: Evidence from the Displaced Worker Survey." *Industrial and Labor Relations Review* 41 (October): 17–29.

_____(1987b). "The Duration of Joblessness Following Displacement." *Industrial Relations* 26 (Fall): 213–26.

Ruhm, Christopher J. (1987a). "The Economic Consequences of Labor Mobility." *Industrial and Labor Relations Review* 41 (October): 30–40.

_____(1987b). "The Extent and Persistence of Unemployment Following Permanent Quits and Layoffs." Mimeographed. Boston: Boston University.

Shapiro, David, and Steven Sandell (1985). "Age Discrimination in Wages and Displaced Old Men." *Southern Economic Journal* 52 (July): 90–102.

Shaw, Kathryn (1987). "Occupational Change, Employer Change, and the Transferability of Skills." *Southern Economic Journal* 53 (January): 702–19.

Topel, Robert (1986). "Job Mobility, Search, and Earnings Growth: A Reinterpretation of Human Capital Earnings Functions." In *Research in Labor Economics,* 10, edited by Ronald G. Ehrenberg, pp. 199–233. Greenwich, Conn.: JAI Press.

_____(1988). "Wages Rise with Job Seniority." Mimeographed. Chicago: University of Chicago.

CHAPTER FIVE

Displacement and Unemployment

PAUL L. SWAIM AND MICHAEL J. PODGURSKY

I. Introduction

An important issue related to worker displacement is the unemployment that may result. The belief that displacement often results in lengthy unemployment is reflected in recent legislation such as the Omnibus Trade Act of 1988, which reformed and expanded federal programs that provide labor-market adjustment assistance to "dislocated" workers.[1] Do many of these workers, in fact, experience long periods of unemployment following displacement? If so, which workers risk lengthy spells? Clearly, the answers to these questions are crucial to an assessment of labor-market policy toward displaced workers.

An analysis of displacement and unemployment is also valuable for assessing the revival of "structural" theories of unemployment. Whereas "turnover" or "frictional" theories of unemployment that emphasize labor-market fluidity and worker choices to quit or refuse jobs found much acceptance in the 1970s (Feldstein 1973), recent trends in the level and composition of unemployment have led some economists to devote increased attention to long-duration unemployment and demand-side factors. In an influential paper, Lilien (1982) identifies increased sectoral shifts in labor demand as the main cause of the rise in the U.S. unemployment rate in the 1970s. He argues, however, that the resulting increase in unemployment is "frictional" and should be viewed as a productive investment in the reallocation of labor. Consistent with Lilien's sectoral shifts hypothesis, Podgursky (1984) and Summers (1986) show that the increase in unemployment has been concentrated

136

among experienced workers and involuntary job losers. They question, however, how smoothly the sectoral reallocation of labor proceeds since the increase is largely attributable to longer duration, rather than more frequent, unemployment spells. Summers also examines state-level data on employment trends by industry and hypothesizes that displacement from high-wage industries is generating a large pool of structurally unemployed, who are slow to move to new jobs in growing industries and occupations. Finally, Murphy and Topel (1987) show that the secular rise in unemployment coincided with a decline in the sectoral mobility of the unemployed. A decreased propensity to change industrial sector is consistent with a structural diagnosis of rising unemployment, but can also be interpreted as evidence against Lilien's sectoral shifts hypothesis. Since none of these studies use data that explicitly identify displaced workers, their conclusions regarding the importance of permanent layoffs and worker immobility for total unemployment are quite tentative.[2]

In this chapter we use data from the January 1984 and 1986 Displaced Worker Surveys to shed light on these questions. This new data source provides a large, nationally representative sample of workers displaced between 1979 and 1985.[3] We find that the unemployment experience of displaced workers is extremely diverse. Although many find jobs quickly following displacement—often with no interruption in work—a substantial group suffer very long spells of joblessness following displacement, often ranging to one year or more. The long-duration jobless also have much larger earnings losses once reemployed. To identify workers at risk of long spells, we estimate multivariate hazard models of jobless spell durations and identify a number of significant demographic and economic covariates. Many of these findings are consistent with frictional or turnover theories of unemployment, but others are more easily reconciled with structural theories.[4]

We then turn to the thorny statistical issue of differentiating between "heterogeneity" and "state dependence" as explanations for long jobless durations. Although seemingly an abstract econometric matter, this distinction has practical implications for labor-market policy. Our tentative findings indicate an important role for state dependence, that is, that the reemployment rate for a worker falls as his or her jobless spells lengthens. If substantiated by future research, this "scarring" effect provides a strong argument for the prompt provision of adjustment assistance following displacement.

Overall, our research indicates the need for caution in generalizing about displacement and unemployment. As a group, displaced workers exhibit high rates of sectoral mobility and many experience little or no unemployment. We also find, however, that a significant minority of displaced workers appear to become structurally unemployed and that long spells of unemployment are somewhat more likely for workers eventually reemployed in a new industry or occupation. Finally, although we identify personal characteristics and labor-market conditions that significantly increase the risk of long jobless spells, much unexplained variation remains. The implications for manpower policy are thus somewhat paradoxical: Prompt and well-targeted adjustment assistance programs would likely yield important equity and efficiency gains, but may be difficult to implement since ex ante identification of displaced workers most in need of assistance may be difficult.

II. The Duration of Joblessness: Preliminary Evidence

In January 1984 and January 1986 all respondents from the roughly 60,000 Current Population Survey (CPS) households were asked whether they or any adult member of their household aged 20 or older had lost a job in the last five years due to "a plant closing, an employer going out of business, a layoff from which . . . was not recalled or other similar reasons." An affirmative response triggered a series of supplemental questions concerning the job loss and subsequent labor-market experience. These largely retrospective questions comprise the Displaced Worker Survey (DWS) and augment the extensive current labor force data provided in the basic monthly CPS.

From the sample of workers responding affirmatively to the initial displacement screening question, we select workers aged twenty to sixty-one who were formerly employed as full-time wage and salary workers in nonagricultural jobs. We also limit our sample to workers who stated that the cause of their displacement was: (1) a plant shutdown, business failure or relocation; or (2) whose employer continued in operation but who lost their jobs due to slack work or otherwise had their jobs eliminated.[5] Finally, we initially limit our sample to workers displaced a year or more prior to the survey date (i.e., 1979–83 and 1981–84 for the two surveys). This targets workers unlikely to be recalled by their former employer. It also guarantees that most workers have completed their initial jobless spell, hence, most of our observations are *complete* rather than *censored*.

In the DWS, interviewers were to ascertain the number of weeks workers were without work and "available" for work following displace-

138

ment. Unlike the familiar measure of unemployment duration in the monthly CPS, the DWS question does not refer to active job search. Thus, a spell of joblessness may include one or more periods of suspended job search and labor force withdrawal. Since Clark and Summers (1979) have shown that the distinction between "unemployed" and "out of the labor force" is problematic for workers who have long or recurrent spells of unemployment, the DWS measure of jobless duration is arguably a better indicator of reemployment difficulties for displaced workers. In order to emphasize this difference, however, we consistently refer to our dependent variable as duration of *joblessness* rather than duration of *unemployment*.

Another difference between our jobless duration measure and standard unemployment duration is the treatment of multiple spells. If displaced workers obtained a temporary job followed by another spell of joblessness, the combined total is reported. Although we have no direct measure of the importance of multiple spells for total jobless duration, it may be substantial. One indication that displacement frequently results in an extended period of employment instability is that 34.8% of the men and 38.8% of the women in the 1986 DWS had held two or more jobs since being displaced. Drawing upon a special January–March 1984 matched CPS datafile we also find that 56.0% of the workers displaced prior to 1983 who were unemployed at the time of the 1984 survey worked in 1983.[6] Ruhm's analysis of PSID data also indicates that displacement frequently results in multiple spells of joblessness (chapter 6 of this volume).

A potential problem with this retrospective data is recall bias. The five-year retrospective data on which this study is based have not been subject to the careful scrutiny of standard CPS measures. It has been shown, however, that the one-year retrospective data on unemployment duration in the annual Work Experience Supplement (WES) to the CPS probably understate unemployment (Bowers 1980; Horvath 1982). This suggests that the DWS understates total jobless duration resulting from displacement. It does not follow, however, that the average duration of reported spells is biased downward, since underreporting may frequently take the form of simply not recalling displacements with short spells of joblessness.[7] A study of response errors in retrospective reports of unemployment in the Panel Study of Income Dynamics is somewhat reassuring in this regard. Mathiowetz and Duncan (1988) find that the extent of reporting error on annual weeks of unemployment is relatively small, although there is substantial error in reporting the timing of unemployment spells within the year, with short spells likely to go unreported.

We note that the DWS question refers to the total weeks of joblessness, hence requests the sort of information apparently most easily recalled.

Finally, although we are interested in the joblessness *caused* by displacement, the DWS more nearly measures the joblessness that *follows* displacement. Reported weeks jobless may thus be upward biased in two ways. First, workers reporting combined durations for two or more spells of joblessness may have included later spells unrelated to displacement. The CPS interviewers' instruction manual indicated that multiple spells should be included only if they are reasonably attributable to the initial displacement (i.e., if the intervening job was "temporary"), but such a determination is clearly rather subjective. Second, even in the absence of displacement these workers might have experienced some time jobless, perhaps due to temporary layoffs or voluntary quits. Unfortunately, the DWS provides no basis for estimating "counterfactual" jobless durations since retrospective information on joblessness was only collected for displaced workers.[8]

With these caveats in mind, we examine the distribution of spell lengths of joblessness in table 1. The weighted tabulations from the 1986 DWS are reported in the top panel of the table and correspond to a population of 3.6 million blue-collar workers (26% female) and 2.9 million white-collar and service workers (48% female) displaced between 1981 and 1984.[9] Weighted displacement totals for 1979–82 from the January 1984 DWS are 4.2 and 2.7 million, respectively, with a similar gender mix. In both surveys, the median duration of joblessness for blue-collar workers is considerably longer than that of white-collar and service workers, and within each occupational group, female exceeds male duration.

For all groups the variation of spell lengths is very large. While many workers secure new jobs relatively quickly, others experience very long spells of joblessness. In the 1986 DWS, for example, 44.2% of male blue-collar workers had fourteen or fewer weeks of joblessness following displacement. On the other hand, 22.5% had more than one year of joblessness following displacement. Even for white-collar men, the group experiencing the least joblessness, 25.0% were without work for more than six months.

While a more complete explanation of this varied experience awaits the development of our multivariate hazard models in the next section, the tabulations in table 2 allow us to discount three tempting hypotheses regarding displaced workers with long spells of joblessness. First, they are not simply workers with high-reservation wages who have chosen to invest more time searching for an especially good job offer. The data in

140

Table 1   **Duration of Jobless Spells Following Displacement**[a]

Weeks of joblessness	Blue-collar			White-collar and service		
	Total	Male	Female	Total	Male	Female
January 1986 DWS (1981–84)						
Total (thousands)	3,611	2,687	924	2,851	1,487	1,364
Percent distribution						
0–14	40.0	44.2	27.5	52.8	57.1	48.2
15–26	14.2	14.0	14.7	17.0	17.9	16.0
27–52	20.2	19.2	23.0	15.4	15.5	15.4
53+	25.7	22.5	34.8	14.8	9.5	20.2
Median weeks	25	20	48	12	12	16
January 1984 DWS (1979–82)						
Total (thousands)	4,150	3,159	991	2,734	1,371	1,371
Percent distribution						
0–14	35.0	36.9	29.0	50.1	55.0	45.2
15–26	13.7	13.8	13.3	13.0	13.5	12.4
27–52	19.2	18.8	20.6	16.7	16.9	16.5
53+	32.2	30.6	37.1	20.2	14.6	25.8
Median weeks	30	26	40	14	12	20

[a]Workers aged twenty to sixty-one displaced from full-time nonagricultural wage and salary jobs. Totals exclude a small number of workers previously employed as household service workers.

columns 1 and 2 show that earnings losses for reemployed workers are much larger for workers with long jobless spells. Blue-collar men with the shortest jobless spells, for example, have a median loss in weekly earnings of just 5% (i.e., a ratio of current to adjusted past earnings of 0.95). Those with a year or more of joblessness, however, have median losses of 29% with 54.7% experiencing losses that exceed 25%. This data on reemployment earnings is, of course, consistent with the hypothesis that workers experiencing long spells of joblessness initially maintained reservation wages that were high *relative* to their postdisplacement earnings capacity. Such long spells of joblessness, however, are difficult to reconcile with job search models that assume expected income maximization unless workers badly overestimate either prevailing wage rates or the offer arrival rate in the labor market segment in which they initially focus their search.[10]

Second, we can also reject the hypothesis that long-term jobless workers are primarily older workers who face job discrimination or who partly retire in the face of displacement. The average age of displaced workers

141

Table 2 **Worker Characteristics by Weeks of Joblessness**[a]

Weeks of joblessness	Wage ratio[b]		Age when displaced		Changed Three-Digit Industry/ Occupation[c]	
	(1) Median	(2) Prob. < .75	(3) Mean	(4) Prob. > 50	(5) (%)	(6) (%)
Male, blue-collar						
0–14	.95	28.6	31.7	7.7	68.5	70.8
15–26	.92	29.3	31.4	8.4	80.7	72.1
27–52	.77	44.7	33.6	10.4	79.2	77.1
53+	.71	54.7	36.2	17.0	80.4	85.8
Female, blue-collar						
0–14	.95	26.8	32.9	6.9	85.3	89.6
15–26	.84	45.2	33.7	11.5	75.3	73.5
27–52	.82	41.6	33.4	11.3	81.5	80.6
53+	.58	66.9	35.4	14.8	85.4	88.7
Male, white-collar and service						
0–14	.99	21.2	32.7	6.8	76.4	63.7
15–26	.96	32.0	34.1	9.5	78.8	76.7
27–52	.81	40.7	33.6	10.8	80.2	78.4
53+	.73	53.2	39.5	21.6	94.5	86.6
Female, white-collar and service						
0–14	1.01	23.0	30.7	4.8	85.4	79.8
15–26	.93	34.5	33.5	9.7	84.0	82.7
27–52	.82	41.6	33.2	9.2	92.1	83.3
53+	.69	60.2	35.7	13.3	94.5	92.9

[a]Workers aged twenty to sixty-one displaced from full-time nonagricultural wage and salary jobs between 1981 and 1984 (January 1986 DWS). Since the results are so similar, the corresponding tabulations for the January 1984 DWS are not reported.

[b]For workers employed in January 1986, ratio of usual weekly earnings on current job to usual weekly earnings on former job adjusted for trend growth of full-time weekly earnings between the year of displacement and January 1986.

[c]Workers employed in January 1986. Column (5) reports percent reemployed in a new industry and column (6) the percent in a new occupation.

with very long jobless spells (one year or more) in column 3 ranges from the mid to upper thirties for the four groups. White-collar men with long spells have the highest mean age, yet just 21.6% are fifty or older and all of the workers in our sample are under age sixty-two. Third, although displaced workers reemployed in different three-digit SIC industries or occupations are more likely to have long jobless spells than those reemployed in the same industry or occupation, displaced workers are hardly immobile. Among reemployed workers with zero to fourteen weeks of joblessness, the share changing industry ranged between 68.5% and 85.4% and the share changing occupation ranged between 63.7% and 89.6%.

Finally, we consider the possibility that many workers reporting long spells of joblessness are weakly attached to the labor force. This seems unlikely for the men in our sample. In the January–March 1984 matched CPS datafile we find that just 10.6% of blue-collar males reporting a year or more of joblessness and 11.3% of the corresponding white-collars males: (1) did not work in 1983 and (2) were out of the labor force in January 1984. Among the blue-collar group, even these labor force drop-outs demonstrated some continuing attachment to the labor force, since 43.1% actively searched for work five or more weeks in 1983.

The issue of labor-force attachment is less clear-cut for the women in our sample. This is particularly true for blue-collar women, over half of whom report more than six months of joblessness. Nonetheless, of women reporting a year or more of joblessness just 36.3% of blue-collar and 38.5% of white-collar and service workers did not work in 1983 and were out of the labor force in January 1984. Among this group, 47.3% of blue-collar and 67.6% of white-collar and service workers cited responsibilities as a homemaker as the major reason for not working in 1983. It should be recalled, however, that these women were formerly full-time workers. In addition, 33.5% of the blue-collar and 24.4% of the white-collar and service women reported family incomes below the poverty level.

III. Model and Estimates

A. Multivariate Hazard Model

In order to test more rigorously for demographic differences in jobless duration, as well as the effect of labor-market and policy variables, we estimate a hazard model of jobless spell durations that is consistent with standard search-theoretic studies of unemployment duration (Mortensen 1986). In this model a jobless spell begins at the time of displacement and ends when a displaced worker receives a sufficiently attractive job offer. Denoting spell lengths with the random variable T, the probability that an on-going jobless spell ends in its tth week is

$$Pr(T \leq t | T > t - 1) = Pr(N(t) \geq 1) \, Pr(W(t) \geq W^r(t) | N(t) \geq 1), \quad (1)$$

where $N(t)$ is the number of job offers received in the tth week, W the maximum offered wage, W^r the worker's reservation wage, and the two

143

right-hand probabilities reflect worker preferences and labor market constraints. For example, frictional theories of unemployment emphasize that unemployment insurance benefits or a high valuation of nonwork activities result in higher reservation wages hence longer expected durations. Structural theories of unemployment typically place greater emphasis on a low offer arrival rate, rather that a high-reservation wage, as the major source of long durations.

Our reduced-form model of jobless duration is specified in terms of the reemployment rate emphasized in job search theory. We assume a hazard function (i.e., instantaneous exit rate into employment) of the form

$$h(t) = \lim_{\Delta t \to 0} Pr\,(t \le T < t + \Delta t | T > t) \,/\, \Delta t = \lambda\,\alpha\,(\lambda\,t)^{\alpha-1}. \tag{2}$$

This implies that T follows a Weibull distribution with "location" parameter λ and "shape" parameter α. The resulting Weibull survivor function, defined by $S(t) = Pr(T > t)$ is

$$S(t) = \exp(-(\lambda\,t)^\alpha). \tag{3}$$

An attractive feature of the Weibull distribution is that it allows us to test for changes in the exit rate from joblessness over time. If $\alpha = 1$, the hazard rate is constant at the value λ and T follows an exponential distribution. If $\alpha < 1$, the hazard rate decreases monotonically with the jobless spell length producing *negative* duration dependence. If $\alpha > 1$, the opposite result obtains (i.e., *positive* duration dependence). Unlike some of the survival time distributions analyzed by Portugal (chapter 7 of this volume), the Weibull distribution imposes monotonic duration dependence patterns that are restrictive and may be inappropriate. Thus, we also estimate lognormal and log-logistic variants of our multivariate hazard model. Unlike the Weibull model, these distributional assumptions accommodate "inverted-U"shaped hazard functions.[11] As is discussed below, all of our major findings proved robust to these variations in distributional form.

Job-search theory implies that the hazard rate varies across individuals according to a number of observable individual characteristics and labor-market conditions. We accommodate independent regressors by adopting the proportional hazards specification, in which the ith individual's hazard function becomes

$$h_i(t) = h(t)\,Q(X_i), \tag{4}$$

where $h(t)$ is the "base-line" Weibull hazard function, X_i a row vector of independent variables for the ith individual, and $Q(.)$ a nonnegative function. An easy way to implement the proportional hazards assumption in the Weibull case is to specify that the location parameter λ is a log-linear function of X_i:

$$\lambda_i = \exp(-X_i \beta), \tag{5}$$

where β is a column vector of coefficients.[12] Since lower hazard rates lead to longer expected duration, variables associated with *positive* β-coefficients imply *longer* jobless spells.

This Weibull regression model is quite flexible and is commonly used in studies of unemployment duration (Lancaster 1979; Solon 1985). It does imply, however, that the hazard rates for two individuals with different X-values differ by the same proportionate amount throughout their jobless spells. Denoting the hazard rates for individuals i and j by h_i and h_j, and using equations (2) and (5):

$$h_i(t)/h_j(t) = \exp(\alpha \, \beta(X_j - X_i)), \tag{6}$$

which is constant for all values of t. Thus, if an independent variable is more important at one stage of a spell of joblessness than another, our proportional hazards specification captures only the average effect throughout the entire spell.[13]

Before proceeding to estimate our multivariate model we must introduce one more complication. The survivor model defined by equations (2)–(5) assumes no unmeasured heterogeneity among workers. Workers with identical observable characteristics (X) are assumed to have identical hazard functions, hence "draw" from the same distribution of jobless spell durations. Workers who are identical in terms of X may, however, have different exit probabilities due to unmeasured attributes (e.g., IQ, motivation, or contacts). If this is the case, workers with higher exit probabilities form a progressively smaller share of the sample as jobless duration increases, while the share of the less-employable workers grows. As a consequence, the *group* hazard rate for survivors falls over time. Unobserved heterogeneity in the sample would thus bias our estimate of α toward zero, producing spurious negative duration dependence (Heckman and Singer 1984). Our estimates of β might also be biased, although in an indeterminate way (Lancaster 1985).

In order to capture such unobserved heterogeneity, we generalize our hazard and survivor functions as follows:

$$h(t|v) = v \, \lambda \, \alpha \, (\lambda \, t)^{\alpha-1}, \tag{2'}$$
$$S(t|v) = \exp[-(\lambda \, t)^\alpha v], \tag{3'}$$

where v is a random variable capturing unmeasured heterogeneity (analogous to the mean-zero additive disturbance in the classical linear regression model) and we have suppressed the individual subscript for brevity. We assume that v follows a gamma distribution with unit mean and variance σ^2. Thus, with no worker heterogeneity, $\sigma^2 = 0$ and we have our simple Weibull model. Larger values of σ^2 imply greater heterogeneity. It follows that our new population survivor function is

$$S(t) = \int_0^\infty S(t|v)f(v) \, dv = (1 + \sigma^2 \, (\lambda t)^\alpha)^{-1/\sigma^2}, \tag{7}$$

where $f(v)$ denotes the gamma density function. Similarly, our population hazard function becomes

$$h(t) = [S(t)]^{\sigma^2} [\lambda \, \alpha \, (\lambda \, t)^{\alpha-1}], \tag{8}$$

where the second term on the right-hand side of equation (8) is the simple Weibull hazard from equation (2). We will also estimate the generalized model defined by equations (7) and (8), which will be termed a "gamma heterogeneity" or GH model.

The independent variables comprising the X-vector are defined in table 3. As equation (1) indicates, this list includes variables that affect the frequency with which job offers are received and the level of workers' reservation wages relative to the distribution of offered wages. In each case we have indicated our *a priori* expectations regarding the sign of the variable. A *positive* coefficient indicates a *higher* probability of "surviving" in a jobless state from one week to the next, and hence a *longer* expected spell of joblessness. In some cases, demand (the frequency and attractiveness of job offers) and supply (reservation wage) factors likely reinforce one another. For example, we expect that age will have a positive sign since *ceteris paribus* many employers will prefer younger over older workers in their hiring decisions and the option of early retirement may encourage some older workers to set high reservation wages. In other cases, these sign expectations reflect our beliefs regarding the relative dominance of demand-side factors. For example, we do not expect blacks and workers with low levels of educational attainment to set low enough reservation wages to offset the preference of employers for whites and better-educated workers.[14]

Since most of these variables are common to applied job search studies we limit our discussion to several less traditional variables of particular relevance for assessing the mobility of displaced workers. If we assume that reservation wages are an increasing function of earnings at the time of displacement, then to the extent that union wages embody nonportable rents we would expect a lower hazard rate for

Table 3   **Description of Variables in the Model**
                     (expected sign in parenthesis)

Variable	Definition
T	Duration of joblessness in weeks (dependent variable) T = reported weeks of joblessness +0.5
AGE	Age in years at time of displacement (+)
EDUCATION	Years of schooling completed (−)
BLACK	1 = black (+)
MARRIED	1 = married (−)
#CHILDREN	Number of children in primary family (?)
LN(OLDWAGE)	Natural log of usual full-time weekly earnings on former job adjusted for trend growth in earnings (?)
TENURE	Years of employment with former employer (+)
UNION%	Industry unionization rate (from Kokkelenberg and Sockell 1985) (+)
SHUTDOWN	1 = Employee lost job due to plant shutdown (−)
UIELIG	1 = Eligible for unemployment insurance benefits (+) Workers were assumed eligible if: (1) they collected UI; or (2) $T < 3$ and tenure ≥ 1.
ADVANCE	Dummy variable indicating whether the worker expected layoff or received advance notification of layoff (−)
UNAREA	Area unemployment rate at the time of displacement. For workers not in a major SMSA, the residual state unemployment rate. From *Employment and Earnings,* various issues. (+)
YEARS	Years since displacement (?)
CRAFT, OPERATIVE, MANAGER, PROFESSIONAL, TECHNICAL, SALES, CLERICAL	Occupation Dummy variables

union workers and hence a positive sign on UNION%.[15] Case studies of mass layoffs and plant shutdowns suggest that as long as a plant remains in operation, many workers maintain unrealistically high expectations regarding recall and thus postpone aggressive job search or other long-term adjustment strategies (e.g., relocation or retraining), or maintain unrealistically high reservation wages. Presumably, this "waiting for recall" effect will be smaller in the case of a plant shutdown as compared to a layoff in which the employer's plant or establishment remained in operation. Thus, our reading of the case study literature leads us to expect a negative sign on a plant shutdown dummy (SHUTDOWN).[16] Finally, we include years since displacement (YEARS) to capture recall bias and the possible effect of cumulated multiple spells.

B. Estimation and Results

One problem that often arises in estimating models of unemployment duration is censoring. As is usually the case in a sample of workers who have experienced a spell of unemployment, some of the workers' jobless spells were still in progress at the January 1984 and January 1986 survey dates. Matters are further complicated by the fact that the DWS measure of joblessness was "top-coded" at ninety-nine weeks for both completed and continuing spells. Excluding from the sample workers with jobless spells in progress or with "top-coded" spells would likely result in sample censoring bias.[17]

We dealt with the problem of censoring as follows. We restricted our sample to workers displaced between 1979 and 1981 in the January 1984 DWS and between 1981 and 1983 in the January 1986 DWS. Since at least two years have passed since displacement, most of these workers have completed their spell of joblessness. Those workers still jobless at the time of the survey have passed the ninety-nine week limit and are identified as censored observations along with workers whose completed spell was ninety-nine weeks or greater. Thus, all workers whose jobless spells were recorded as ninety-nine weeks are treated as censored observations.[18]

Maximum likelihood estimates of the parameters of our duration models and related statistics are presented in table 4. For each occupation-sex subsample, we estimate two versions of our survival model. The column labeled model (1) presents estimates for the simple Weibull model defined by equations (2)–(5) above. The column labeled model (2) presents estimates for the gamma heterogeneity (GH) model defined by equations (7) and (8). The estimates of the shape parameter α and the heterogeneity parameter σ^2 are presented near the end of table 4. Recall that σ^2 is the variance of unmeasured worker heterogeneity (v). This means that the null hypothesis $\sigma^2 = 0$ states that there is no worker heterogeneity. This null hypothesis is rejected at a 1% significance level for three of the four subsamples, and at 1.4% for the fourth (white-collar men). Hence the discussion that follows focuses primarily on the model (2) estimates, although, with the exception of the shape parameter α, these do not differ greatly from the simple Weibull estimates.

Recall that the β-coefficients measure the impact of the independent variables on expected weeks of joblessness, with a positive coefficient indicating that increases in the variable increase expected duration. In most cases, the β-coefficients take their expected signs, although

148

Table 4

Estimated Parameters of Jobless Duration Models[a]

Model:	Blue-Collar Male (1) β̂	Blue-Collar Male (2) β̂	Blue-Collar Male X̄	Blue-Collar Female (1) β̂	Blue-Collar Female (2) β̂	Blue-Collar Female X̄	White-Collar and Service Male (1) β̂	White-Collar and Service Male (2) β̂	White-Collar and Service Male X̄	White-Collar and Service Female (1) β̂	White-Collar and Service Female (2) β̂	White-Collar and Service Female X̄
CONSTANT	2.678** (5.41)	2.290** (4.11)	—	5.185** (5.57)	4.632** (4.06)	—	3.121** (4.32)	2.917** (3.75)	—	4.707** (6.40)	3.829** (4.59)	—
AGE	.013** (3.32)	.010* (2.23)	36.5	.003 (.52)	-.002 (.22)	38.3	.026** (4.56)	.025** (4.10)	37.4	.033** (5.73)	.030** (4.81)	36.6
EDUCATION	-.117** (-6.69)	-.122** (-6.45)	11.7	-.119** (-4.38)	-.180** (-5.59)	11.5	-.032 (-1.50)	-.034 (-1.50)	13.8	-.110** (-4.14)	-.111** (-3.63)	12.9
BLACK	.828** (5.89)	.886** (6.07)	.087	.683** (4.03)	.589* (3.12)	.160	.481* (2.26)	.500* (2.19)	.059	1.026** (4.99)	1.104** (5.24)	.105
MARRIED	-.350** (-3.70)	-.360** (-3.50)	.764	.196 (1.48)	.146 (.92)	.662	-.380** (-3.03)	-.406** (-2.92)	.710	.111 (.97)	.149 (1.17)	.604
#CHILDREN	.005 (.16)	-.001 (-.04)	1.07	.104 (1.73)	.068 (1.03)	.920	-.042 (-.94)	-.028 (-.57)	.886	.224** (3.79)	.201** (3.15)	.784
LN(OLDWAGE)	.077 (.96)	.097 (1.09)	5.92	-.330* (-2.07)	-.201 (-1.06)	5.47	-.135 (-1.15)	-.136 (-1.10)	6.03	-.387** (-3.20)	-.372** (-2.71)	5.57
TENURE	.027** (4.31)	.028** (4.32)	5.54	.038** (2.63)	.042** (2.72)	4.60	.023* (2.25)	.025** (2.41)	4.73	.010 (.75)	.008 (.60)	3.72
UNION%	.014** (7.24)	.014** (6.81)	36.7	.022** (5.47)	.026** (5.98)	29.8	.009** (3.32)	.009** (3.14)	22.7	.006* (1.99)	.007 (1.84)	19.9
SHUTDOWN	-.400** (-5.79)	-.457** (-5.94)	.497	-.328** (-2.65)	-.423** (2.89)	.544	-.411** (-4.10)	-.463** (-4.27)	.506	-.403** (-3.61)	-.430** (-3.43)	.537
UIELIG	.189* (2.32)	.281** (2.95)	.814	.166 (1.13)	.217 (1.21)	.791	-.036 (-.31)	-.053 (-.40)	.777	-.246* (-2.06)	-.226 (-1.64)	.715
ADVANCE	-.005 (-.07)	-.017 (-.08)	.519	-.135 (-1.14)	-.087 (.63)	.524	.034 (.34)	-.054 (-.50)	.493	.022 (.20)	.001 (.01)	.541
YEARS	.095* (2.21)	.105* (2.22)	3.36	.113 (1.47)	.074 (.81)	3.42	-.012 (-.21)	-.013 (-.20)	3.37	.053 (.79)	.093 (1.23)	3.31
UNAREA	.097** (7.13)	.105** (7.13)	8.44	.085** (3.37)	.108** (3.86)	8.20	.064** (3.15)	.070** (3.20)	7.97	.113** (4.88)	.140** (5.55)	7.94

Table 4 (Continued)

Model:	Blue Collar						White Collar and Service					
	Male			Female			Male			Female		
	(1) β̂	(2) β̂	X̄	(1) β̂	(2) β̂	X̄	(1) β̂	(2) β̂	X̄	(1) β̂	(2) β̂	X̄
CRAFT	-.284** (-2.82)	-.304** (-2.72)	.407	.128 (.58)	-.025 (-.09)	.204	—	—	—	—	—	—
OPERATIVE	-.061 (-.61)	-.041 (-.31)	.424	.035 (.18)	-.074 (-.32)	.680	—	—	—	—	—	—
MANAGER	—	—	—	—	—	—	-.149 (-.80)	-.121 (-.59)	.248	.099 (.54)	.076 (.36)	.179
PROFESSIONAL	—	—	—	—	—	—	-.140 (-.70)	-.098 (-.44)	.177	.127 (.61)	.144 (.59)	.113
TECHNICAL	—	—	—	—	—	—	.123 (.57)	.112 (.46)	.089	.000 (.00)	.153 (.49)	.060
SALES	—	—	—	—	—	—	-.191 (-1.03)	-.151 (-.74)	.252	-.061 (-.31)	.044 (.20)	.148
CLERICAL	—	—	—	—	—	—	.226 (1.18)	.196 (.93)	.139	.007 (.04)	.147 (.79)	.347
shape α (std. error)	.692** (.02)	.786** (.03)	—	.742** (.03)	1.041 (.08)	—	.707** (.02)	.812** (.05)	—	.657** (.02)	.821** (.06)	—
heterogeneity σ²	—	.346** (3.70)	—	—	1.240** (4.10)	—	—	.314* (2.47)	—	—	.630** (3.43)	—
log likelihood	-3,916.8	-3,907.3	—	-1,207.5	-1,192.8	—	-1,813.9	-1,808.7	—	-1,854.5	-1,844.8	—
Sample size	2,135	2,135	2,135	737	737	737	964	964	964	997	997	997
Simulations for an average worker[b]												
Median spell	22.6	18.1	—	46.0	25.9	—	12.3	10.0	—	20.7	13.9	—
E(T)	49.1	33.1	—	90.6	36.2	—	25.9	17.6	—	41.0	24.1	—
Pr(T > 52)	.289	.201	—	.465	.235	—	.145	.069	—	.279	.126	—

[a]Model (1) is the basic proportional hazards Weibull specification, while model (2) incorporates gamma heterogeneity. (See the text.) Both models were estimated by maximum likelihood. (t-values in parenthesis except where otherwise noted.)

[b]Simulated values calculated from the estimated survival curves evaluated at the means of the independent variables.

*, ** = reject null hypothesis at 5% and 1% level of significance, respectively.

significance levels vary considerably across the four groups. For blue-collar males, by far the largest of the four subgroups, eleven of fifteen variables are statistically significant and all of the significant variables take their expected sign. Across the four subgroups, the most consistently significant variables are age, education, race, tenure, union membership, plant shutdown, and the area unemployment rate.

Before discussing specific coefficients, it is helpful to note that the magnitude as well as the sign of the β-coefficients is meaningful. For any particular covariate X_i, β_i is the effect of a unit change in X_i on the natural logarithm of the predicted mean jobless spell. Thus, $(\exp(\beta_i) - 1)$, which for small changes is closely approximated by β_i, gives the proportionate effect of X_i on the expected jobless spell.[19] For example, each additional year of age increases expected jobless spell length by approximately 1% for blue-collar males, 2.5% for white-collar males, and 3% for white-collar females.

Many of the statistically significant variables have sizeable effects on the expected duration of joblessness. Among blue-collar males, for example, each additional year of schooling reduces jobless duration by 11.5%. Education has a potent effect for the other subgroups as well, except for white-collar males. The latter is in part due to the fact that some of the effect of education is picked up by the occupation dummies. When the model is reestimated without the occupation dummies, the education coefficient becomes slightly larger in absolute value ($-.042$) with a slightly larger t-value (1.92), but is still much smaller than for the other three groups.

The race dummy (BLACK) registers a very powerful effect for all four groups. A blue-collar black male has an expected jobless spell 143% longer than a similar white worker. The magnitude of this coefficient is very large for all of the other subgroups as well. This is a clear indication that, on average, blacks fare much worse than whites following displacement.

The effects of family structure differ for men and women. Marital status (MARRIED) reduces duration for males, suggesting that family responsibilities tend to reduce reservation wages or that more employable men are selected into marriage. The presence of children at home (#CHILDREN), however, has no additional effect on male duration. In contrast, married women have longer durations than single women, perhaps due to the (typically) higher earnings of their spouses. Women with children at home also tend to have longer jobless durations, consistent with child care and market work being closer substitutes for women than for men.

151

Tenure and union membership on the former job tend to prolong the jobless spell. A likely explanation is workers' reluctance to lose job specific rents on the former job. Whether they reflect specific training, the fact that workers with high tenure have better job matches, or non-market-clearing wage premiums, larger rents apparently induce workers to restrict their job search in hopes of an eventual recall by their former employer. The strong negative effect of the plant shutdown dummy (SHUTDOWN) is also consistent with this "waiting for recall" hypothesis. Male blue-collar workers displaced due to plant shutdowns, hence less likely to anticipate eventual recall, have an expected spell 37% shorter than that of a worker laid-off by an employer whose plant remained in operation. A similar effect is present for the other three groups.[20]

Consistent with job-search theory, eligibility for unemployment insurance benefits (UIELIG) significantly increases joblessness for blue-collar males. This variable is, however, insignificant for the other three samples. Similarly, the dummy for advance knowledge of job loss (ADVANCE) is always insignificant. These, surprisingly weak findings probably reflect the relative paucity of DWS data on UI entitlements and the length and credibility of advance notice (Swaim and Podgursky 1988, 1990). It should also be recalled that our proportional hazards specification does not allow for the fact that these policy variables clearly affect the hazard function most at relatively early stages of a jobless spell.

Labor-market demand conditions also strongly influence adjustment. In particular, the duration effect of higher local rates of unemployment (UNAREA) is substantial. For blue-collar males, an incremental percentage point of area unemployment raises expected duration of joblessness by 11%. Male blue-collar duration tends to be more sensitive to area labor market conditions than does male white-collar and service, and for white-collar workers female duration is considerably more sensitive to local demand conditions than male. These differences are consistent with labor mobility studies showing that blue-collar and female workers tend to be less geographically mobile than white-collar and male workers (Greenwood 1985).

We also estimated lognormal and log-logistic variants of model (1) and obtained β-coefficients for the independent variables that are very similar to those reported in table 4. In terms of sign, size, and significance, the maximum likelihood coefficients for the two white-collar samples are consistent for all of the independent variables for all three distributional models. Two minor discrepancies are present, however, for the blue-collar samples: All three distributional models indicated that older blue-collar men have longer jobless durations, but the effect is not significant, at the 5% level, for the lognormal and log-logistic models. Similarly, higher earnings on the prior job always reduces duration for blue-collar women, but the effect is not significant, at 5%, for the lognormal and log-logistic models. A further confirmation of the robustness of our results is provided by the log-likelihood statistics, which indicate a similar "fit" for all three distributional models.[21]

C. Heterogeneity and Duration Dependence

Finally, we turn to the parameter governing the behavior of the exit rate over time. As expected, the GH estimate of α is larger than the simple Weibull estimate. Nonetheless, the point estimates of α are considerably less than unity and the null hypothesis that $\alpha = 1$ is rejected at a 1% significance level for the GH model in three of the four subsamples.[22] This means that *individual* exit rates from joblessness decline as jobless spells progress. A likely explanation for "true" negative duration dependence, is that the experience of joblessness *itself* reduces the employability of the worker. This "scarring" may reflect the physical and psychological effects of unemployment on the worker (e.g., loss of self-esteem and self-confidence, alcoholism, mental illness) and stigmatization by potential employers. Such an interpretation is consistent with case studies of plant closings, and psychological and sociological studies of unemployed workers.[23]

Negative duration dependence has obvious implications for policy. To adopt a medical metaphor, the dislocation illness worsens if untreated. This implies that timely provision of adjustment assistance for displaced workers is likely important. Evaluation studies of dislocated worker programs have identified early intervention as an important factor in the successful provision of adjustment assistance (United States Congress, Office of Technology Assessment, 1986 and United States Department of Labor, 1986). Our findings provide further support for this conclusion.[24]

It is possible that our heterogeneity correction is inadequate so that our GH results exaggerate the importance of early intervention. As is now widely recognized, precise differentiation between duration dependence and heterogeneity is difficult (Lancaster and Nickell 1980; Heckman and Singer 1984). A related concern is that the degree of negative duration dependence in the postdisplacement hazard function is exaggerated by our failure to account for the role of predisplacement search in generating very short durations (Swaim 1988). It should also be noted that the importance of heterogeneity suggests that cost-effective targeting of early interventions may be difficult to achieve, since ex ante identification of workers likely to experience long spell of joblessness may be quite imprecise. Whatever the relative importance of heterogeneity and state dependence, however, the conclusion is that a long-term jobless worker has very poor reemployment prospects.

The decline in the reemployment rate that occurs as weeks of joblessness increase produces a highly skewed distribution of completed spell lengths. The last three rows of table 4 illustrate this skewness by comparing median and mean jobless spells, and calculating the probability that a spell exceeds one year for an average worker. In all four groups, mean spell durations are about 50% higher than median and there exists a high risk of protracted joblessness. For example, mean and median weeks of joblessness for blue-collar males are 33.1 and 18.1, while an average member of this group has a 20.1% likelihood of a year or more of joblessness. Of course, the variability of outcomes is even greater if we compare workers who differ in terms of observable characteristics, such as race and education, or the unobserved heterogeneity term (v).[25]

Finally, while we have emphasized the difference between our jobless measure and standard unemployment duration measures, it is nonetheless interesting to contrast these average jobless spells for displaced workers with estimates of completed unemployment spells in two recent studies. Sider (1985) estimates average unemployment duration for 1979 to 1981 to be 11.9 weeks. Using gross flow data, however, Bowers (1980) estimates the mean spell to be 9.8 weeks.[26] These comparisons suggest that the average displaced worker has much greater difficulties in job search than an average unemployed worker.

D. Structural Versus Turnover Interpretations

Were a substantial number of these displaced workers structurally unemployed? Workers are usually considered structurally unemployed if they experience lengthy unemployment as a result of a mismatch between supply and demand for particular skills in a local labor market (Ehrenberg and Smith 1985, pp. 497–98). Persistent excess supply, in turn, presupposes substantial worker immobility and relative wage rigidity in the face of demand shifts.[27] Structural unemployment is usefully contrasted with turnover or frictional unemployment, wherein workers with incomplete information regarding potential employers periodically invest in searching for a good job match. This job search time is measured as unemployment, but is generally economically productive and unlikely to reflect severe economic hardship.

154

Our results indicate that both structural and turnover factors are at work. Turnover models predict that most unemployment spells are short and that groups of workers for whom the cost of job search is low will set relatively high reservation wages, hence experience longer spells of joblessness. This may explain the tendency for women, older workers, and workers qualifying for unemployment insurance to return to work more slowly. A number of our findings, however, do not easily fit such an interpretation. For example, it is not clear why workers with low educational credentials, blacks, or workers living in areas with high unemployment rates should adopt job search strategies that result in a high probability of a year or more of joblessness. Furthermore, our data show that, as a group, workers with long spells of joblessness face bleak reemployment prospects and large earnings losses once reemployed. A structural interpretation of these results seems more convincing.

Our differentiation between structural and turnover factors is somewhat impressionistic, since we have not provided a rigorous theoretical framework for dividing total unemployment into turnover and structural components. Furthermore, our reduced-form hazard model summarizes the overall reemployment process, but does not decompose the determinants of reemployment rates into the supply- and demand-side factors emphasized in turnover and structural theories, respectively. Nonetheless, our qualitative analysis suggests that both sets of factors play important roles in determining postdisplacement joblessness. Our structural interpretation of some postdisplacement joblessness also does not address the "reasonableness" of the type of jobs for which these long-duration jobless workers are searching. It does, however, suggest that much of the time spent without a job is both personally and socially unproductive, and may well cause considerable economic hardship.

Finally, the long spells of joblessness experienced by workers in our sample are not purely a cyclical phenomenon. For example, the probability that an average male blue-collar workers is jobless for more than a year is .201 (table 4, bottom row). If we recompute this probability for the same worker in a local labor market with an unemployment rate of just 4%, the one year and longer share drops to a lower, but still substantial .099. The corresponding probabilities of more than twenty-six weeks of joblessness are .392 and .259, respectively. The conclusion that economic growth leaves significant pockets of long-term joblessness is also borne out for the other three subsamples, and in a recent study comparing New England, with its relatively low unemployment rates, to the country at large (Podgursky and Swaim 1986).

155

IV. Conclusion

A widely-cited essay characterized the labor market of the late 1960s and early 1970s as follows:

> The picture of a hard core of unemployed workers who are not able to find jobs is an inaccurate description of our economy and a misleading basis for policy. A more accurate description is an active labor market in which almost everyone who is out of work can find his usual type of work in a relatively short time (Feldstein 1973, p. 5).

While this may have been an accurate description of the predominant experience fifteen years ago, and indeed still fits the experience of many unemployed today, it does not fit the experience of the approximately eight million workers displaced from full-time nonagricultural jobs between 1979 and 1984 who have been the focus of this study. While some of these workers secured new jobs relatively quickly, others experienced many months of joblessness and large reductions in weekly earnings when they eventually became reemployed. The traditional textbook description of structural unemployment thus better fits the labor market experience of many of these displaced workers than frictional or turnover models of unemployment.

In order to better understand this varied experience, we estimated a multivariate hazard model of joblessness spell durations, which allowed us to test whether reemployment rates differ by demographic group, and whether labor market and policy variables influence reemployment. We found that black and female workers have much lower reemployment rates, hence much longer expected spells of joblessness following displacement. Greater education significantly improves reemployment prospects, while high area unemployment rates increase the expected duration of joblessness, particularly for blue-collar and female workers. High tenure and union membership on the old job, as well as the prior employer remaining in operation, are associated with long durations. We also find that the group—and probably the individual—reemployment rate from joblessness falls as weeks of joblessness rise. As a consequence, long-term jobless workers have very poor reemployment prospects. Some of these differences are consistent with frictional or turnover models of unemployment, but others strongly suggest that some displaced workers are trapped in labor markets with persistent excess supply.

Our analysis of jobless duration leads us to conclude that a sizeable minority of these workers have considerable adjustment difficulties. In the language of current labor-market policy, many displaced workers become "dislocated." The adequacy of existing income support programs

156

for these workers and their families is an important topic for future research. Our findings also suggest that dislocated worker adjustment assistance under the Economic Dislocation and Worker Adjustment Assistance Act might best be targeted to blue-collar workers, workers with below-average education, minorities and women, and communities with above-average rates of unemployment. If negative duration dependence accounts for much of the fall in group reemployment rates over time, prompt adjustment assistance may be especially important.

NOTES

1. The Omnibus Trade Act contained sections amending both JTPA Title III and Trade Adjustment Assistance, the two most important federal programs designed specifically to assist displaced workers. The amendments to JTPA Title III, often referred to as the Economic Dislocation and Worker Adjustment Assistance Act of 1988 (EDWAAA), are substantial and include a large increase in authorized funding levels. Although $980 million were authorized for fiscal year 1989, just $284 million were appropriated. The Bush administration has, however, requested that 1990 appropriations be increased to $400 million. See Addison (chapter 1 of this volume) and Leigh (chapter 9 of this volume) for more extensive discussions of manpower programs for displaced workers.

2. Jacobson (1987) and Crosslin et al. (1986) show that some displaced workers maintain strong ties to their former employer and industry. Since neither study analyzes nationally representative samples of displaced workers, the generality of their results is hard to assess.

3. Earlier studies of displacement and unemployment that use data from the Displaced Worker Surveys include Addison and Portugal (1987), Podgursky and Swaim (1987a), Kruse (1988), and Kletzer (1988).

4. The data used in this study relate to the period of high unemployment between 1979 and 1985, hence do not fully reflect the reduction in unemployment in the mid- to late-1980s, which may represent a reversal of the upward secular trend in the unemployment rate. Preliminary analysis of the 1988 Displaced Worker Survey suggests that displacement continues to be an important source of long-duration unemployment (Swaim 1989).

5. The omitted categories are completion of a seasonal job, self-employed business failure, and "other." For further description of these surveys see Flaim and Sehgal (1985) and Horvath (1987). Unlike these authors, we do not limit our sample to workers with three or more years of tenure with the former employer.

6. Almost half of the displaced workers identified in the January CPS/DWS were reinterviewed in the March CPS, which contains the Annual Work Experience Survey. We are grateful to Robert McIntire of the BLS for constructing this matched file for us.

7. Akerlof and Yellen (1985) argue that survey respondents in the WES tend not to recall unemployment spells that were of little economic or psychological consequence.

8. Estimating counterfactual jobless spell durations for displaced workers raises

157

difficult conceptual issues. For example, should it be assumed that the reduction in labor demand that caused the displacement did not occur, or that it did occur but wages or other conditions of employment adjusted so as to avoid permanent layoffs? In short, should the counterfactual comparison be to healthy or sick employers? See Hamermesh (chapter 3 of this volume) for a model of the relationship between demand shifts and changes in employment conditions, including the probability of plant shutdowns. Ruhm (chapter 6 of this volume) uses PSID data to construct control groups for his analysis of postdisplacement unemployment and earnings loss.

9. These tabulations make use of the Census Bureau population weights provided with the CPS datafile.

10. For further analysis of the link between long duration joblessness and earnings loss in the 1984 DWS see Addison and Portugal (1989).

11. Of course, the lognormal and log-logistic also place strong restrictions on the shape of the hazard function. We adopt the Weibull model as our base case since it accommodates positive, negative, and zero duration dependence and is more easily generalized to accommodate heterogeneity.

12. In general, the assumption that the location parameter is a log-linear function of the independent variables produces an accelerated failure-time model. If the base-line hazard function is Weibull, however, the resulting model also satisfies the proportional hazards property of equation (4). Thus the lognormal and log-logistic variants of our model are accelerated failure-time but not proportional hazards models. See Portugal (chapter 7 of this volume) and Swaim and Podgursky (1990, appendix 1) for more extensive discussions of these distinctions.

13. This is the problem of time-varying covariates. Solon (1985) and Swaim and Podgursky (1990) estimate rather different models incorporating such effects.

14. These expectations reflect our "structuralist" prior that workers viewed as relatively undesirable employees often receive *fewer* rather than *less remunerative* job offers. They also reflect the fact that we are controlling for earnings on the previous job and believe that displaced workers are likely to give considerable weight to past earnings when setting initial reservation wages.

15. If nonunion employers prefer not to hire workers with a history of union membership, union workers will also receive fewer job offers.

16. Katz (1986a) shows that laid-off workers with higher (subjective) probabilities of recall are less aggressive searchers. An offsetting factor is that complete plant shutdowns may produce greater disequilibrium in local labor markets. We have tried to control for this effect by including the area unemployment rate at the time of displacement (UNAREA) in the model.

17. What is described here is sometimes termed "right-censoring." "Left censoring" occurs when a spell begins prior to the measurement period. All spells of joblessness in the DWS began during the years under consideration, hence are not left-censored. These jobless spells are, however, left-censored measures of total search time for workers receiving advance notice, if they began searching for new jobs before their old jobs ended. See Addison and Portugal (chapter 8 of this volume) and Swaim and Podgursky (1990) for alternative treatments of predisplacement search.

18. The nature of the independent variable required another adjustment in our estimation procedure. Survivor models such as that defined in equations (2)–(5) generate only positive spell durations, but a number of workers in our sample reported zero weeks of joblessness following displacement. This is due in part to the fact that roughly one-half of our sample had some advance knowledge of the layoff, thus began job search prior to

termination. Since the DWS duration variable is integer-valued, zero spells may also result from truncation of fractional weeks of joblessness. We adjust for this by defining our dependent variable T as 0.5 + reported jobless weeks.

19. This property is easily demonstrated for the continuous case. The mean of a Weibull random variable with parameters λ and α is $E(J) = (1/\lambda\alpha) \Gamma(1/\alpha)$, where $\Gamma(.)$ is the gamma function. Differentiating with respect to X_i yields $d\,E(J)/dX_i = \beta_i E(J)$. Thus, β_i is the proportionate effect on $E(J)$ of an infinitesimal increase in X_i.

20. Alternately, employers may use partial layoffs to weed out less productive workers. We doubt that the plant shutdown dummy variable is serving as a proxy for unmeasured differences in worker quality since it is not significantly associated with postdisplacement earnings (Podgursky and Swaim 1987b).

21. The likelihood statistics do not provide a ranking of the three distributional assumptions that is consistent across the four subsamples. Overall, the lognormal specification seems to fit the data better than the Weibull or log-logistic models. Since our model (2) estimates in table 4 indicate that unobserved heterogeneity is important, we prefer our GH specification to any of these models. Nonetheless, the robustness of our coefficient estimates across these simple distributional models is reassuring and consistent with more extensive studies of distributional assumptions for jobless spells in the 1984 DWS (Swaim and Podgursky 1988) and unemployment spells in the 1983 wave of the PSID (Portugal, chapter 7 in this volume).

22. The exception is blue-collar women, who have a σ^2 value double that for white-collar women and nearly four times that for men. The particular importance of heterogeneity for this group is consistent with the our discussion of labor force attachment, where we hypothesized that the female blue-collar sample is most contaminated by long duration jobless who are only minimally engaged in job search. This is also the smallest of the four subsamples.

23. See Hurst and Shepard (1986) and Bluestone and Harrison (1982, chapter 3). In contrast, job search models usually predict constant or rising exit rates due to constant or falling reservation wages. Negative duration dependence thus indicates that reservation wages fail to fall fast enough to offset declines in either offered wages or the frequency of job offers.

24. The importance and *rapid onset* of negative duration dependence is confirmed by the lognormal and log-logistic variants of model (1) despite the fact that the former imposes and the latter accommodates "inverted-U" shaped hazard functions, which first rise and then fall. The modal point, after which negative duration begins, was attained in less than 0.01 weeks for the lognormal model in all four subsamples. Three of the four log-logistic models indicated monotonically negative duration dependence, while the fourth indicated a "inverted-U" hazard function with the mode at 0.09 weeks.

25. The simple Weibull results, which do not hold ν fixed, indicate much greater right skewness. The skewness is not an artifact of our choice of a Weibull duration model, since a Weibull with a sufficiently large α is not right skewed. This skewness is also clearly visible in table 1 and for simulations using the lognormal or log-logistic variants of model (1).

26. This is the unweighted average for the years 1979–1981 reported in Sider (1985, p. 467). Estimates based on gross flow data for 1979 are reported in Bowers (1980, p. 24). Unpublished estimates for 1980 and 1981 were provided by Bowers.

27. Efficiency wage theories provide a promising explanation for the persistence of non-market-clearing wages, hence the possibility that some unemployed queue-up for rationed, high-wage jobs (Katz 1986b).

159

REFERENCES

Addison, John T., and Pedro Portugal (1987). "The Effect of Advance Notification of Plant Closings on Unemployment." *Industrial and Labor Relations Review* 41 (October): 3–16.

———(1989). "Job Displacement, Relative Wage Changes, and Duration of Unemployment." *Journal of Labor Economics* 7 (July): 281–302.

Akerlof, George A., and Janet Yellen (1985). "Unemployment Through the Filter of Memory." *Quarterly Journal of Economics* 100 (August): 747–73.

Bluestone, Barry, and Bennett Harrison (1982). *The Deindustrialization of America.* New York: Basic Books.

Bowers, Norman (1980). "Probing the Issues of Unemployment Duration." *Monthly Labor Review* 103 (July): 23–32.

Butler, Richard J., and James B. McDonald (1986). "Trends in Unemployment Duration Data." *Review of Economics and Statistics* 68 (November): 545–57.

Clark, Kim B., and Lawrence H. Summers (1979). "Labor Market Dynamics and Unemployment: A Reconsideration." *Brookings Papers on Economic Activity* 1:13–60.

Crosslin, Robert L., James S. Hanna, and David W. Stevens (1986). "The Permanence of Dislocation: 1979–83 Evidence." Research Report, National Commission for Employment Policy (June).

Ehrenberg, Ronald G., and Robert S. Smith (1985). *Modern Labor Economics,* second edition. Glenview, Ill.: Scott, Foresman and Company.

Feldstein, Martin (1973). "The Economics of the New Unemployment." *Public Interest* 53 (Fall): 3–42.

Flaim, Paul O., and Ellen Sehgal (1985). "Displaced Workers of 1979–1983: How Have They Fared?" *Monthly Labor Review* 108 (June): 3–16.

Greenwood, Michael J. (1985). "Human Migration: Theory, Models, and Empirical Studies." *Journal of Regional Science* 13 (June): 397–433.

Heckman, James J., and Burton Singer (1984). "Econometric Duration Analysis." *Journal of Econometrics* 24:63–132.

Horvath, Francis (1982). "Forgotten Unemployment: Recall Bias in Retrospective Data." *Monthly Labor Review* 105 (March): 40–43.

———(1987). "The Pulse of Economic Change: Displaced Workers of 1981–85." *Monthly Labor Review* 110 (June): 3–12.

Hurst, Joe B., and John W. Shepard (1986). "The Dynamics of Plant Closings: An Extended Emotional Roller Coaster Ride." *Journal of Counseling and Development* 64 (February): 401–5.

Jacobson, Louis (1987). "Labor Mobility and Structural Change in Pittsburg." *APA Journal* (Autumn): 438–48.

Katz, Lawrence (1986a). "Layoffs, Recall and the Duration of Unemployment." NBER Working Paper #1825 (January).

———(1986b). "Efficiency Wage Theories: A Partial Evaluation." In *NBER Macroeconomics Annual: 1986,* edited by Stanley Fischer. Cambridge, Mass.: MIT Press.

Kletzer, Lori Gladstein (1988). "Determinants of Re-employment Probabilities of Displaced Workers: Do Workers Displaced from High-Wage Industries Have Longer Durations of Unemployment?" Mimeographed. Williamstown, Mass.: Williams College.

Kokkelenberg, Edward C., and Donna R. Sockell (1985). "Union Membership in the United States: 1973–1981." *Industrial and Labor Relations Review* 38 (July): 497–543.

Kruse, Douglas (1988). "International Trade and the Labor Market Experience of Displaced Workers." *Industrial and Labor Relations Review* 41 (April): 402–17.

Lancaster, Tony (1979). "Econometric Methods for the Duration of Unemployment." *Econometrica* 47 (July): 939–56.

———(1985). "Generalized Residuals and Heterogenous Duration Models." *Journal of Econometrics* 28 (Annals, 1): 155–69.

Lancaster, Tony, and Stephen Nickell (1980). "The Analysis of Re-Employment Probabilities for the Unemployed." *Journal of the Royal Statistical Society* 143:141–65.

Lilien, David M. (1982). "Sectoral Shifts and Cyclical Unemployment." *Journal of Political Economy* 90 (August): 777–93.

Mathiowetz, Nancy A., and Greg J. Duncan (1988). "Out of Work, Out of Mind: Response Errors in Retrospective Reports of Unemployment." *Journal of Business and Economic Statistics* 6 (April): 221–9.

Mortensen, Dale T. (1986). "Job Search and Labor Market Analysis." In *Handbook of Labor Economics,* Vol III, edited by O. Ashenfelter and R. Layard. Amsterdam: Elsevier Science Publishers.

Murphy, Kevin M., and Robert H. Topel (1987). "The Evolution of Unemployment in the United States: 1968–1985." In *NBER Macroeconomics Annual: 1987,* edited by Stanley Fischer. Cambridge, Mass.: MIT Press.

Podgursky, Michael (1984). "Sources of Secular Increases in the Unemployment Rate, 1969–82." *Monthly Labor Review* 107 (July): 19–25.

Podgursky, Michael, and Paul Swaim (1986). "Plant Shutdowns and Job Displacements: How Do New England Workers Fare?" *New England Economic Indicators,* (February): A3–A5.

———(1987a). "Duration of Joblessness Following Displacement." *Industrial Relations* 26 (Fall): 213–26.

———(1987b). "Job Displacement and Earnings Loss: Evidence from the Displaced Worker Survey." *Industrial and Labor Relations Review* 41 (October): 17–29.

Sider, Hal (1985). "Unemployment Duration and Incidence: 1968–82." *American Economic Review* 75 (June): 461–72.

Solon, Gary (1985). "Work Incentive Effects of Taxing Unemployment Benefits." *Econometrica* 53 (March): 295–306.

Summers, Lawrence H. (1986). "Why is the Unemployment Rate So Very High Near Full Employment?" *Brookings Papers on Economic Activity* 2:339–83.

Swaim, Paul (1988). "The Hazards of Modeling Survivor Data with Zero Spells: The Case of Advance Notice." *American Statistical Association 1988 Proceedings:* 454–58.

———(1989). "Worker Displacement in the 1980s: An Overview of Recent Trends." In *The Worker in Transition: Technological Change,* edited by T. J. Kozik and D. G. Jansson. New York: ASME Press.

Swaim, Paul, and Michael Podgursky (1988). "The Distributional Shape of Unemployment Duration: A Reconsideration." Mimeographed. Amherst, Mass. University of Massachusetts.

———(1990). "Advance Notice and Job Search: The Value of an Early Start." *Journal of Human Resources* 25 (Spring):147–78.

United States Congress (1986). Office of Technology Assessment. *Plant Closing Advance Notice and Rapid Response—Special Report.* OTA-ITE-321. Washington, D.C.: G.P.O. (February).

United States Department of Labor (1986). Secretary of Labor's Task Force on Economic Adjustment and Worker Dislocation. *Economic Adjustment and Worker Dislocation in a Competitive Society.* Washington, D.C.: G.P.O. (December).

CHAPTER SIX

The Time Profile of Displacement-Induced Changes in Unemployment and Earnings

CHRISTOPHER J. RUHM

I. Introduction

Workers are typically unemployed for an extended period of time follow-ing plant closures or permanent layoffs and often are forced to accept large pay cuts in order to obtain new jobs. A minority procure new positions paying higher wages than prior to displacement and a still smaller percentage (mostly those with advance notice) are able to avoid unemployment altogether.[1] Much less is known about the time profile of adjustment patterns.

There are a number of reasons to be interested in the extent, timing, and persistence of displacement-induced changes in earnings and unem-ployment. Policy choices depend critically on whether postdisplacement changes are transitory or persistent. For example, if earnings changes are short-lasting, job search assistance and training, which result in improved initial placements, are unlikely to yield permanent benefits. Conversely, the arguments for increased placement assistance and re-training may be strengthened by a pattern of transitory unemployment and persistent wage changes.

The time profile is also important from a theoretical viewpoint. Hamermesh (1987b) has used information on *predisplacement* seniority-wage profiles to study the awareness of workers and firms to the possibil-ity of future layoffs. Similarly, data on the distribution and permanence of postdisplacement joblessness adds to our understanding of the rela-tive contributions of demand and supply factors in explaining aggregate unemployment.

The consequences of labor displacement could vary over time for several reasons. Wages and employment stability will decrease prior to terminations if temporary layoffs and cost-containment measures are initially used by firms in an (unsuccessful) attempt to prevent permanent reductions in force. Earnings losses may be most severe immediately following reemployment if workers initially obtain job-specific training or receive relatively low wages during short-lasting probationary periods. Alternatively, the loss of seniority-wage premiums or industry rents may imply more permanent reductions. Joblessness falls when new positions are obtained but may also remain higher than predisplacement levels if the new employment is less stable than the old.

Despite the proliferation of recent research studying the consequences of labor displacement, relatively little is known about the adjustment time profile. One reason is that the main data sources used in this work, the Displaced Worker Supplements (DWS) to the Current Population Survey, are not well designed to provide information on the timing of changes in earnings or unemployment.[2] The problems with the DWS are threefold. First, no detail is available on wage growth or joblessness prior to dislocations. Second, retrospective data is lacking on nondisplaced workers. As a result it is not possible to construct an appropriate control group using this data.[3] Third, when data from only a single supplement is used, there is perfect collinearity between the time since displacement (until the survey) and the year of the job termination. Consequently, persistence effects can not be separated from the impact of economic conditions at the date of job loss.[4]

These shortcomings can be overcome by using panel data. Interestingly, although "first generation" studies investigating the economic consequences of labor mobility, during the late 70s and early 80s, generally utilized longitudinal data—particularly the National Longitudinal Surveys (NLS) or Panel Study of Income Dynamics (PSID)—they obtained almost no information on either the timing or permanence of the changes.[5] The interpretation of the limited evidence gathered on the time profile is also questionable. For example, Jacobson (1984) argued that because 40% to 50% of peak reductions in annual average earnings were eliminated over a two-year period, losses were largely transitory. This ignores the possibility that a portion of the decrease is short-lasting, with the remainder being much more permanent. In the opposite vein, Podgursky and Swaim (1987b) claim that most of the initial drop in earnings persists for at least five years. These findings are obtained using DWS data, however, and so are subject to collinearity problems discussed above. In addition, the estimated "catch-up" coefficients show no clear time pattern and are always statistically insignificant in their preferred specification.

This chapter uses data on periods prior and subsequent to (potential) displacements from the Panel Study of Income Dynamics. A careful attempt is made to control for both observable and difficult to observe heterogeneity and a consistent framework is developed for investigating the extent and timing of changes in both weekly wages and unemployment.[6] The analysis reveals three primary findings. First, most of the extensive joblessness that follows involuntary layoffs is transitory. Second, postdisplacement earnings changes are both diverse and long lasting. Workers obtaining new positions at higher pay maintain the increases for several years, whereas those accepting lower initial earnings fail to recover their losses over even a substantial period of time. Third, unemployment begins to increase *prior* to the permanent job loss and there is some evidence that relative wages also start to decline before the date of displacement.

II. Estimation Framework

A general framework for investigating the time profile of changes in earnings or unemployment, associated with job displacement occurring at time t, is

$$Y_{i,t+n} = \mathbf{X}_{i,t}\alpha + D_{i,t}\beta + \epsilon_{i,t+n}, \tag{1}$$

where Y is the dependent variable, $\mathbf{X}$ a vector of observable characteristics, D a dummy variable indicating whether person i is displaced from a job at time t, and ϵ is the regression disturbance term.[7] Exposition can be simplified by deleting the individual subscript, calling the year of displacement time 0, and rewriting equation (1) as

$$Y_n = \mathbf{X}_0\alpha + D_0\beta + \epsilon_n, \tag{1'}$$

where n is positive (negative) for years subsequent to (preceding) the permanent job loss. The dependent variables considered in this chapter are the natural log of real weekly wages, the change in log wages, and the number of weeks of calendar year unemployment. The displacement variable indicates permanent involuntary job terminations occurring in year zero.[8]

The earnings equations can be estimated using a linear regression model. When unemployment is the dependent variable, however, truncation at zero weeks requires the use of an alternative technique such as

164

TOBIT. In this case, Y represents a latent (unobserved) variable indicating potential unemployment, with actual unemployment defined by

$$Y^* = \begin{matrix} Y \\ 0 \end{matrix}, \quad \text{if } \epsilon \begin{matrix} > \\ \leq \end{matrix} -\mathbf{X}_0\alpha - D_0\beta.$$

The TOBIT coefficients show the marginal impact of the regressors on the latent variable Y. The predicted effects of covariates on actual unemployment are obtained from

$$E(Y^*|\mathbf{Z}) = \Phi(.)\mathbf{Z}\delta + \sigma\phi(.), \tag{2}$$

where $\mathbf{Z}$ and δ are vectors of regressors ($\mathbf{X}$ and D_0) and coefficients (α and β), and $\Phi(.)$ and $\phi(.)$ are the c.d.f. and density function of the standard normal distribution, evaluated at $\mathbf{Z}\delta/\sigma$.[9]

Estimates of equation (1) provide consistent estimates of $\hat{\alpha}$ and $\hat{\beta}$ if the error term is orthogonal to the included regressors ($E[D_0|\epsilon] = E[\mathbf{X}|\epsilon] = 0$). This requires the vector of independent variables to control for all types of individual, firm, or economy-wide heterogeneity that affect the probability of displacement, a condition that is unlikely to be fulfilled. For example, job terminations will be more likely in firms facing declining product demand or for workers paid high wages relative to their marginal revenue product. If the covariates fail to completely account for these factors, the regressions will overstate the negative impact of permanent job terminations, by confounding the impacts of displacement and unobserved heterogeneity. Put differently, even were dislocation avoided at time 0, these individuals would face higher probabilities of subsequent temporary or permanent layoffs and slower relative wage growth in future periods than randomly chosen job stayers.

One way of controlling for this heterogeneity is to find a comparison group whose unobserved characteristics are closer to those of workers displaced in year 0 than is the sample of all nondisplaced workers. A promising choice is persons involuntarily terminating jobs after the end of the observation period.[10] Since displaced workers are followed for four years subsequent to the loss of jobs, this involves comparing them to observably similar persons dislocated in period 5. The model estimated is thus of the form

$$Y_n = \mathbf{X}_0\alpha + D_0\beta + D_5\gamma + \epsilon_n. \tag{3}$$

If the conditional expectation of the error term is the same for persons displaced in years 0 and 5 ($E[\epsilon|D_0] = E[\epsilon|D_5]$), $\hat{\beta}$ and $\hat{\gamma}$ will have identical biases. $\hat{\beta} - \hat{\gamma}$ then shows the true effect of displacement and $\hat{\gamma}$ indicates the impact of unobserved heterogeneity. If unobserved differences are only partially controlled for, $\hat{\beta} - \hat{\gamma}$ generally provides an upper bound of the displacement effect. We should note, however, one important situation where these estimates may *understate* the impact of dislocation. If adjustment begins *prior* to permanent layoffs, $\hat{\gamma}$ will combine displacement and heterogeneity effects for the years immediately preceding time 5 displacements (i.e., years 3 and 4). Coefficient estimates of $\hat{\gamma}$ from only the earlier periods ($t - 2$ through $t + 2$) should therefore be used to measure the differences associated with unobserved heterogeneity.

Sample selection bias is present in the earnings regressions if reemployment probabilities depend on potential wages. To correct for this, the standard two-stage procedure for obtaining consistent estimates is used. The first stage involves estimating a probit equation where the dependent variable takes a value one if the individual reports earnings in the period considered and zero otherwise. The inverse Mill's ratio (which is essentially a weighting factor based on the probability of reemployment) from this regression is then included as an additional regressor in the second-stage ordinary least squares earnings equation.[11] Because this correction procedure places fairly strict restrictions on the distributions of the error terms in the two equations, the results of single-stage OLS regressions (without an inverse Mill's ratio) are also included. The estimated displacement coefficients are extremely robust to the specification chosen.[12]

III. Data and Sample

Data is obtained for head of households from the 1969 to 1980 waves of the Michigan Panel Study of Income Dynamics (PSID). Individuals are classified as displaced or nondisplaced in the five base years 1971 through 1975 and followed over the two years preceding and four years subsequent to that period. For example, if 1974 is the base year (time 0), information on unemployment and wages is collected for the 1972 through 1978 calendar years (periods minus 2 through plus 4, respectively). A dummy variable is also constructed to indicate individuals who are displaced in year 5 but not in year 0.[13]

Household heads are included in the sample if they are between the ages of twenty-one and sixty-five in year 0, participate in the labor force during some part of periods 0 through 4, and report earnings during either year $t - 2$ or $t - 1$. These restrictions limit the analysis to individuals with fairly strong labor force attachments and ignore potential effects of displacements on retirement.[14]

Three types of dependent variables are used in the analysis. UN_n and W_n refer, respectively, to the number of weeks of unemployment and the natural log of real weekly wages in year n (where n takes the values -2 through 4). Wage changes, denoted by ΔW_n, show the change in log wages between time n and $t - 2$ (thus $\Delta W_n = W_n - W_{-2}$). Period $t - 2$ was chosen as the comparison year because relative wages may decline immediately prior to displacements.[15]

The vector of independent variables includes: labor market experience, education, marital and ethnic status, sex, age, city size, job tenure, blue-collar and professional occupations, employment in a manufacturing industry, and the survey year. In all cases, the regressors apply to characteristics at period 0 and are dichotomous. For instance, the occupation variables refer to the employment sector in the base year, regardless of any previous or subsequent changes. Workers are defined to be displaced at period 0 if they lose jobs because of layoffs or plant closings and fail to return to the original employers by the end of year 2.

Table 1 shows mean values of selected variables. Workers losing jobs in year 0 tend to be younger, less experienced, less educated, less frequently married, and have much lower job seniority than nondisplaced persons. They are more likely to be nonwhite, male, and to work in blue collar jobs or manufacturing industries. They earn an average of 18 percent less per week, in the year prior to the separation, and are unemployed approximately 7 extra weeks over the preceding two years. These patterns are similar to those obtained using nationally representative data from the DWS.[16]

Variable averages for workers displaced in year 5 are generally intermediate between those of period 0 job losers and nondisplaced workers. This suggests that at least a portion of *observed* heterogeneity is accounted for by using these persons, rather than random job stayers, as the comparison group. Evidence presented below indicates that most, if not all, *unobserved* heterogeneity is controlled for as well.

IV. Predisplacement Employment Conditions

This section briefly examines how wages and unemployment vary, *prior to the base year*, with individual, firm, and economy characteristics, as well as displacement status. These estimates show the association between the nondisplacement regressors and weekly earnings, the wage

167

Table 1 **Sample Means By Displacement Status**

Variable	Not displaced	Displaced in year zero	Displaced in year five
Personal			
Age	40.41 yrs.	37.39 yrs.	38.73 yrs.
Experience	20.78	17.61	19.60
Education	11.40	10.54	10.66
Married	82.29 %	79.82 %	80.29 %
Female	12.68	11.90	10.71
Nonwhite	30.75	40.51	33.09
Predisplacement job			
Tenure (years):			
< 1	13.79 %	37.95 %	21.18 %
1–3	24.07	29.82	26.28
3–9	29.03	23.19	26.52
10–19	21.07	7.53	17.03
≥ 20	12.04	1.51	9.00
Blue-collar	52.79 %	73.19 %	65.94 %
Manufacturing	28.25	31.63	32.60
Professional	26.41	14.61	17.76
Log wage[a]	5.223	5.027	5.130
Unemployment[b]	2.37 wks.	9.27 wks.	4.64 wks.
N	11,793	664	411

[a]Natural log of (real) weekly wages at $t - 1$.
[b]Total weeks of unemployment in $t - 2$ and $t - 1$.

growth rate, or the level of joblessness.[17] They also indicate whether the unobserved characteristics of persons losing jobs in period 0 and period 5 are similar to each other and to those of random nondisplaced workers.

Columns (1) and (2) of table 2 present coefficient estimates from regressions where the dependent variable is the log of real wages in years $t - 2$ and $t - 1$. Columns (3) and (4) show corresponding results for TOBIT regressions on weeks of unemployment. Finally, column (5) displays coefficients for changes in log wages between $t - 2$ and the base year.

The nondisplacement regressors generally have the expected signs and so receive only brief mention. Experience, education, and job tenure are all associated with higher wages and lower levels of unemployment. Whites, married persons, and professional workers earn more and are unemployed less than their counterparts. Blue-collar employment is associated with significantly elevated joblessness and manufacturing work with higher pay. Females and persons residing outside large cities

Table 2 **Wages and Unemployment Prior to Displacement**

	W_{-2}	W_{-1}	UN_{-2}	UN_{-1}	ΔW_0
Exp (≤ ten years)	−.174	−.130	.73	2.21	.064
	(15.69)	(11.66)	(.64)	(1.85)	(7.27)
School (≤ twelve years)	−.200	−.208	.99	−.38	−.012
	(18.12)	(18.80)	(.69)	(.24)	(1.42)
Married	.176	.200	−2.29	−4.42	1.3E−3
	(9.79)	(11.14)	(1.34)	(2.40)	(.09)
Nonwhite	−.323	−.307	−.48	−1.27	4.3E−3
	(32.73)	(31.14)	(.47)	(1.27)	(.01)
Female	−.379	−.356	−2.27	−4.51	.013
	(18.18)	(17.16)	(1.18)	(2.07)	(.81)
Age (>fifty-five years)	−.181	−.192	−1.69	.32	−.038
	(10.51)	(11.17)	(.66)	(.14)	(2.74)
City size:					
>100,000	.149	.138	1.41	.98	−.010
	(13.63)	(12.61)	(1.11)	(.77)	(1.18)
<25,000	−.187	−.185	−1.03	−.05	4.2E−3
	(14.90)	(14.77)	(.71)	(.03)	(.42)
Job tenure (years):					
1–3	.125	.116	−13.90	−5.32	−.051
	(9.48)	(8.80)	(11.42)	(4.16)	(4.65)
4–9	.208	.174	−19.03	−7.33	−.068
	(15.82)	(13.25)	(13.80)	(5.52)	(6.12)
10–19	.240	.213	−20.17	−8.99	−.078
	(16.56)	(14.72)	(12.28)	(5.39)	(6.39)
≥ 20	.184	.181	−19.40	−10.74	−.049
	(11.01)	(10.86)	(9.31)	(4.85)	(3.62)
Blue-collar	−.017	−.019	6.86	9.12	.019
	(1.44)	(1.64)	(4.97)	(6.17)	(1.74)
Manufacturing	.102	.103	.45	−.79	−2.9E−3
	(10.95)	(11.02)	(.42)	(.73)	(.37)
Professional	.304	.317	−8.81	−8.33	.022
	(23.82)	(24.82)	(4.72)	(4.23)	(1.92)
$DISP_0$	−.028	−.053	6.00	14.17	−.100
	(1.50)	(2.84)	(5.39)	(13.05)	(3.82)
$DISP_5$	−.014	−.040	2.94	5.13	−.038
	(.61)	(1.74)	(2.10)	(3.50)	(2.09)
$DISP_0 - DISP_5$	−.014	−.013	3.07	9.05	−.062
	(.48)	(.46)	(2.00)	(5.87)	(2.09)
Mills					.299
					(1.24)
$\Phi(\hat{\beta}\bar{X}/\sigma)$			.125	.146	

Absolute values of *t*-statistics in parentheses.

Note: Wage regressions estimated by ordinary least squares, weeks of unemployment by TOBIT. Controls for the survey year are also included in regressions. $\Delta W_0 = W_0 - W_{-2}$. (If W_{-2} is not available, wage changes are calculated using W_{-1} as the base.)

receive lower wages but are unemployed less often than males or city dwellers. Workers older than fifty-five earn substantially below their younger counterparts, once experience and job tenure are controlled for, whereas earnings grow faster for younger workers and those with low seniority.

If workers displaced in years 0 and 5 have similar unobserved characteristics *and* a period sufficiently prior to either termination is chosen that the latter has no effect on employment conditions, wages and unemployment of the two types of workers should be similar, once observables are controlled for. Coefficients on $DISP_0 - DISP_5$ therefore provide tests of the joint hypothesis that unobservables are similar and displacement effects are negligible in the year considered. Parameter estimates that differ significantly from zero indicate *either* the failure to fully control for heterogeneity (i.e., the two categories of job leavers have different unobserved characteristics) *or* that the displacement has already begun to have an effect in the year studied.

Workers displaced in year 0 earn a statistically insignificant 1.4% less than year 5 job losers in period $t - 2$ (see column 1).[18] The coefficient on $DISP_0 - DISP_5$ implies that they are also unemployed an average of one-half extra week in that year (column 3).[19] Although the unemployment effect is statistically significant, these small differences reveal that the unobserved characteristics of the two groups are fairly similar. In addition, evidence presented in sections V and VI suggests that relative wages begin to decline and joblessness to increase more than two years prior to the date of displacement. This suggest that most, if not all, of the disparities remaining at $t - 2$ result from impending period 0 displacements, rather than uncontrolled for heterogeneity.

The statistically significant coefficients on $DISP_5$ indicate that, compared to job stayers, workers displaced in period 5 possess unobserved characteristics associated with reduced wages and increased unemployment. For example, they earn 3.9% less than nondisplaced workers and are unemployed 0.7 weeks more in year $t - 1$. This indicates the importance of difficult to observe heterogeneity and suggests the inadequacy of using random nondisplaced workers as a control group for measuring the impact of involuntary terminations.

V. The Time Profile of Unemployment

Table 3 provides information on the time profile of unemployment. The coefficients indicate the predicted impact of period 0 and 5 perma-

Table 3   Weeks of Unemployment by Period Zero and Period Five Displacement Status

Dependent variable	Coefficient		
	$DISP_0$	$DISP_5$	$DISP_0 - DISP_5$
UN_{-2}	.856	.370	.486
	(4.34)	(1.47)	(2.00)
UN_{-1}	2.822	.681	2.141
	(13.05)	(3.50)	(5.87)
UN_0	8.771	.635	8.136
	(24.99)	(3.59)	(14.62)
UN_1	4.234	.816	3.418
	(16.00)	(3.71)	(7.57)
UN_2	1.950	.441	1.509
	(8.60)	(2.00)	(4.15)
UN_3	1.750	1.376	.374
	(7.76)	(5.45)	(.97)
UN_4	1.472	2.813	−1.341
	(7.09)	(9.96)	(3.17)

Absolute value of t-statistics in parentheses.

Note: Coefficients show predicted changes in weeks of unemployment obtained from TOBIT regressions, which include variables controlling for: experience, education, marital and ethnic status, sex, age, city size, industry and occupation, job tenure, and the survey year.

nent layoffs on weeks of unemployment for the years $t - 2$ through $t + 4$ and are obtained from TOBIT regressions of equation (3). Differences between persons dislocated in period 0 and nondisplaced workers are statistically significant in all seven years and show a clear pattern. Unemployment rises slightly prior to the layoff, peaks in the year of displacement, and then falls fairly rapidly. The additional joblessness associated with base year job terminations is four days in $t - 2$, approximately three weeks the next year, almost nine weeks at time 0, four weeks in period 1, and less than two weeks in years 2 through 4 (see column 1).

There is clear evidence that joblessness increases *prior* to displacement. The coefficient on $DISP_0$ rises in the years preceding time zero, from 0.86 weeks at $t - 2$ to 2.82 weeks at t − 1. The corresponding increment to $DISP_5$, as the year 5 permanent layoff approaches, is from 0.44 weeks at time 2 (three years before the separation) to 2.81 weeks in period 4 (one year prior to the job loss). The evidence that adjustment begins more than two years before the termination also suggests that the positive coefficient on $DISP_0 - DISP_5$ at $t - 2$ results from the impending

171

base year displacements, rather than unobserved differences between the treatment and control groups.

Workers losing jobs in year 5 are unemployed two to four days more per year than nondisplaced individuals between $t - 2$ and $t + 2$. This suggests that failure to control for unobserved heterogeneity will lead to an overstatement of the effects of displacements on unemployment. Nonetheless, the vast majority of the unemployment differential between displaced and nondisplaced workers results from the job termination itself. Assuming that the coefficients on $DISP_5$, in years $t - 2$ through $t + 2$, provide good estimates of the impact of unobserved heterogeneity, the true displacement effect exceeds eight weeks in period 0, 3.5 weeks in period 1, and is significantly positive in all seven years.[20]

The evidence, however, also strongly indicates the transitory nature of the elevated joblessness. For example, displaced workers are unemployed only 1.75 and 1.5 weeks more than nondisplaced individuals in years 3 and 4, respectively. If heterogeneity explains one-half week of this additional joblessness, the impact of the displacement falls to 1.25 and 1 week in these two years. This is less than one-sixth and one-eighth as large as the initial (time 0) effect.

Additional information on the persistence of unemployment for persons displaced at time 0 is provided in table 4. The sum of weeks of unemployment in years 0 and 1 is used as the measure of initial joblessness and is denoted as WKS_0.[21] Rows 1 through 6 show the relationship between WKS_0 and total weeks of unemployment in periods 3 and 4 (denoted as WKS_3). The remaining three rows indicate results of TOBIT regressions which control for observed characteristics as well as WKS_0.

Approximately one-fifth (21.7%) of displaced workers move into new positions without experiencing intervening unemployment in years 0 or 1. These persons are out of work for substantially less time in periods 3 and 4 than the four-fifths of individuals suffering some initial unemployment; WKS_3 is positive for only 22.9% of the former group versus 45.5% of the latter (see column 1). Similarly, the likelihood that WKS_3 exceeds six, thirteen, or twenty-six weeks is less than half as large for workers with no initial unemployment as for those with positive weeks. For instance, the probability that WKS_3 is greater than 13 is 0.083 if WKS_0 equals zero but 0.225 if WKS_0 is positive (column 3).

More surprising, however, is the complete absence of a relationship between early and subsequent joblessness among workers with some initial unemployment. Although WKS_3 exceeds six months less often when WKS_0 is between one and six weeks than when it is seven or greater, workers with shorter initial joblessness are actually more likely

Table 4 **Unemployment in Periods Two Through Four as a Function of Unemployment in Year Zero and One**

	Probability WKS_3 greater than[a]			
Conditional on WKS_0 equals[b]	0	6	13	26
0	22.9%	13.9%	8.3%	3.5%
1–6	49.2	34.2	19.2	5.8
7–13	41.8	30.6	22.4	10.2
14–26	46.1	33.6	23.4	10.2
≥ 26	46.0	36.2	24.1	13.8
All	40.6	29.6	19.4	8.9
Regression coefficient on WKS_0:				
UN_2	.088			
	(6.00)			
UN_3	.031			
	(2.09)			
UN_4	.030			
	(2.69)			

[a] $WKS_3 = UN_3 + UN_4$.
[b] $WKS_0 = UN_0 + UN_1$
Note: Regression Coefficients obtained from estimates of $UN_n = \mathbf{X}_0\alpha + WKS_0\beta + \epsilon_n$. *T* statistics in parentheses.

to experience some subsequent unemployment and are more often out of work for between one and thirteen weeks in periods 3 and 4 than their counterparts (see rows 2 through 5). Similarly, there is only a weak correlation between WKS_0 and WKS_3 among persons unemployed more than seven weeks in years 0 and 1, despite the complete lack of controls for individual or firm characteristics.[22]

Equally noteworthy is the general brevity of unemployment experiences three and four years after displacement. Only 41% of individuals displaced in period 0 are unemployed at any point during the two years, 72% of these for six weeks or less (row 6). WKS_3 exceeds three months for fewer than one in five period 0 job losers and is greater than six months for only one in ten.[23] Even where WKS_0 exceeds six months, over half of workers experience no unemployment in years 3 and 4 and less than a quarter are jobless more than three months (row 5).

Rows 7 through 9 indicate the persistence of postdisplacement unemployment, after controlling for observable characteristics. These estimates are obtained from TOBIT regressions of

$$UN_n = \mathbf{X}_0\alpha + WKS_0\beta + \epsilon_n, \tag{4}$$

where n is equal to 2 through 4 and the sample is restricted to workers permanently laid off in year 0. The coefficients displayed in the table are equal to $\Phi(.)\hat{\beta}$, where $\Phi(.)$ is evaluated at the regressor means. They indicate the predicted increase in future unemployment when WKS_0 rises by one week. Again there is almost no evidence of persistent unemployment. An additional week out of work, in year 0 or 1, correlates with an increase of less than half a day at time 2 and under one-seventh of a day in periods 3 or 4. As shown in the next section, this transitory joblessness contrasts starkly with the extended duration of wage changes.

VI. Wage Changes

Job displacement is associated with significant reductions in relative wages. Table 5 shows results of earnings regressions, where the dependent variable is the change in log wages. Coefficients on $DISP_0$, $DISP_5$, $DISP_0 - DISP_5$, and the inverse Mill's ratio (if any) are reported. The predicted impact of displacement on the percentage growth in wage *levels* can be calculated as $e^\beta - 1$, where $\hat{\beta}$ is regression coefficient of interest. Model (a) contains estimates from a single-stage OLS regression; model (b) includes the inverse Mill's ratio from a first-stage probit reemployment equation, as a correction for sample-selection bias. With the exception of the base year, the Mill's coefficient is small and values for $DISP_0$ and $DISP_5$ are virtually identical in the two models. The positive Mill's coefficient in year 0 implies that the expected weekly wages of employed workers are 33.6% above those of their nonemployed counterparts. This indicates that high earners obtain new positions more rapidly than others following displacements. However, given the large standard error on the Mill's coefficient, this result should be interpreted cautiously.

Postdisplacement wage losses are large and lasting. The expected weekly earnings of workers losing jobs at time 0 decline 9.5%, between t − 2 and the base year, relative to their nondisplaced peers (using model b estimates). This understates the loss in earnings potential, however, since the average weekly wage during period 0 partially reflects the higher pay received on the preseparation job. For example, for individuals displaced in July, the average wage reflects the more than half the year worked in the predisplacement position. Changes measured through time 0 fail to capture the impact of subsequent slowdowns in earnings growth. As a result, the relative wage reduction increases to 12.6% in year 1 and to between 13% and 14% over the next three years (column 1). All coefficients on $DISP_0$ are statistically significant.

Table 5   **Wage Changes By Displacement Status**

Dependent variable	Model	Coefficient			
		$DISP_0$	$DISP_5$	$DISP_0 - DISP_5$	Mills
ΔW_0	(a)	−.074	−.035	−.039	
		(4.94)	(1.94)	(1.70)	
	(b)	−.100	−.038	−.062	.290
		(3.82)	(2.09)	(2.09)	(1.24)
ΔW_1	(a)	−.142	−.030	−.112	
		(9.02)	(1.54)	(4.65)	
	(b)	−.135	−.029	−.106	−.045
		(8.47)	(1.48)	(4.38)	(2.92)
ΔW_2	(a)	−.145	−.030	−.114	
		(8.78)	(1.52)	(4.53)	
	(b)	−.145	−.030	−.115	2.6E−3
		(8.70)	(1.52)	(4.53)	(.17)
ΔW_3	(a)	−.142	−.076	−.066	
		(8.36)	(3.64)	(2.52)	
	(b)	−.141	−.076	−.065	−.012
		(8.14)	(3.62)	(2.45)	(.70)
ΔW_4	(a)	−.147	−.121	−.026	
		(8.18)	(5.50)	(.94)	
	(b)	−.152	−.122	−.030	.028
		(8.33)	(5.53)	(1.08)	(1.61)

Absolute values of t-statistics in parentheses.

Note: Coefficients show predicted changes in log wages from regressions that include the same independent variables as in table 2. Model (b) also includes the inverse Mill's ratio obtained from a first-stage probit reemployment regression.

A portion of this reduced wage growth is caused by unobserved differences between displaced and nondisplaced workers. For example, the weekly wages of year 5 job losers, as measured by ΔW_0 through ΔW_2, decrease 2.9% to 3.7%, relative to equivalent job stayers, between $t - 2$ and periods 0 through 2 (column 2). Attributing this differential to unobserved heterogeneity, base year displacements are associated with a 6% wage loss in the year they occur and a reduction of at least 10% over the next four years. The stability of coefficients on $DISP_0$ between periods 1 and 4 is quite striking and provides strong evidence that earnings losses persist over time.

The coefficients on $DISP_5$ also show that wage growth begins to decline prior to displacement. Where the wages of nondisplaced workers and period 5 job losers grow at approximately the same rate between periods 0 and 2, the relative wages of the latter group decline 4.4% in each of years 3 and 4. The total loss during these two years (8.7%) is

Table 6 **Distribution of Wage Changes for**
Displaced and Nondisplaced Workers

	Wage changes of displaced and nondisplaced workers ($\Delta\omega_1$)			
Displacement status	$< -.25$	$-.25$ to $-.1$	$-.1$ to $.1$	$> .1$
None	11.5%	12.2%	31.8%	44.5%
Displaced in year zero	29.8	18.4	19.4	32.4
Displaced in year five	12.7	11.4	37.0	38.9

Note: ω_n refers to the level of weekly wages at year n.

60% of the maximum difference between time 0 job losers and nondisplaced workers. Further, the evidence that the deterioration begins more than two years before the period 5 separation suggests that the 1.4% wage disparity, at time $t - 2$, between workers displaced in year 0 and those laid-off in period 5 (shown in table 2) results from the impending terminations of the former individuals rather than because of unobserved differences between the two groups. This provides additional support for methodological approach employed in this paper.

Additional evidence on the variance and persistence of wage changes is contained in tables 6 and 7. Table 6 shows percentage changes in wage *levels* between periods $t - 2$ and $t + 1$ ($\Delta\omega_1$) for job losers and nondisplaced workers.[24] Table 7 provides more detailed information on the earnings changes of workers displaced in the base year and indicates the high persistence of these changes (both gains and losses).

The variance in wage growth, as measured by $\Delta\omega_1$, is significant for all types of workers but largest of all for those displaced in period 0. Thirty percent of this group suffer 25% or larger earnings reductions and almost half (48.2%) lose 10% or more (table 6, row 2). This compares to equivalent losses for 11.5% and 23.7% of nondisplaced workers and 12.7% and 24.1% of period 5 job losers respectively (rows 1 and 3). Nonetheless, lower pay is a far from universal consequence of permanent job loss. The weekly wages of nearly a third (32.4%) of dislocated workers grow at least 10% over the period—versus 44.5% of job stayers and 38.9% of persons displaced in year 5.

The first eight rows of table 7 indicate the probabilities that $\Delta\omega_2$ through $\Delta\omega_4$ are greater than 0.1 or less than -0.25, conditional on $\Delta\omega_1$. Initial and subsequent earnings growth is highly correlated. For example, the probability of "large" (greater than 25%) losses is over 60% in

Table 7　　　　　　　**Persistence of Wage Changes for Workers
Displaced at Year Zero**

	$\Delta\omega_2$	$\Delta\omega_3$	$\Delta\omega_4$
$Pr(\Delta\omega_n < -.25)$:			
All	28.9%	25.2%	25.5%
$\Delta\omega_1 < -.25$	61.6	51.0	45.0
$-.25 \leq \Delta\omega_1 < -.1$	23.8	21.3	25.4
$\Delta\omega_1 > .1$	10.2	9.8	14.0
$Pr(\Delta\omega_n > .1)$			
All	37.5	39.6	38.4
$\Delta\omega_1 < -.25$	10.6	17.2	16.7
$-.25 \leq \Delta\omega_1 < -.1$	23.0	23.8	20.5
$\Delta\omega > .1$	68.8	68.4	66.1
Coefficient on ΔW_1 in earnings regressions	.650	.544	.523
	(18.71)	(15.52)	(13.34)

Note: ω_n refers to the level of weekly wages at year n.

year 2 and gradually falls to 45.0% by year 4 for displaced workers with "large" reductions through year 1 (row 2). By contrast, only 10% to 14% of persons with "moderate" (10% or greater) initial wage increases suffer comparable losses in years 2 through 4 (row 4). The conditional probabilities of receiving raises of 10% or more in the later years are reversed. Workers are four to six times as likely to earn 10% above predisplacement pay levels in periods 2 through 4 if $\Delta\omega_1$ is greater than .1 than if it is less than $-.25$ (see rows 8 and 6).

To check whether the persistence of earnings changes results from observable individual characteristics which are correlated with accelerated or depressed wage growth, row 9 displays regression estimates of

$$\Delta W_n = \mathbf{X}_0\alpha + \Delta W_1\beta_n + \epsilon_n \tag{5}$$

for n equal to 2 through 4. $\hat{\beta}_n$ shows the correlation between initial and subsequent wage changes, after controlling for observable heterogeneity. The coefficient values indicate that 65% of the initial wage change persists to year 2 and 52.3% through time 4.

Even more striking is the duration of a substantial portion of the initial earnings change. Although $\hat{\beta}_n$ does decline with time since displacement, most of the reduction occurs in the first few periods. For example, if the correlation of expected wage changes between periods m and n is estimated as $\rho_{m,n} = \hat{\beta}_m/\hat{\beta}_n$, the autocorrelation coefficients between adjoining time periods are .65, .84, and .96 for $\rho_{1,2}$, $\rho_{2,3}$, and $\rho_{3,4}$, respectively. Assuming that the autocorrelation remains constant after period 3 ($\rho_{n,n+1} = .96$ for $n \geq 3$), 50.2% of the initial wage change lasts through year 5 and 40.9% through year 10. This suggests extremely high persistence of wage changes and lasting personal costs of displacement for those workers initially accepting pay cuts.

VII. Conclusions

This chapter has examined the time profile of displacement induced changes in employment and wages. The four main results can be summarized as follows. First, workers typically experience a small increase in unemployment and a moderate reduction in wage growth rates prior to involuntary job terminations. For example, expected joblessness increases by one-half to three weeks annually in the years immediately preceding the loss of jobs.

Second, postdisplacement unemployment is extensive but generally transitory. The average increase during the first two years is approximately three months. This declines to around one week annually after three years. Further, there is no relationship between the durations of initial and subsequent unemployment for individuals out of work for some period of time following the original job loss.

Third, postdisplacement wage changes are both diverse and lasting. Where the real weekly wages of almost half of all dislocated workers fall 10% or more, immediately after reemployment, roughly one-third increase their pay by an equivalent amount. These early gains or losses are highly correlated with future changes. Over 50% of the initial increase or reduction is predicted to continue five years after displacement and 40% through the tenth year.

Fourth, failure to control for heterogeneity between displaced and nondisplaced workers results in an overestimate of the adverse impacts of economic dislocation. For example, even had they been able to avoid the permanent loss of jobs in year 0, displaced workers would be predicted to experience one-half week of extra unemployment per year above that of a random group of job stayers.

These findings have important implications for both theory and policy. Reductions in relative wages and employment stability occurring *prior* to displacements indicate a partial response to market pressures but one that is inadequate to prevent the job terminations. The combination of transitory joblessness and more permanent wage changes is consistent with models requiring (possibly extended) unemployment for

178

efficient job search. If employed search were equally efficient, we would expect workers to quickly accept new (low-wage) positions with continued search occurring after the initial reemployment. This would be likely to result in short unemployment durations and a low correlation between initial and subsequent wage changes.

Extended initial unemployment and persistent wage changes might also be expected in efficiency wage models with rationing of high-paying jobs and in theories stressing "wait unemployment." Conversely, the findings are not supportive of models emphasizing the rapid equilibration of labor markets or the equivalence of quits and layoffs. In these theories, the experiences of displaced and nondisplaced workers should be similar, once heterogeneity is controlled for.

The results also indicate that programmatic assistance for displaced persons may be seriously misdirected.[25] Given the permanence of postdisplacement wage changes, more attention may need to be paid to the problems associated with initial reemployment in low-wage jobs. Particularly troubling is the lack of current support for basic skills training that exceeds twenty-six weeks duration. Similarly, the extended initial spell duration of postseparation joblessness frequently implies the exhaustion of unemployment benefits and suggests that the needs of the long-term unemployed are currently being underserved.

A number of changes could simultaneously increase assistance to displaced workers presently receiving inadequate support, while improving system incentives. One possibility would involve a combination of (1) delaying the payment of first unemployment insurance benefits until the fifth week of joblessness and (2) increasing the maximum duration of benefits from twenty-six to thirty-nine weeks. A longer waiting period substantially reduces program costs (since most unemployment spells are of fairly short duration), gives workers who can easily find new jobs increased incentive to quickly search for them, and reduces the unemployment insurance subsidy to firms extensively using temporary layoffs. The cost savings from not paying benefits during the first month of unemployment can then be used to increase assistance to the long-term unemployed, primarily displaced workers with unfavorable employment options, by providing more extended unemployment insurance.

Training incentives could be improved by requiring recipients to share in the costs of training and by making government guaranteed loans, modeled on existing student loan programs, available to workers receiving extended training. Cost-sharing is useful because it encourages individuals to self-select into those types of training that are expected to be most beneficial (or to avoid training altogether when little benefit is

179

expected). The guaranteed loans, if they covered living expenses as well as program costs, would make productive training available to liquidity-constrained displaced workers.[26]

It is appropriate to conclude this chapter on a cautionary note. The costs of displacement are frequently measured by changes in the levels of wages or unemployment that follow the permanent loss of jobs. As shown above, however, employment conditions frequently deteriorate prior to the termination. Thus, unless a period sufficiently before displacement is used as the basis for comparison, the costs of the dislocation will be understated. In addition, the size of expected changes frequently depends on the initial position of the displaced worker. For example, persons paid low wages before the layoff will generally suffer relatively small reductions in earnings as a result of it. For these individuals, however, the loss of jobs may be costly not because it leads to large decreases in pay but rather because it prevents them from obtaining the employment stability needed for subsequent career growth. Understanding how displacement impacts low-wage workers is an important topic for future research.

NOTES

1. See Ruhm (1987, 1989a, 1991a); Podgursky (1987a,b); Addison and Portugal (1987); Kletzer (1986); and Hamermesh (1987a) for evidence.

2. Recent analysis using the DWS includes: Flaim and Sehgal (1985); Horvath (1987); Podgursky and Swaim (1987a,b); Addison and Portugal (1987); Kruse (1988); Kletzer (1986); Ehrenberg and Jakubson (1989); Seitchik (1988); and several chapters in this book.

3. This problem, which is quite serious but has been virtually ignored by researchers using the DWS, is discussed in considerable detail in Ruhm (1991a). The best attempt to construct a control group using DWS data is by Madden (1988). She matches workers dislocated in 1983 with persons not involuntarily terminating jobs in that year. This overcomes part but not all of the problem.

4. This collinearity can potentially be avoided by using data from several waves of the DWS.

5. Typically this research involved comparing either earnings or unemployment in a single time period prior and subsequent to mobility. Examples of this type of study include: Antel (1985); Black (1980); Bartel and Borjas (1981); Blau and Kahn (1981a, 1981b); Borjas (1981, 1984); Jacobson (1984); and Mincer and Jovanovic (1981).

6. Some aspects of the adjustment profile were investigated in two of my earlier studies (Ruhm 1987, 1991b).

7. This assumes that displacement only affects the regression intercept. Slope effects could be captured by interacting D and $\mathbf{X}$.

8. Separations are considered to be permanent if the individual does not return to the firm within two calendar years of the termination.

9. The effect of a marginal change of the jth regressor is $\Phi(.)\lambda_j$, which is simply the TOBIT coefficient times the probability of a nonzero dependent variable. Infra-marginal changes, such as those occurring when a dummy variable switches from 0 to 1, must be calculated directly from equation (2) above. See Maddala (1983) for further discussion.

10. Future job changers have also been used to control for unobserved heterogeneity by Ruhm (1988) and Mincer (1986).

11. The second-stage model estimated is

$$Y_n = \mathbf{X}_0\alpha + D_0\beta + D_5\gamma + [\hat{\phi}/\hat{\Phi}]\lambda + \epsilon_n.$$

$\hat{\phi}$ and $\hat{\Phi}$ are obtained from the first-stage probit equation. If the error terms in the underlying reservation and market wage equations are joint normally distributed, $\hat{\lambda}$ equals $E(\epsilon_n|Y > 0)$. See Heckman (1976) for further discussion.

12. This occurs partly because of the small proportion of displaced workers who are unemployed during entire survey years. For example, only 2.6% to 5.7% of workers terminated in period zero fail to report wages in years zero through four. This compares with unemployment rates exceeding 25% in the January 1984 Displaced Worker Supplement (which uses information on employment status at a point in time).

13. Thus, when 1974 is the base year, this variable indicates persons not displaced in 1974 who are permanently laid-off from jobs in 1979.

14. Regressions on a dichotomous retirement variable indicate no increases in retirements for dislocated workers in the PSID.

15. If wage information was unavailable at $t - 2$ (which occurred in just over 1 percent of cases), wage changes were calculated as $\Delta W_n = W_n - W_{-1}$.

16. See Flaim and Sehgal (1985) or Horvath (1987) for evidence.

17. Since a structural model has not been constructed, the direction of causation can not be inferred.

18. Predicted differences in wage *levels* for the $j$the parameter are estimated from $\exp[\beta_j] - 1$, where β_j is the regression coefficient from the log wage equation.

19. Unemployment differentials can not directly ascertained from the coefficients of the TOBIT regressions. They are obtained by the change in expected unemployment, specified in equation (2), which occurs when the relevant dummy variable switches from 0 to 1 (with $\Phi(.)$ and $\phi(.)$ evaluated at the regressor means).

20. Because the unemployment of time five job losers begins to rise prior to the date of the permanent layoff, the coefficient on $DISP_0 - DISP_5$ is negative in year four. This does not imply that the year zero displacement effect has completely dissipated by this period.

21. Unemployment at period one is included because some terminations occur near the end of calendar year zero, in which case a substantial portion of the initial spell of joblessness carries over to the next year.

22. The Pearson correlation coefficient between WKS_0 and WKS_3 for all workers displaced in period zero (including those with WKS_0 equal to 0) is 0.1109.

23. This contrasts with extensive initial unemployment. WKS_0 surpasses thirteen weeks for 45.5% of displaced workers and exceeds six months for 26.2%.

24. ω is used to indicate weekly wage *levels*, as opposed to W, which denotes the natural log of wages. Table 6 displays percentage wage changes only for workers reporting

181

wages in year *n*. Since displaced workers are somewhat more likely than others to be unemployed during the entire year, their relative wage losses are slightly understated.

25. Unemployment insurance is the most important source of support for displaced workers. The two largest targeted programs during the eighties have been Title III of the Job Training Partnership Act and Trade Assistance Adjustment.

26. I discuss in detail how an integrated set of changes could improve assistance for displaced workers in Ruhm (1989b).

REFERENCES

Addison, John T., and Pedro Portugal (1987). "The Effect of Advance Notification of Plant Closings on Unemployment." *Industrial and Labor Relations Review* 41:3–16.

Antel, John J. (1985). "Costly Employment Contract Renegotiation and the Labor Mobility of Young Men." *American Economic Review* 79:976–91.

Bartel, Ann P., and George J. Borjas (1981). "Wage Growth and Turnover: An Empirical Analysis." In *Studies in Labor Markets,* edited by Sherwin Rosen. Chicago: University of Chicago Press.

Black, Matthew (1980). "Pecuniary Implications of On-The-Job Search and Quit Activity." *The Review of Economics and Statistics* 62:222–29.

Blau, Francine D., and Lawrence M. Kahn (1981a). "The Causes and Consequences of Layoffs." *Economic Inquiry* 19:270–95.

———(1981b). "Race and Sex Differentials in Quits Among Young Workers." *Industrial and Labor Relations Review* 34:270–95.

Borjas, George J. (1981). "Job Mobility and Earnings Over the Lifecycle." *Industrial and Labor Relations Review* 34:365–76.

———(1984). "Race, Turnover, and Male Earnings." *Industrial Relations* 2:73–89.

Ehrenberg, Ronald G., and George H. Jakubson (1987). "Advance Notice of Plant Closings: Does It Matter?" *Industrial Relations* 28:60–71.

Flaim, Paul O., and Ellen Sehgal (1985). "Displaced Workers of 1979–83: How Well Have They Fared." *Monthly Labor Review* 108:3–16.

Hamermesh, Daniel S. (1987a). "What Do We Know About Worker Displacement in the U.S." Working Paper #2402, Cambridge, Mass.: National Bureau of Economic Research.

———(1987b). "The Costs of Worker Displacement." *Quarterly Journal of Economics* 52:51–75.

Heckman, James J. (1976). "The Common Structure of Statistical Models of Truncation, Sample Selection and Limited Dependent Variables and a Simple Estimator for Such Models." *Annals of Economic and Social Measurement* 5:475–92.

Horvath, Francis W. (1987). "The Pulse of Economic Change: Displaced Workers of 1981–5." *Monthly Labor Review* 110: 3–12.

Jacobson, Louis S. (1984). "A Tale of Employment Decline in Two Cities: How Bad Was the Worst of Times?" *Industrial and Labor Relations Review,* 37:557–69.

Kletzer, Lori G. (1986). "Employment and Earnings Outcomes of Permanent Job Loss: Results from the January 1984 BLS Displaced Worker Survey." Mimeograph, Williamstown, Mass.: Williams College.

Kruse, Douglas L. (1988). "International Trade and the Labor Market Experience of Displaced Workers." *Industrial and Labor Relations Review* 41:402–17.

Maddala, G.S. (1983). *Limited Dependent and Qualitative Variables in Econometrics.* New York: Cambridge University Press.

Madden, Janice F. (1988). "The Distribution of Economic Losses Among Displaced Workers: Measurement Methods Matter." *Journal of Human Resources* 23:93–107.

Mincer, Jacob (1986). "Wage Changes in Job Changes." Working Paper #1907, Cambridge, Mass.: National Bureau of Economic Research.

Mincer, Jacob, and Boyan Jovanovic (1981). "Labor Mobility and Wages." In *Studies in Labor Markets,* edited by Sherwin Rosen. Chicago: University of Chicago Press.

Podgursky, Michael, and Paul Swaim (1987a). "Duration of Joblessness Following Job Displacement." *Industrial Relations* 26:213–26.

———(1987b). "Job Displacement and Earnings Loss: Evidence From the Displaced Worker Survey." *Industrial and Labor Relations Review* 41:17–29.

Ruhm, Christopher J. (1987). "The Economic Consequences of Labor Mobility." *Industrial and Labor Relations Review* 41:30–42.

———(1989a). "Do Long Tenure Workers Have Special Problems Following Job Displacement." *Economic Development Quarterly.*

———(1989b). "Labor Displacement in the United States." Paper prepared for the National Planning Association.

———(1991a). "Displacement Induced Joblessness." *Review of Economics and Statistics,* forthcoming.

———(1991b). "Are Workers Permanently Scarred by Labor Displacements?" *American Economic Review,* forthcoming.

Seitchik, Adam (1988). "Labor Displacement Within the New Family Economy." Unpublished Ph.D. dissertation, Boston, Mass.: Boston University.

CHAPTER SEVEN

Duration Models of Unemployment

PEDRO PORTUGAL

I. Introduction

In this Chapter we employ data from the 1983 wave of the PSID to investigate the distributional shape of unemployment duration.[1] To this end, three principal empirical strategies are deployed. First, within the framework of an accelerated failure time model, we test which of the parametric models widely used in the unemployment duration literature best fits the data, examine the sensitivity of the arguments in the duration equation to distributional assumptions, and, finally, compare the different estimates of the predicted duration of unemployment.

Our second empirical strategy involves the use of parametric proportional hazards models. As in the first exercise, our aim is to assess which of the various parametric specifications best fits the data, inter alia.

The final strategy is to compute the simple Cox semiparametric regression model, which is distribution free with respect to the baseline hazard. Here we examine not only the effects of the variables on the probability of escaping from unemployment but also test the proportionality assumption itself; namely, that the effects of the variables are linearly related to the logarithm of the hazard rate.

Researchers in the field have often uncritically assumed that unemployment duration or hazard rates follow a particular distribution. We show how this assumption can lead to potentially important biases in parameter estimates, the predicted duration of unemployment, and the shape of the hazard function.

An attempt is made to distinguish between the two models simply on the basis of the proportionality assumption rather than on the existence of a unique hazard function. That said, it remains entirely possible that the data might still conform to a mixed proportional hazards–accelerated failure time model. Investigation of this possibility is the subject of future research.

II. Statistical Models

Two duration models are specified. The first is an accelerated failure time model (see, for example, Kalbfleisch and Prentice 1980; Lawless 1982), and the second is a proportional hazards model (see Kiefer 1988). Beginning with the former, the relation between unemployment duration and its determinants can be expressed.

$$\log_e T = X\beta + \sigma\omega, \tag{1}$$

where X is a matrix of explanatory variables, σ is a scale parameter, and ω is a disturbance term. Thus, the accelerated failure time model assumes that the logarithm of unemployment duration is linearly related to its covariates. Also, the underlying baseline survival function, depicting the probability of remaining unemployed for given X, is determined by the distribution of the error term.

For the purposes of the current exercise we implement an estimation procedure that is flexible enough to accommodate a variety of shapes of the distribution function for the error term in equation (1) and by implication for the duration of unemployment and for the hazard function $[f(t)/1 - F(t)$, where $f(t)$ is the probability density function and $F(t)$ is the distribution function], which indicates the probability of reemployment given the existing spell length of unemployment.

A distribution function that meets the bill is the extended generalized gamma (Farewell and Prentice 1977; Addison and Portugal 1987). The probability density function (pdf) for the error term in this case is the log gamma distribution, defined as

$$|q|(q^{-2})^{q^{-2}} \exp\left[q^{-2}(q\omega - \exp q\omega)\right]/\Gamma(q^{-2}), \qquad \text{for } q \neq 0$$
$$(2\pi)^{-1/2} \exp(-1/2\omega^2), \qquad \text{for } q = 0, \tag{2}$$

where Γ denotes the gamma function and q the shape parameter. The extension of the model derives from the fact that q is allowed to be negative, corresponding to situations in which $-\omega$ has the pdf defined in equation (2) for $q > 0$. It can be seen that the limiting case, $q = 0$, is the standard normal density function.

185

Within this generalized specification, a number of different distributions can be defined:

$q = 1$ implies a Weibull distribution for unemployment duration and an extreme value distribution for ω;

$q > 0$, $\sigma = 1$ implies a gamma distribution for unemployment duration and a log gamma distribution for ω;

$q = 0$ implies a lognormal distribution for unemployment duration and a normal distribution for ω;

$q = -1$ implies a reciprocal Weibull distribution for unemployment duration and an extreme value distribution for ω;

$q = \sigma = 1$ implies an exponential distribution for unemployment duration and a standard extreme value distribution for ω;

$q = 1$, $\sigma = \frac{1}{2}$ implies a one-parameter Rayleigh distribution for unemployment duration, and;

$q = 1/\sqrt{2}$, $\sigma = 1/\sqrt{2}$ implies a one parameter chi-square distribution for unemployment duration.

For purposes of comparison we also include a nonspecial case, that implies a log-logistic distribution function for unemployment duration and a logistic distribution for the error term.

Each special case (and the log-logistic) allow for different shapes of the hazard function. For three of the cases the shape of the hazard function is already incorporated into the distribution. Thus, for the exponential, the Rayleigh, and the chi-square distributions there is implied constant, monotonically increasing, and monotonically declining hazard rates, respectively. For the lognormal, which is a two-parameter case, an inverse U-shaped hazard function is implied. For the remaining cases, other than the generalized gamma (and the log-logistic), the shape of the hazard function depends on the parameter estimates; q for gamma, and σ for Weibull and the reciprocal Weibull. In the case of the gamma distribution, $q > 1$ implies a U-shaped hazard rate, and an inverse U-shaped function for $q < 1$. For the Weibull and reciprocal Weibull cases, $\sigma > 1$ implies monotonically decreasing and $\sigma < 1$ monotonically increasing hazard rates. For the generalized gamma all the above possibilities are recognized. (Finally, for the log-logistic, $\sigma \geq 1$ implies a monotonically decreasing hazard function, and $\sigma < 1$ implies in inverse U-shaped hazard function.)

Turning now to the proportional hazards model, the relation between the escape rate from unemployment and its determinants may be written

$$\log_e \lambda(t) = \log_e \lambda_o(t) + X\beta', \tag{3}$$

where $\lambda_0(t)$ is an arbitrary baseline hazard function. The β' vector can be estimated without imposing any assumptions as to the baseline function via the Cox proportional hazards model (Cox 1972). Accordingly, this estimator is termed semiparametric. For the parametric specification, however, some assumption has to be made regarding the baseline hazard. A distribution that fits the flexibility requirement is the generalized Weibull (Turner, Hazelrig, and Blackstone 1982). The derivative of the cumulative hazard function can be written

$$\lambda(t) = \left[\left(1 + \left(\frac{t}{\tau} \right)^\gamma \right)^{1/\alpha} - 1 \right]^{\eta-1} \cdot \left[1 + \left(\frac{t}{\tau} \right)^\gamma \right]^{(1-\alpha)/\alpha} \cdot \left(\frac{t}{\tau} \right)^{\gamma-1} \frac{\gamma\eta}{\tau\alpha} \cdot \left[\mu(X,\beta') \right] (4)$$

This flexible specification allows for a *very large* number of special cases, only five of which are estimated here. Each special case is defined by the restrictions placed on the parameters:

Variant I—$\gamma = 1$; $\eta = 1$
Variant II—$\gamma = 1$; $\tau = 1$; $\eta = 1$
Variant III (Weibull)—$\gamma = 1$; $\tau = 1$; $\eta = 1$
Variant IV (Exponential)—$\gamma = 1$; $\tau = 1$; $\alpha = 1$; $\eta = 1$
Variant V (Rayleigh)—$\gamma = 1$; $\tau = 1$; $\alpha = 1$; $\eta = 2$.

We note parenthetically that the Weibull distribution obeys the assumptions of both the accelerated failure time and proportional hazards models.

For the special cases considered a monotonically declining hazard rate is implied if either α or η exceed unity, and a monotonically increasing hazard rate for values of α or η below unity. Estimates for yet more general variants of the generalized Weibull proved computationally cumbersome and, for this data set, intractable. This outcome also obtained for simpler, more restrictive models such as the Gompertz and generalized Gompertz, both of which are also special cases of the generalized Weibull.

III. The Data

The data employed in this empirical inquiry are drawn from the 1983 PSID. We restrict our attention to male workers because information is complete only for heads of households. Our sample comprises male workers between the ages of eighteen and sixty-four separated from nonagricultural employment and economically active at the time of the survey.

187

In order to construct the unemployment duration variable only the last recorded spell of unemployment is utilized. Moreover, a distinction is drawn between temporary layoffs and permanent separations. The determinants of unemployment are likely to differ as between these two sources of job loss, being demand driven for temporary layoffs and mediated by both supply (i.e., search) and demand influences for the permanently separated. As a practical manner, the permanently separated include quits (the omitted category in the subsequent regression estimates), individual layoffs and fires, mass layoffs associated with plant closings, and an amorphous category comprising seasonal and temporary work cessations, and unemployment associated with labor-market entries.

The unemployment duration data are right-censored for those workers who are still unemployed, for those reporting a spell length of unemployment of ninety-eight weeks (at which point the data are top coded), and for those who do not report a precise spell length of unemployment beyond noting that it exceeds eight weeks. This censoring of the data was accommodated in the specification of the likelihood function. For the accelerated failure time model the likelihood function takes the following form:

$$L(\sigma,q,\beta) = \sum_{i=1}^{n} \delta_i [\log_e f(\omega_i;q) - \log_e \sigma] + \sum_{i=1}^{n} (1 - \delta_i) \log_e \left[1 - F(\omega_i;q)\right] \quad (5)$$

where $\delta_i = 0$ indicates a censored observation. For the proportional hazards model, the likelihood function is written

$$L(\alpha, \tau, \eta, \beta') = \Sigma \ \delta_i \log_e [\lambda \ (t_i, X_i, \alpha, \tau, \eta, \beta')]$$
$$- \Sigma \ H \ (t_i, X_i, \alpha, \tau, \eta, \beta'), \quad (6)$$

where λ is the hazard function, and H ($\cdot$) is the integrated hazard corresponding to λ.

IV. Findings

Results for the accelerated failure time model are given the tables 1 and 2 for permanently separated and temporarily laid-off workers, respectively. Beginning with the former, it can be seen that in the preferred specification, the extended generalized gamma, the "individual" variables tend to be significant. Thus, schooling reduces unemployment duration while being nonwhite serves dramatically to increase duration. The experience variable, picking up the length of employment history,

188

Table 1 The Distributional Shape of Unemployment Duration, Accelerated Time to Failure Model, Permanently Separated Workers

Distribution:	Extended generalized gamma	Weibull	Gamma	Lognormal	Reciprocal Weibull	Exponential	Rayleigh	Chi-square	Log-logistic
School	-.094	-.088	-.085	-.095	-.081	-.084	-.057	-.087	-.099
	(.001)	(.002)	(.001)	(.001)	(.006)	(.001)	(.000)	(.000)	(.001)
Experience	.012	.012	.011	.012	.013	.011	.005	.010	.011
	(.135)	(.108)	(.105)	(.135)	(.167)	(.105)	(.190)	(.104)	(.177)
Nonwhite	.439	.388	.366	.437	.436	.364	.218	.368	.448
	(.002)	(.006)	(.003)	(.002)	(.003)	(.004)	(.001)	(.002)	(.002)
Married	-.105	-.169	-.150	-.109	-.038	-.162	-.126	-.138	-.096
	(.504)	(.255)	(.251)	(.485)	(.814)	(.230)	(.071)	(.273)	(.535)
CUN	.065	.086	.079	.067	.042	.082	.065	.076	.070
	(.007)	(.000)	(.000)	(.005)	(.067)	(.001)	(.000)	(.000)	(.004)
Layoff	.599	.520	.494	.598	.568	.486	.262	.504	.626
	(.000)	(.000)	(.000)	(.000)	(.000)	(.001)	(.000)	(.000)	(.000)
Close	.564	.580	.557	.569	.464	.554	.368	.558	.629
	(.008)	(.003)	(.001)	(.007)	(.033)	(.002)	(.000)	(.001)	(.003)
Other	.288	.426	.403	.301	.095	.411	.287	.391	.370
	(.197)	(.035)	(.024)	(.170)	(.673)	(.025)	(.002)	(.024)	(.101)

Table 1 (Continued) The Distributional Shape of Unemployment Duration, Accelerated Time to Failure Model, Permanently Separated Workers

Distribution:	Extended generalized gamma	Weibull	Gamma	Lognormal	Reciprocal Weibull	Exponential	Rayleigh	Chi-square	Log-logistic
MSA1	.250	.329	.308	.260	.044	.313	.225	.302	.335
	(.159)	(.057)	(.042)	(.136)	(.797)	(.047)	(.007)	(.038)	(.053)
MSA2	.095	.170	.153	.101	.025	.162	.134	.141	.102
	(.565)	(.264)	(.257)	(.534)	(.879)	(.241)	(.056)	(.279)	(.535)
MSA3	-.029	-.001	-.000	-.026	-.093	.003	.039	-.004	-.026
	(.899)	(.998)	(.999)	(.906)	(.687)	(.986)	(.670)	(.982)	(.904)
Constant	3.126	3.478	3.444	3.152	2.654	3.483	3.607	3.398	3.117
	(.000)	(.000)	(.000)	(.000)	(.000)	(.000)	(.000)	(.000)	(.000)
$\hat{\sigma}$	1.414	1.099	1	1.400	1.506	1	.5	$1/\sqrt{2}$	.814
	[.068]	[.047]		[.055]	[.058]				[.036]
$\hat{q}$	-.065	1	.859	0	-1	1	1	$1/\sqrt{2}$	
	[.187]		[.110]						
χ^2_g	—	59.85	—	.12	22.2	1.64	258.15	1.91	—
χ^2_{G}	—	—	43.48	—	—	4.47	254.41	16.37	—
Loglikelihood	-790.10	-806.42	-808.16	-790.17	-799.77	-808.96	-1056.72	-809.12	-793.75
$\hat{U}$	31.19	35.45	34.84	31.44	28.8	35.58	40.91	33.82	32.01
$\hat{S}$	.588	.401	.391	.411	.414	.392	.298	.393	.410

Notes: p-values provided in round brackets, standard errors in square brackets

Table 2   The Distributional Shape of Unemployment Duration, Accelerated Time to Failure Model, Temporarily Laid Off Workers

Distribution:	Extended generalized gamma	Weibull	Gamma	Lognormal	Reciprocal Weibull	Exponential	Rayleigh	Chi-square	Log-logistic
School	-.008	.007	-.005	-.007	-.005	.008	.021	.003	-.011
	(.810)	(.825)	(.868)	(.835)	(.88)	(.778)	(.158)	(.912)	(.743)
Experience	-.017	-.023	-.009	-.019	-.009	-.023	-.020	-.023	-.022
	(.041)	(.001)	(.233)	(.016)	(.262)	(.000)	(.000)	(.000)	(.008)
Nonwhite	-.061	-.189	-.022	-.078	-.022	-.196	-.277	-.157	-.035
	(.682)	(.181)	(.860)	(.603)	(.873)	(.136)	(.000)	(.227)	(.827)
Married	-.017	.016	-.021	-.012	-.021	-.017	.047	.008	-.059
	(.928)	(.930)	(.894)	(.949)	(.903)	(.916)	(.579)	(.960)	(.772)
CUN	.058	.066	.046	.061	.046	.065	.056	.064	.060
	(.007)	(.002)	(.022)	(.005)	(.034)	(.001)	(.000)	(.001)	(.008)
MSA1	.549	.571	.490	.556	.488	.572	.545	.571	.568
	(.008)	(.003)	(.005)	(.008)	(.009)	(.002)	(.000)	(.001)	(.010)
MSA2	.187	-.060	.244	.149	.243	-.072	-.202	-.011	.203
	(.331)	(.736)	(.126)	(.434)	(.162)	(.664)	(.017)	(.946)	(.301)
MSA3	.172	.204	.126	.178	.126	.202	.183	.193	.230
	(.463)	(.374)	(.527)	(.451)	(.561)	(.343)	(.113)	(.353)	(.361)
Constant	1.293	1.890	.825	1.421	.818	1.919	2.213	1.808	1.509
	(.010)	(.000)	(.080)	(.003)	(.100)	(.000)	(.000)	(.000)	(.002)
$\hat{\sigma}$	1.190	1.079	1	1.193	1.094	1	.5	$\surd 2$	.716
	[.051]	[.049]		[.050]	[.050]				[.034]
$\hat{q}$	-.229	1	-.901	0	-1	1	1	$\surd 2$	
	[.234]		[.221]	[.050]	[.050]				
$\chi^2_{\hat{q}}$	—	49.17	1030.51	.92	17.30	8.58	223.55	2.62	—
χ^2_G	—	—	—		—	2.59	220.07	7.0	—
Loglikelihood	-479.18	-493.67	-485.98	-479.67	-484.05	-495.11	-708.37	-491.82	-489.18
$\hat{U}$	5.91	7.53	4.73	6.18	5.07	7.98	13.67	7.62	6.21
$\hat{S}$	.494	.478	.521	.491	.502	.465	.312	.465	.491

Notes: p-values provided in round brackets, standard errors in square brackets

narrowly fails to achieve significance at conventional levels. The labor-market variables, including the source of separation, are also statistically significant; higher county unemployment rates leading to significantly longer spells of unemployment, and employer-initiated separations producing much higher unemployment than voluntary quits (the omitted category). The variables indexing the size of the metropolitan area in which the separations occurred, however, are uniformly insignificant.

For the temporarily laid-off, we obtain the not unexpected finding that neither schooling nor race are significant. (Indeed, there is even some indication that nonwhites now have lower unemployment.) The likely explanation for the failure to observe significant coefficients on the education and race arguments is that neither search nor discrimination are involved in the case of temporary layoffs. Also unsurprising is the significantly negative effect of experience on duration, reflecting as it does priority for recall. County unemployment rates are again found to be of importance in mediating the spell length of unemployment; higher local unemployment rates serving to lengthen unemployment duration. It can also be seen that workers laid off in large metropolitan areas have significantly longer spells of unemployment. This outcome reflects sample composition. Because we observe only the metropolitan area in the event that temporary layoffs occur, it follows that the greater job opportunity effect obtaining in larger MSAs is masked.

For both samples of permanently separated and temporarily laid-off workers it emerges that the special case that best approximates the extended generalized gamma is the lognormal distribution. The chi-square *summary statistic* for the lognormal is very small and statistically insignificant. All the other special cases are rejected both in terms of the chi-square test and the likelihood ratio. In general, distributions with one free parameter perform badly, especially the Rayleigh, although we note that the chi-square distribution outperforms the more widely used Weibull distribution. All the other two-parameter distributions perform better than the Weibull. Finally, note that the log-logistic, although not a special case, approximates quite well the behavior of the lognormal distribution.

With respect to the sensitivity of the parameter estimates to distributional assumption it can be seen that, for relatively small deviations from the general distribution, little change in the coefficients is observed. But the Rayleigh distribution reminds us rather forcefully that a misspecified distribution can produce dramatic changes in magnitudes.

Since the lognormal distribution implies an inverse U-shaped hazard function, it follows that arbitrary selection of one of the other special

192

cases that assume monotonic behavior will lead the investigator to draw inaccurate inferences about duration dependence.

At the foot of tables 1 and 2 are given the predicted median duration of unemployment and the predicted survival rate (at the observed level of unemployment) for each distribution. Reflecting our earlier discussion, there are important differences across distributions. A further breakdown of these results for five quantiles of each distribution is given in appendix table A-2.

Turning next to the proportional hazards model, results for which are provided in tables 3 and 4, we observe that the parameters are consistent in relative magnitude and sign with those obtained from the accelerated failure time model. Of course, the signs are reversed since we are now considering the determinants of the escape rate from unemployment rather than those of unemployment duration. Again, the Rayleigh distribution is a source of marked distortion. For the two samples of permanently separated and temporary laid-off workers, the three-parameter distribution (Variant I) dominates each of the other special cases, although it is not statistically different from the two-parameter distribution (Variant II). Again, the Weibull distribution is rejected as are the special cases represented by the exponential and Rayleigh distributions.

The final two rows of Tables 3 and 4 provide predicted hazard rates (for current t) and corresponding survival rates. Vary small differences are apparent for the special cases of the proportional hazards model, with the obvious exception of the Rayleigh distribution, and this outcome also obtains for the five sample quantiles reported in appendix table A-3.

Having discussed results for the parametric proportional hazards model, we next consider the performance of the semiparametric form; namely, the proportional hazards general linear model (Cox procedure). Results of this exercise are given in table 5. Again, it can be seen that even though the baseline hazard is not considered the individual coefficients closely resemble those provided in the previous tables. In other words, smooth departures from the most flexible distribution do not substantially affect the parameter estimates. A more telling result, however, is the rejection of the proportionality assumption, as indicated by the Z-test statistics (for six out of eleven variables in the case of permanent separations, and for six out of eight variables with respect to the temporarily laid-off equation). The rejection of proportionality for the large majority of variables calls into question most of the results given in Tables 3 and 4, and further undermines the results for the Weibull distribution and its special cases reported in Tables 1 and 2.

Table 3   **The Distributional Shape of Unemployment Duration, Parametric Hazards Model, Permanently Separated Workers**

Distribution: Variable	Variant I	Variant II	Variant III (Weibull)	Variant IV (Exponential)	Variant V (Rayleigh)
School	.075	.074	.076	.081	.111
	(.004)	(.005)	(.004)	(.002)	(.000)
Experience	−.011	−.011	−.011	−.011	−.008
	(.116)	(.118)	(.119)	(.119)	(.258)
Nonwhite	−.349	−.347	−.352	−.363	−.429
	(.007)	(.007)	(.006)	(.005)	(.000)
Married	.150	.151	.155	.163	.252
	(.274)	(.273)	(.260)	(.235)	(.075)
CUN	−.082	−.081	−.084	−.089	−.138
	(.000)	(.001)	(.000)	(.000)	(.000)
Layoff	−.497	−.492	.499	−.513	−.556
	(.000)	(.000)	(.000)	(.000)	(.000)
Close	−.576	−.571	−.586	−.615	−.814
	(.002)	(.002)	(.001)	(.001)	(.000)
Other	−.408	−.404	−.416	−.442	−.623
	(.029)	(.031)	(.027)	(.018)	(.001)
MSA1	−.279	−.271	−.286	−.300	−.440
	(.076)	(.078)	(.072)	(.059)	(.009)
MSA2	−.133	−.136	−.137	−.145	−.258
	(.340)	(.341)	(.330)	(.299)	(.071)
MSA3	−.039	−.037	−.040	−.046	−.133
	(.828)	(.835)	(.832)	(.803)	(.477)
Constant	−1.064	−2.767	−3.054	−3.379	−7.113
		(.000)	(.000)	(.000)	(.000)
$\alpha^{\dagger}$	.250	.181	1	1	1
	(.001)	(.023)			
γ	1	1	1	1	1
τ	1.790	1	1	1	1
	(.001)				
η	1	1	−.097	1	2
			(.026)		
Loglikelihood	−1650.20	−1652.21	−1654.80	−1657.44	−1901.10
h	.025	.025	.025	.026	.028
$\hat{S}$	.597	.596	.600	.609	.702

†The *estimated* parameters for α, τ, and η are in logarithmic form.

Note, however, that one should be wary of abandoning the proportionality assumption in the absence of tests for possible nonlinearities and interaction effects between the variables. Such tests fall outside the scope of the present analysis. Moreover, rejection of the proportionality

194

Table 4   The Distributional Shape of Unemployment Duration, Parametric Hazards Model, Temporarily Laid Off Workers

Distribution: Variable	Variant I	Variant II	Variant III (Weibull)	Variant IV (Exponential)	Variant V (Rayleigh)
School	−.005	−.006	−.007	−.009	−.044
	(.864)	(.836)	(.792)	(.745)	(.150)
Experience	.019	.019	.021	.022	.039
	(.004)	(.003)	(.002)	(.007)	(.000)
Nonwhite	.145	.154	.173	.194	.549
	(.272)	(.242)	(.189)	(.139)	(.000)
Married	−.011	−.016	−.020	−.023	−.098
	(.941)	(.924)	(.906)	(.890)	(.564)
CUN	−.055	−.056	−.059	−.063	−.108
	(.005)	(.004)	(.003)	(.001)	(.000)
MSA1	−.467	−.491	−.530	−.574	−1.090
	(.009)	(.007)	(.004)	(.002)	(.000)
MSA2	.022	.033	.051	.067	.401
	(.890)	(.842)	(.759)	(.683)	(.012)
MSA3	−.167	−.163	−.170	−.184	−.343
	(.434)	(.446)	(.429)	(.396)	(.144)
Constant	.638	−1.397	−1.730	−1.904	−4.423
	(.686)	(.001)	(.000)	(.000)	(.000)
$\alpha^\dagger$	.463	.204	1	1	1
	(.213)	(.007)			
γ	1	1	1	1	1
τ	1.87	1	1	1	1
	(.138)				
η	1	1	−.079	1	2
			(.082)		
Loglikelihood	−952.21	−953.32	−956.23	−957.80	−1172.51
h	.101	.100	.099	.099	.091
$\hat{S}$	.509	.511	.522	.536	.691

$\dagger$The *estimated* parameters for α, τ, and η are in logarithmic form.

assumption does not necessarily imply acceptance of the assumption of the accelerated failure time model; namely, the assumed loglinear relation between the duration of unemployment and its determinants. To proceed further a modified Box-Cox transformation model might be implemented; modified, that is, so to accommodate censoring and distributional assumptions.

Given the similarities between the two broad models in terms of the magnitude and significance of the parameters, the distinction between the assumptions of those models does not appear overly critical. What is

Table 5 **Proportional Hazards, General Linear Model, Permanently Separated and Temporarily Laid Off Workers**

	Permanently separated	Z-test	Temporarily laid off	Z-test
School	.077	−6.30*	−.002	−2.37*
	(.003)		(.942)	
Experience	−.011	1.02	.018	−3.70*
	(.124)		(.007)	
Nonwhite	−.332	2.90*	.135	5.21*
	(.008)		(.305)	
Married	.126	4.13*	−.026	−3.61*
	(.349)		(.877)	
CUN	−.071	−3.76*	−.053	−2.47*
	(.001)		(.007)	
MSA1	−.281	−.71	−.436	.06
	(.071)		(.017)	
MSA2	−.155	−3.00*	.034	4.59*
	(.261)		(.838)	
MSA3	−.034	.28	−.146	1.83*
	(.853)		(.489)	
Layoff	−.457	6.41*	—	
	(.000)			
Close	.489	.61	—	
	(.006)			
Other	−.358	−1.48	—	
	(.053)			
χ^2	72.38		19.09	
S	.575		.478	

*denotes significance of Z-test at .05 level.

Note: the Z-test is a modified version of that suggested by Nagelkerke *et al.* (1984).

much more critical than model specification is the distributional assumption made within each model.

Finally, let us consider the vexed question of duration dependence. The *nonparametric* hazard (and survival) rates provided in table 6 indicate initially rising escape rates from unemployment (up to eight weeks for the permanently separated sample, and up to thirteen weeks in the case of the temporarily laid off) followed by decreasing escape rates. These crude results receive support in the preferred special case of the accelerated failure time model—namely, the lognormal distribution—and are further supported by the log-logistic regression. No such inference can be drawn from the generalized Weibull specifications, which point to monotonically declining hazard rates.

Table 6   **Nonparametric Survival and Hazard Rates**

	Permanently separated		Temporarily laid off	
Week	$\hat{S}$	h	$\hat{S}$	h
1	.977	.023	.827	.189
2	.952	.026	.704	.162
3	.919	.036	.645	.087
4	.850	.078	.547	.164
5	.836	.017	.531	.030
6	.811	.030	.472	.118
7	.800	.013	.455	.036
8	.745	.072	.389	.159
9	.736	.012	.365	.063
10	.727	.013	.345	.058
11	.721	.008	.334	.030
12	.696	.036	.291	.132
13	.663	.049	.255	.139
14	.654	.014	.238	.071
15	.644	.014	.234	.015
16	.633	.018	.223	.047
17	.597	.059	.195	.140
18	.582	.026	.195	—
19	.576	.010	.191	.019
20	.568	.014	.187	.020
21	.560	.014	.165	.128
22	.552	.014	.153	.071
23	.550	.004	.153	—
24	.542	.015	.146	.053
25	.536	.011	.142	.028
26	.487	.100	.121	.159
27	.487	—	.121	—
28	.478	.019	.117	.038
29	.475	.005	.112	.039
30	.459	.035	.103	.083
31	.457	.005	.103	—
32	.454	.005	.085	.200

IV. Conclusions

Two broad lines of consideration are warranted: one economic and the other more narrowly statistical. Beginning with the former, the distinction between permanently separated and temporarily laid-off workers appears to be a valid one. But although the effects of the variables differ as between samples, it is interesting to note that the same underlying distribution obtains in each case. Relatedly, unobserved heterogeneity does *not* appear to have a substantially differential impact on the results, which finding carries the potentially important implication that chance

197

rather than choice drives the unobservables. Let us amplify this point in the following manner. From a search-theoretic perspective, we can identify three potential sources of unobserved individual heterogeneity influencing the arrival rate of job offers, the wage offer distribution, and the costs of search. Of these, search costs and wage offers are unlikely to play an important role in the case of temporary layoffs. Thus, if permanent separations and temporary layoffs have much the same underlying hazard functions, an argument can be made that the two groups of workers face similar arrival rates of job offers. It is in this sense that we say that chance rather than choice dominates the unobservables.

We also find that the labor-market variables (area unemployment and size of metropolitan statistical area [MSA]) operate in similar fashion across the samples. A final economic result is that negative duration dependence only obtains in the case of longer-term unemployed workers.

Much attention has been focused on the role of unobserved individual heterogeneity, without correction for which duration analysis will tend to be biased toward accepting negative duration dependence in the data. Consideration of this issue has consumed considerable research resources. Unfortunately, however, the literature offers no guidance as to the choice of an appropriate correction for unobserved individual heterogeneity and to this extent much of the debate has distracted attention away from other important questions of model specification that do have solutions.

The statistical issues are as follows. First, the distinction between the proportional hazards and accelerated failure time models is apparently not critical in analyzing the effect of individual arguments. More critical is the arbitrary selection of the underlying distribution within each broad model. Two-parameter distributions do not imply severe distortion in individual coefficients as compared with the more general distributions. The single parameter case(s) do, however, lead to major distortions. The important differences have to do with duration dependence and predicted unemployment and hazard rates. It is these differences that underline the requirement to work with flexible distributions. Second, an important research agenda is indicated by the present analysis. One pressing need is to implement nonparametric models that are robust in the presence of unobserved heterogeneity (Heckman and Singer 1984). Another is the ability to develop models that jointly accommodate the assumptions of each broad model investigated here. A final necessary development is the implementation of models with mixed hazard functions.

APPENDIX

Table A-1 **Definition and Values of Variables**

Variable	Permanently separated		Temporarily laid off	
	Mean	Standard deviation	Mean	Standard deviation
T—duration of unemployment in weeks	28.36 (37.46)	25.19	10.41 (7.16)	12.34
School—number of years schooling completed	11.77	2.32	11.05	2.31
Experience—number of years actually employed	8.87	8.49	11.92	9.39
CUN—county unemployment rate	8.42	2.79	9.37	3.37
Nonwhite—blacks and hispanics = 1, 0 otherwise	.46		.37	
Married—married = 1, 0 otherwise	.74		.85	
Layoff—individual separations from permanent jobs = 1, 0 otherwise	.48			
Close—workers displaced by reason of plant closure or relocation = 1, 0 otherwise	.12			
Other—workers laid off from seasonal or temporary work, etc. = 1, 0 otherwise	.11			
MSA1—metropolitan statistical area ≥500,000 population = 1, 0 otherwise	.25		.15	
MSA2—metropolitan statistical area ≥100,000 <500,000 population = 1, 0 otherwise	.26		.18	
MSA3—metropolitan statistical area ≥ 50,000 <100,000 population = 1, 0 otherwise	.10		.10	
N	566		307	

Note: figures in parenthesis indicate percentage of censored observations.

Table A-2   Predicted Duration of Unemployment for Selected Quantiles by Sample, Accelerated Failure Time Model

Group/quantile	Extended generalized gamma	Weibull	Gamma	Lognormal	Reciprocal Weibull	Exponential	Rayleigh	Chi-square	Log-logistic
Permanently separated									
.05	3.18	2.03	3.19	3.15	3.19	2.63	0.22	5.92	2.92
.25	12.13	13.50	15.18	12.27	10.18	14.78	6.83	20.06	13.12
.50	31.29	35.50	34.89	31.54	28.93	35.62	39.64	37.35	32.10
.75	81.83	76.06	68.81	81.07	108.81	71.24	158.56	60.96	78.53
.95	334.59	177.45	150.56	315.34	1460.94	153.95	740.46	105.14	352.96
Temporarily laid off									
.05	.92	.45	1.10	.87	1.02	.59	.03	1.65	.75
.25	2.68	2.91	2.39	2.76	2.38	3.31	.79	5.60	2.82
.50	5.90	7.51	4.73	6.17	5.07	7.97	4.59	10.42	6.19
.75	13.52	15.87	11.01	13.80	13.27	15.94	18.35	17.02	13.61
.95	48.34	36.43	54.92	43.90	87.55	34.44	85.70	29.35	51.08

Table A-3 Predicted Hazard Rates for Selected Quantiles by Sample, Proportional Hazards Model

Group/quantile	Variant I	Variant II	Variant III (Weibull)	Variant IV (Exponential)	Variant V (Rayleigh)
Permanently separated					
.05	.008	.008	.009	.010	.002
.25	.014	.014	.015	.016	.008
.50	.021	.020	.021	.022	.019
.75	.032	.032	.032	.031	.035
.95	.059	.058	.057	.056	.085
Temporarily laid off					
.05	.046	.049	.052	.053	.007
.25	.072	.073	.076	.077	.017
.50	.098	.097	.097	.094	.052
.75	.123	.121	.116	.117	.131
.95	.174	.173	.166	.163	.297

NOTES

I should like to thank John T. Addison for his encouragement and assistance in the preparation of this essay.

1. For a more extensive discussion of the distributional shape of unemployment duration using data from both the PSID and the Displaced Worker Surveys, see Portugal (1989).

REFERENCES

Addison, John T., and Pedro Portugal (1987). "On the Distributional Shape of Unemployment Duration." *Review of Economics and Statistics* 68 (August): 520–26.

Cox, David R. (1972). "Regression Models and Life Tables." *Journal of the Royal Statistical Society* Series B 34 (May/August): 187–202.

Farewell, Vern T., and Ross L. Prentice (1977). "A Study of Distributional Shape in Life Testing." *Technometrics* 19 (February): 69–76.

Heckman, James J., and Burton S. Singer (1984). "Econometric Duration Models." *Journal of Econometrics* 24 (January/February): 63–132.

Kalbfleisch, John D., and Ross L. Prentice (1980). *Statistical Analysis of Failure Time Data.* New York: Wiley.

Kiefer, Nicholas M. (1988). "Economic Duration Data and Hazard Function." *Journal of Economic Literature* 26 (June): 646–79.

Lawless, Jerald F. (1982). *Statistical Models and Methods for Lifetime Data.* New York: Wiley.

Nagelkerke, N. J. D., J. Oosting, and A. A. M. Hart (1984). "A Simple Test for Goodness of Fit of Cox's Proportional Hazards Model." *Biometriks* 40 (June): 483–86.

Portugal, Pedro. (1989). "Two Essays in Unemployment." Unpublished doctoral dissertation. Columbia: University of South Carolina.

Turner, Malcolm E., Jane B. Hazelrig, and Eugene H. Blackstone (1982). "Bounded Survival." *Mathematical Biosciences* 59:33–46.

CHAPTER EIGHT

Advance Notice

JOHN T. ADDISON AND PEDRO PORTUGAL

I. Introduction

Legislation seeking to provide workers with advance notification of their impending redundancy raises interesting theoretical and practical questions. At the former level of inquiry, one has presumably to ask why it is necessary to mandate notice; alternatively put, under what circumstances is the market, left to its own devices, unlikely to produce an optimal quantity of advance notification? At the practical level, one would seek to identify the effects of mandating notice on the unemployment (and earnings) development of displaced workers. These are the principal themes investigated in the present chapter. The context of our discussion is of course the recent passage of the Worker Adjustment and Retraining Notification Act (WARN) as a result of which the United States has now joined the ranks of the majority of industrialized nations that mandate prenotification of collective dismissals.[1]

II. U.S. Legislation

Although the United States has lagged other nations in legislating prenotification rights, there has been no lack of congressional activism in this area. Thus, plant closing legislation has come before every Congress since 1973, with more than forty bills having been introduced in the last decade.[2] But it was not until 1985 that a bill succeeded in being reported out of a full committee of either House. In November of that year, the first version of the bill ("The Community and Dislocated Worker Notification Act," H.R. 1616) was narrowly defeated by a vote of 208 to 203. The bill would have required employers of fifty or more full-time employees (at a single site) to provide ninety-days' notice of employment loss. This notice interval was to be activated when the employment loss at any site constituted either 30% of the employees or fifty employees (whichever was the greater) during any thirty-day period, or one hundred or more employees over the same interval.[3]

The closeness of the vote on this particular piece of legislation has to be seen against the backdrop of earlier initiatives that went far beyond notification rights. The abortive 1979 National Employment Priorities Act, for example, sought to penalize firms that ceased operation for any reason. Under the Act, firms were required to give up to two years' notice of their plans to relocate or close. Employees were to be given fifty-two weeks of severance pay, amounting to 85% of their average wages, after allowing for earned income, unemployment insurance benefits, and trade-adjustment assistance. Additionally, dislocated employees were to be offered reemployment at other plants for up to three years, without loss of wages or fringes. Moreover, the firm was obliged to pay the community in which it was located an amount equal to 85% of one year's taxes; and if the firm in question was in the process of moving its operations overseas it had to pay the federal government an amount equal to 300% of one year's total lost taxes.[4]

A further diminution in the reach of legislation would appear to explain the success of the most recent initiative. In July 1987, the Senate passed the Trade Bill (S.1420), appended to which were advance notification provisions.[5] As a result of a conference agreement (designed to reconcile differences between separate legislation in the Senate and House of Representatives) in April 1988, the terms of the original Senate amendment were left largely intact. The final legislation, the Worker Adjustment and Retraining Notification Act (Public Law 100-379), was enacted into law on 4 August 1988 after the president decided not to veto it and became effective 4 February 1989. Under the terms of the Act, sixty-days' prenotification is required of a plant closing that results in employment loss of at least 50 employees at a single site of employment, or a (mass) layoff of more than six months duration that results in an employment loss for 50 or more employees if 33% of the workforce at a site of employment are affected or that results in an employment loss for 500 employees in which case the one-third rule does not apply. Employment loss is calculated over a thirty-day interval. (Note that the legislation also provides for the determination of a plant closing or mass layoff based on an aggregation of smaller employment losses over a ninety-day period unless these are the result of separate and distinct actions, although mass layoffs of 50 to 499 employees must still affect 33% of the employees at a particular employment site.) Only those employers with 100 or more full-time employees are covered by the legislation, and only employees working at least twenty hours a week who have at least six-months' tenure are to be included in calculating the number of employees who have experienced an employment loss. Furthermore, employees are deemed not to have suffered an employment loss in the event that they have been offered transfers within a reasonable commuting distance from their current job, have accepted transfer to any of the employer's facilities, or have been rehired by a purchaser of the business.

Note, too, that notice is not required if the closing is a shutdown of a temporary facility or the mass layoff results from the completion of a particular project where the affected employees were hired on the understanding that the job was limited to the duration of the facility or project. Lockouts, not intended to evade the requirement of the act, are similarly excluded.

A reduction of the notification period applies in the case of faltering companies and unforeseeable business circumstances. The former escape route requires that the employer be actively pursuing measures that would avoid or indefinitely postpone the closing. Moreover, the employer must reasonably believe that he has a realistic opportunity of obtaining the necessary capital or business *and* that giving notice would militate against the success of the endeavor. Unforeseeable business circumstances associated with natural disasters, unexpected termination of business contracts, and dramatic changes in business conditions (prices, costs, and orders) also permit closings or mass layoffs before the end of the full-notice period.

Notice has to be given to each representative of the affected employees or, in the absence of any such representative, to each employee. Moreover, the bill also provides for third-party notice; specifically, to the state's dislocated worker unit (designated or created under Title III of the Job Training Partnership Act) (see chapter 1) and the chief elected official of the local government affected by the closing or mass layoff. In the event that more than one unit of local government is involved, the employer has simply to notify that unit to which he has paid the highest taxes over the year preceding notice.

Remedies for violation of the notice requirement are as follows. First, with respect to employees, damages are equivalent to one day's

205

pay and the value of related fringe benefits for each day of the violation. The amount owed by the employer is reduced by any earnings or fringes paid during the violation period. Second, failure to notify the relevant state agency may result in a fine of up to $500 a day for each day of the sixty-day period that notice was not given, subject to a maximum penalty of $30,000. The penalty does not apply where the employer pays each affected employee the full amount for which he is liable to that employee within three weeks of the shutdown or layoff. In short, the employer can buy out this notice obligation to the individual and the "community" by paying the sixty-day value of wages and fringes.

With one exception, the rights and remedies provided under the advance notification provisions do not preempt or displace rights and remedies provided under other statutes or contractual agreements. That exception concerns the notice period that is to run *concurrently* with intervals established under state law or contract. Details of extant state and local legislation on plant closings are provided in table 1, only two of which set notice intervals greater than that established under the existing law.

Despite the apparent modesty of WARN vis-à-vis its precursors, employer opposition to its terms has been no less vigorous than on earlier occasions.[6] Why is this? In part, the opposition can be traced to the additional costs of doing business imposed by prenotification, to include litigation costs stemming from potential ambiguities in the legislation (e.g., what constitutes a "reasonable commuting distance"?). Arguably more important than these costs, however, is a fear among employers that the successive moderation of plant closing legislation over the years since 1973 is a chimera or tactical diversion. Indeed, employer resistance may be yet more deeply seated than this, having a basis in recent congressional activism in the area of mandated benefits.[7]

III. Why Legislate?

There is very little dispute about the efficacy of advance notification, where this is voluntarily agreed to by the parties to the individual or collective contract. Rather, the debate hinges on the question of mandating notice. The case against rests on what may be termed an "everything is optimal" depiction of labor market reality. Prenotification of impending redundancy is conventionally viewed as part of a "payment bundle" that can be freely negotiated between the employer and the worker; just one element in a total compensation package that includes

Table 1   State and Local Legislation on Plant Closings

	Maine	Wisconsin	Hawaii	Massachusetts	Philadelphia, Penn.	Vacaville, Calif.
Enacted	1971; amended 1973, 1975, and 1983	1976; amended 1984	1987	1984	1982	1984
Coverage	≥ 100 employees	≥ 100 employees	≥ 50 employees	All firms receiving funding from five designated state agencies must "agree to accept" certain voluntary standards of corporate behavior	≥ 50 employees	All firms who relocate to this development area who receive at least $1,000 in local financial aid and where employment loss ≥ 35 permanent employees
Notification	Director, State Bureau of Labor; plus employees and municipality if out of state move	State Department of Industry, Labor, and Human Resources; affected employees, unions, and municipal and county governments	State Director, Labor and Industrial Relations; affected employees	Director, Employment Service; employees and unions	Director, Philadelphia Commerce Department; employees and unions	City Council
Period of notice	60 days	60 days	45 days	"At least 90 days or equivalent benefits"	60 days	At least 3 months and typically one year
Severance pay	One week's pay for each year of service where employee has worked for the firm for at least three years			No formal stipulation but employer to provide for 90 days of health insurance coverage after plant closing, jointly financed by the employer and the displaced worker		

Table 1 (Continued)   State and Local Legislation on Plant Closings

	Maine	Wisconsin	Hawaii	Massachusetts	Philadelphia, Penn.	Vacaville, Calif.
Exemptions	Natural calamities or unforeseen circumstances." Employer exempted from severance pay requirement where it has an "express contract" with its employees providing for severance pay.					
Penalties	$500 fine for failing to notify coupled with state enforcement of severance pay provisions	$50 per worker	Affected employees have the right to sue the firm for damages; employer subject to fine equal in value to three months' wages and benefits measured across all laid-off workers.	Contractual	Court enforcement to prevent closure if notice not given. In case of closure, the courts can award damages of up to 60 days wages to each employee.	Contractual

both pecuniary and a variety of nonmoney benefits. Workers seek to maximize the size of the payment bundle; if they value prenotification rights, then this will enter the package of benefits and will presumably be reflected in a lower wage, ceteris paribus. In the market, we will observe some contracts in which notice is given and others where it is not. In the former case, the costs to employers will tend to be small relative to the gains to employees, thus providing scope for the beneficial trade. On the other hand, where the costs to employers are relatively large and the benefits to workers relatively small, we should not expect to observe notice clauses in individual and collective contracts. Firms that can provide notice most cheaply will attract workers who value notice, and those for whom notice is costly will attract workers who value it less. Legislating notice would largely be irrelevant in one sector and detrimental in the other (which is not to say that firms that do provide notice will not find common cause with analogous others in supporting mandated notice since this will impose costs on their competitors). In the absence of constraints on the trades that may be undertaken, on which more below, the suggestion is that the privately optimal incidence and quantity of notice will result from voluntary trades. *Vulgo:* there is no scope for policy activism, leave all well alone.

The case for is often presented in equally stark terms: workers do not in fact possess sufficient information to make the trades envisaged by the market model. Only dimly aware that their jobs are in jeopardy, workers will not take into account the full costs of displacement and continue to make investments in inappropriate skills. Facing positive costs, however, the employer will not find it to his advantage to impart his private information. In short, maximizing choices are not observed because of the implausibly high informational requirements of the voluntary exchange process. In this milieu, so the argument runs, there is indeed scope for third-party intervention to ensure that the employer internalizes other than his or her own private costs. This rationalization for regulation is not without costs because in the first instance the employer has to pay without the benefit of any offsetting trade. The increase in employment adjustment costs inevitably means that there will be some reduction in employment offered by the system on net. Proponents of advance notification argue that the costs are small compared with the benefits.

There exists a wide body of evidence suggesting the presence of positive wage differentials for differences in unemployment risk. Thus, we observe compensation for differences in industry cyclicality, for firm-specific and systematic risks of unemployment, for both temporary and permanent layoffs, and for the incidence and/or duration of unemployment (Abowd and Ashenfelter 1981; Topel 1984; Adams 1985; Li 1986; and Hamermesh and Wolfe 1986). What is at issue is the magnitude of the differential and hence the degree to which wages compensate for unemployment risk. This is because work by Murphy and Topel (1987), in particular, has suggested that fully two-thirds of the compensation estimated using cross-sectional date is illusory and reflects unobserved heterogeneity in workers' earnings capacities. An appropriate conclusion, subject to the caveat that worker insurance can never be complete, would appear to be that although one can perhaps dispense with the pathological view of worker information there may indeed be significant constraints on the ability of workers to trade off wages for an instrument capable of limiting their exposure to unemployment risk.

Some such constraints, albeit in a rather different conceptual framework, are analyzed by Deere and Wiggins (1988) in whose treatment some positive level of notice is a feature of *all* optimal contracts. Since we do not in practice observe notice clauses in all employment contracts, a crucial feature of the authors' analysis is contractual failure. It is this that provides the rationale for mandating notice.

The notion that it is efficient for firms to give their employees some warning of the timing of plant closure exploits the argument that both parties to the employment contract invest in specific assets generating quasi-rent flows that are voided on termination of the employment relation. These investments include search costs and shared firm-specific human capital. A decision by one party to sever the job match impacts adversely on the other by raising search costs and wasting training investments. Moreover such decisions have important externalities, on which more below.

At its simplest level, however, Deere and Wiggins's model envisages (homogeneous) workers searching across heterogeneous firms in the quest for a productive match. Having located a job, the search process continues but this time on the job. Workers are supposed to know the likelihood that plans for a shutdown will be activated but not the actual point of closure. It is argued that as long as the firm knows about the closing in advance, and that it takes time for workers to locate a suitable job match upon displacement, some positive amount of notice will be given. Familiarly, the efficiency of notice turns on the costs and benefits of the instrument.

The worker gains from prenotification because of a reduction in the spell length of joblessness. He will accept an alternative job offer that would otherwise have been declined. On notification, the worker is assumed to search more intensively for work *and* lower his reservation wage. Both factors reduce the probability that the worker will experience unemployment. The cost to the employer, on the other hand, is the lost output sustained as a result of a successful search.

The optimal length of notice in this model is determined by equating the marginal costs and benefits of prenotification. For the worker, the marginal benefit of an additional day's notice is the increased probability of locating an acceptable job multiplied by the gain from finding a job today *less* the expected gains from notice tomorrow. Although the increase in the probability of finding another job is assumed constant over the notice interval, the net gain from taking the job on the day of notice, rather than embarking on increased search one day later, is assumed to decline. With one day's notice, for example, the marginal benefit conditional on finding a job is the avoidance of the median spell of joblessness experienced by displaced workers. With much longer periods of notice, however, the marginal gain shrinks since the worker is assumed to be under less pressure to search at the point of notice. For the employer, the marginal cost of an incremental day's notice is the change in the quit rate (identical to the increased probability that the worker finds a job) multiplied by the output loss from a quit today *less* the expected loss from notice tomorrow. Such output losses may be viewed as increasing pari passu with the notice interval; the marginal cost of one day's notice conditional on a new match being one day's sacrificed output, that for a second day's notice being two days' output, and so on. More accurately, if the heightened probability of a worker quit is denoted by Δq, the total cost of one day's notice is Δq, and that of two days notice is $2\Delta q + \Delta q\,(1 - Dq)$, with the result that the marginal cost of the two days' notice is $2\Delta q - (\Delta q)^2$. In other words, the marginal cost of notice in practice increases less than proportionately with the notice interval because of job finding on other than the day of notice. With marginal benefits that remain positive as the notice interval declines and tend to zero as that interval increases, and marginal costs that rise with the notice interval and that are zero in the absence of notice, Deere and Wiggins conclude that some positive level of notice will be a feature of all efficient contracts.[8]

To reinforce the conclusion that some amount of notice is efficient, Deere and Wiggins then introduce search costs and specific training investments. The basic idea is that turnover and investment decisions affect the value of a job match over its life and that a worker who expects to receive notice will exhibit different behavior from one who does not. Specifically, that worker will have less tendency to quit. Reduced quit behavior obviously influences the expected duration of the match and hence the incentive of both sides to invest in productivity augmenting job specific assets. Workers who fail to receive notice will evince higher quit rates than their notified counterparts, at least up to the formal communication of notice. Thereafter, notified workers may be expected to quit at somewhat higher rates than are typical of nonnotified workers. Deere and Wiggins argue that, since the notice interval is considerably shorter than the actual and expected life of the job match, factors that improve the net economic value of the match dominate and ensure the Pareto optimality of notice. Indeed, on this model, absence of notification may be viewed as prejudicial to the viability of marginal firms.

Unfortunately, there is a problem of time-inconsistency in all of this. Thus, a firm that promises to give notice obtains the benefit of a more stable labor force and reduced employment costs irrespective of whether or not it actually delivers on its promise. Since the ex post cost of giving notice is a higher turnover rate, what factors inhibit the firm from reneging? It is here that the substantive contribution of Deere and Wiggins lies. In the conventional contracts literature, employer malfeasance is circumscribed by reputation effects. A firm that reneges on its promise to prenotify workers of their impending displacement will suffer as remaining workers and potential workers adjust their behavior accordingly. Remaining workers will alter their quit behavior and replacement workers will require a premium for selecting into the firm. Reliance investments will not be made and the reduced value of existing and future job matches will ultimately threaten the survival of the firm. But, as Deere and Wiggins note, what is the relevance of the reputation effects mechanism if the firm is going out of business? In these circumstances the provision of notice is manifestly a time-inconsistent strategy. Of course, if the firm in question is merely permanently laying off a proportion of its workforce or, if closing, is part of a multiplant entity the gains to both parties of advance notification remain largely intact.

And what of contractual remedies, do these not surmount the time inconsistency of notice? Here Deere and Wiggins draw an important distinction between individual and collective contracts in limiting opportunistic behavior by the employer and reserve an important role for unions often neglected in contract theory. Despite the appeal of individual contracts, they are not only costly to reach but also and more importantly costly to enforce. Moreover, the remaining assets of a firm in closure may be trivial and, even where substantial, may be much dissipated by rent-seeking behavior that characterizes ostensibly more efficient class action type suits.

Now the introduction of a "hostage" or a performance bond into the individual contract, activated by failure to notify, would seem at face value to provide a solution to the problems associated with nonspecific contracts and thereby limit employer malfeasance. The employer now ostensibly faces a credible threat, a tangible punishment that may be leveled against it in the event of default. But, Deere and Wiggins cogently argue, such hostages are unlikely to escape adjudication by the courts either because they are not credible ab initio or because they are subject to duplication (that is, the selfsame hostage is pledged to analogous others).

Both situations they argue are transformed in the presence of collective action. Unions reduce the costs of negotiating an explicit notice agreement and in enforcing contracts. They also prevent competitive rent seeking in the pursuit of contractual remedies and provide a more credible threat in circumstances where few assets are available. Similarly, unions assist in the negotiation, policing, and disposition of contractual hostages. The downside risk is that, although facilitating the provision of optimal levels of prenotification, unions may have other effects that reduce the firm's share of the match and reduce levels of capital investment, inter alia (Addison and Hirsch 1989; Hirsch 1989).

In sum, Deere and Wiggins argue convincingly that problems of time-inconsistency may help explain why one does not observe comprehensive notice provisions in voluntary trades. Collective bargaining may overcome opportunistic behavior, and reputation effects alone may be sufficient where the firm closes one unit of a multiplant operation or engages in mass layoffs that still leave a (considerable) proportion of the work force employed. Alternatively put, advance notice provisions are altogether less likely among workers who are party to individual contracts or employed in single-plant firms.

Thus we have a case for mandatory notice—the vexed question of the appropriate length of which is taken up below—as a means of circumventing the time-inconsistency problem in individual contracts and in situations where reputation effects are lacking. An additional effect of notice would take the form of reducing the incentive to join unions.

Another case for mandating notice would apply even in those situations where reputational effects and contractual remedies are sufficient to generate the privately optimal quantity of advance notification. There may be circumstances in which privately optimal arrangements are not socially optimal. Thus, for example, the presence of unemployment insurance (UI) benefits could artificially reduce the costs to employees of not receiving notice, thereby producing too little notification *and*

213

inefficient quits in the system as a whole. Trades that otherwise might be agreed to may not be worthwhile in the presence of an unemployment subsidy. Here we relax the assumption of Deere and Wiggins's model that all contracts will provide notice, though not the assumption of optimizing behavior, since it is an unnecessary feature of that model that interior solutions will necessarily obtain. (More accurately, the decision to bargain over notice is conceptually distinct from the optimal length of notice.) If the UI system is viewed as inviolable, a second-best case for mandated notice arises.

In the light of the foregoing, a reasonable case can be made for the proposition that markets do not necessarily provide the privately (or socially) optimal level of notice. (Additional arguments based on adverse selection and externalities are offered by Summers [1989].) But it is one thing to argue that we will observe suboptimal notice provisions in private contracts, quite another to formulate an appropriate public standard. The costs and benefits of providing notice will vary from situation to situation. Legislation typically does not take this diversity into account. Clearly, prenotification limits flexibility, namely the need to make rapid decisions in the face of fluctuating market conditions. This problem may be expected to be most acute in the case of small firms, which may not in practice have sufficient lead time to comply with the uniform standards set under legislation. For this reason, it is reassuring that such firms have been exempted under WARN. The U.S. legislation also allows for a reduction in the notice interval in the cases of unforeseeable business circumstances and faltering companies actively engaged in a fight for survival. The latter gateway is interesting precisely because mandated notice may be expected to decrease the likelihood that buyers of the firm's product will place new orders, that banks will supply credit, that suppliers will continue to supply services, and that the firm will be able to sell the enterprise to potential buyers (Ehrenberg and Jakubson 1988). In other words, shutdown pressures or "pinch points" in the life of a business that might otherwise be successfully circumnavigated may become binding in the presence of a nondiscretionary notice standard. Of these arguments, the U.S. Congress, Office of Technology Assessment (1986b) reports that the loss of access to credit is among the principal concerns of businessmen. Loss of credit may again be a special problem for smaller companies. And, if an analogy may be drawn between going out of business and the preannounced termination of a product line, then the loss of consumers may be a potent private cost of notice.

We thus observe some flexibility in the U.S. legislation, but the sixty-day notice standard remains a thorny issue. A preferred solution, and one suggested first by Deere and Wiggins, would be to establish some lower bound notice interval as a default value and allow the parties to negotiate around this standard. In other words, if the parties failed to negotiate an alternative notice interval, the legislated standard would apply. Now a lower bound notice interval is still a matter of guesswork. But it should not be taken as defined by supposedly best practice codes set under voluntary agreements, but should in part reflect the behavior of firms that currently do not give notice but would do so absent constraints on contracting. In the next section we investigate inter alia, the periodicity of notice under pre-WARN contracts in order to get a sense of whether a sixty-day notice is "excessive." Ultimately, however, the private and social benefits of notice have to considered alongside the private costs imposed on employers. To be sure, if as theory would lead us to expect, advance notification significantly reduces the joblessness that accompanies displacement, then savings to the public purse will accompany private gains. Moreover, advance notice may also enhance the effectiveness of existing manpower instruments and state reemployment schemes if they can be activated prior to or at least shortly after the point of layoff. In the process, firms may even realize cost savings in experience-rated UI taxes.[9] Again, social and private gains will obtain if workers respond to prenotification by switching from investments that only have a payoff in what is a failing enterprise into skills that are more general and hence portable. But at all times the costs of legislation to employers have to be borne in mind. Reductions in the overall level of employment offered by the system because of the impact of increased employment adjustment costs on existing enterprises and potential entrants translate in some yet-to-be measured way private costs into social costs. Benefits to workers are more easily identified than costs to employers. Pending improved analysis of the latter, the most obvious conclusion would appear to be that policy be applied in an experimental manner.

IV. Empirical Evidence

In this section, we first examine descriptive material on the incidence and length of notice under individual and collective contracts. Next, we consider the effects of notice on unemployment duration in the wake of displacement, and the erosion of its effects through time. We also consider limited evidence pertaining to advance notification and subsequent earnings. Finally, we examine the vexed question of the endogeneity of notice with a view to generalizing the findings to a regime of mandated notice.

The Incidence and Extent of Notice

Until very recently, and despite continuing attempts to legislate a notice standard, very little information was available on the incidence, still less the periodicity, of notice under voluntary exchange. With the publication of the displaced worker supplements to the January 1984, 1986 and 1988 Current Population Surveys and investigations conducted by the General Accounting Office (GAO), however, the data situation has improved considerably. Nevertheless, some ambiguity still attaches to the empirical evidence.

Of the two main data sets, the GAO material has certain advantages in that it contains information on actual length of notice at establishment level, contractual data on agreed length-of-notice (where applicable), the types of reemployment assistance offered displaced workers, and union presence, inter alia. The displaced worker survey (DWS), on the other hand, tells us whether or not the *individual* received formal notice or expected the coming redundancy. Until the 1988 survey, the DWS contained no information on the length of notice, which has therefore to be inferred, and did not distinguish between formal notice and mere expectation of an impending closure or mass layoff. Moreover, no micro information continues to be available on the presence of a union, the union status of the worker, firm size, and single- versus multiplant operation. Studies using the DWS that seek to include such factors as establishment size and unionization have perforce had to use industry averages. The offsetting strength of the DWS, on the other hand, is that it contains detailed information on the personal characteristics of displaced workers and their labor market experience following displacement (see chapter 2). Another issue is of course that the GAO data are not publicly available. We know of only one study that exploits this data set, although a number of researchers have apparently gained access to this material. Given recent research on union *density* at the individual firm level (Hirsch 1989), which can be matched to the GAO establishment data, analysis of the displaced worker problem may turn increasingly to this data set. In the interim, however, our consideration of this material is largely confined to cross tabulations.

The nature of the DWS having been discussed earlier, we focus here on the GAO survey of establishments (U.S. Congress, General Accounting Office 1987). To determine the extent of business closures and permanent layoffs, the GAO surveyed a national sample of 2,600 establishments stratified by geographic area, industrial group, and number of employees that, based on a comparison of Dun and Bradstreet records for end 1982 and 1984, appeared to have closed or experienced a serious layoff (defined as a reduction in employment at the establishment during 1983 and 1984 of at least 20%, or a minimum of 200 workers in the case of establishments with more than 1,000 employees[10]). The sample comprised 2,400 establishments employing one hundred or more employees, and 200 establishments with fifty to ninety-nine employees.

Each establishment was then contacted to determine whether it had in fact closed or experienced a significant permanent layoff. Only 600 establishments actually fell into these categories over the sample frame, the balance merely reflecting changes in ownership. The rates of closure and layoff subsequently reported in the GAO analysis were determined from the verified sample and the total number of establishments in the United States from Bureau of Census data. Data on the extent of notice *and* assistance provided displaced workers were obtained from a sample of 376 establishments employing one hundred or more workers.

The GAO report that a little over 30% of establishments failed to provide any notice at all. The median length of notice was only 7 days. As shown in table 2, less than 20% of establishments provided their workers with more than 30-days' notice and only 5% gave more than 90 days. Not shown in the table are the less than 2% of establishments giving more than 180-days' notice. Establishments that ceased operations were more likely to provide longer notice than establishments with major layoffs—one-third of establishments that closed down gave more than 30-days' notice

Table 2   **Extent of Advance Notification by Source of Job Loss,
GAO Estimates**

Length of notice	All establishments	Shutdowns	Mass layoffs
Zero	32	29	32
1–14 days	34	20	38
15–30 days	15	16	15
31–90 days	14	25	11
≥ 91 days	5	10	4

Source: U.S. Congress, General Accounting Office (1987), Tables VII.6 and VII.11, pp. 78–79.

as compared with only 15% of establishments in the case of mass layoffs. [Individual data from the 1984 and 1986 displaced worker surveys indicate that 52.5% and 52.1% of the displaced either received formal notice or otherwise anticipated their impending displacement. Moreover, incidence of notice was more pronounced in the case of plant shutdowns than permanent layoffs generated by slack work: 54.4% (54.2%) versus 50.2% (48.8%) percent for the 1984 (1986) survey(s).]

At this point we should perhaps note some discrepancy between the GAO findings, and those of a recent Conference Board study (Berenbeim 1986), which points to altogether longer periods of notice. Specifically, the Conference Board study reports that only 13% of establishments failed to provide notice, 41% gave between 1- and 90-days' notice, and no less than 25% gave 181 or more days' notice. Part of the discrepancy between the two studies clearly reflects the less representative nature of the sample of firms in the Conference Board study: the companies selected were the largest in seven industry categories and the response rate was only 27%. (It will be recalled that the firms questioned in the GAO study were from a stratified random sample of establishments from a national database and the figures quoted above are based on a 78% response rate.) Note, too, that the Conference Board data refer to plant closings, and as we have seen shutdowns are associated with greater notice than major layoffs.

Returning to the GAO findings, it is reported that unionized establishments are more likely to provide notice than their nonunionized counterparts. Less than 20% of establishments with a union present failed to give notice to their blue-collar workers compared with 40% of the establishments without union representation; corresponding values for white-collar workers were 21% and 31%, respectively. But in both cases, particularly the latter, differences between the union and non-union firms appear to erode quickly after the zero notice interval. Around 30% of establishments with union representation that experienced a closure or permanent layoff had a union contract with an advance notice requirement. The contractual length of notice ranged from 1 to 120 days, with a mean of 32 days. Less than one-half of the establishments surveyed were unionized.

GAO cross tabulations of notice by establishment size do not in general produce significant differences between medium-sized (100 to 249 employees) and large (≥ 250 employees) plants, although the tendency is for notice intervals to be longer for the latter. In the case of blue-collar workers, however, medium-sized establishments are significantly more likely to fail to give notice than their larger counterparts

Table 3   Percentage of Establishments Offering Reemployment and
Other Assistance, by Notice Interval and Broad Occupational Status

Benefit	All workers		Blue-collar		White-collar	
	≤30 days	>30 days	≤30	>30	≤30	>30
Income maintenance	42	70*	39	73*	55	77*
Continued health insurance	36	47	36	47	45	59
Continued life insurance	18	36*	19	35**	25	48*
Early retirement	10	27*	8	26*	16	29**
Relocation assistance	10	36*	9	28*	17	49*
Counseling	16	39*	17	33**	20	51*
Occupational training	1	7**	2	12**	1	6
Job search assistance	28	48*	29	42	35	62*
Combination of income, health, counseling, and job search	11	25**	10	24**	16	35*

Note: * and ** denote significant differences at the .05 and .10 levels, respectively.

Source: U.S. Congress, General Accounting Office (1987), Tables VII.28, VII.29, VII.30, pp. 84–85.

(35% versus 23%). Moreover, major differences between the two establishment size groupings emerge when we consider the assistance provided displaced workers. Large firms are significantly more likely to provide income maintenance, continuation of health and life insurance coverage, early retirement, counseling, and job search assistance than their smaller counterparts. These results appear to be dominated by differences in treatment accorded white-collar workers in medium-sized and larger establishments.

Although there are few signs of significant differences in the type of assistance offered displaced workers by source of job loss, there are major differences by length of notice. As indicated in table 3 most types of assistance are more likely to be extended to workers when the notice interval exceeds thirty days. This is true for both white-collar and blue-collar workers. Unfortunately, further breakdown of these results by plant size and union presence is not available. Taken alone, union presence appears to have little material influence on the provision of assistance.

Interestingly, reemployment assistance is dominated by other forms of support. Income maintenance benefits (provided by 45% of establishments) are the most pervasive form of assistance, followed by continued health insurance coverage (37%) and only then by job search assistance

219

(31%), and job counseling (20%). Occupational training is provided by only 2% of all establishments. In general, white-collar workers are significantly more likely than their blue-collar counterparts to receive both placement and financial assistance, though the ranking of benefits is roughly the same in both cases. Reemployment assistance is uniformly higher for plant closings than mass layoffs, but not significantly so in the cross tabulations offered by the GAO.

On the basis of these findings, some will choose to conclude, as did the GAO itself, that workers are provided with inadequate notice and support in the fact of displacement. Others will conclude that even the watered-down notice requirements established under WARN are still overambitious, exceeding as they appear to do the mean reported periods of notice provided under voluntary contracts. But there is no magic in the figures for either antagonist or proponent of mandated notice benefits. In the first place, the provision of simple cross-tabulations does not address the analytics of prenotification, that is, the costs and the benefits of the instrument. In the second place, the figures are also imprecise. One potentially important issue here in the light of notice intervals that may in practice extend considerably beyond those set under contract is the distinction between specific and general notice. The GAO data reviewed above relate to periods of *specific notice,* namely those situations in which the individual is presented with the exact date of his or her termination. *General notice,* which is defined as prenotification of unspecified duration, is more consistent with the information supplied in the DWS. Periods of general notice would appear to exceed those of specific notice by a considerable margin. A recent study by Brown (1987) of layoffs in seven states, and which reports even shorter periods of specific notice than the GAO, points to general notice intervals averaging forty-six days as compared with only eighteen days of specific notice. As we shall see, analysis of DWS data to *infer* notice intervals can produce even higher estimates of the notice interval.

Empirical Analyses

Econometric analysis of advance notification has focused on its unemployment effects. The impact of the instrument on subsequent earnings development has received altogether less attention. We begin our discussion with a review of unemployment and unemployment duration studies, and note some refinements to the basic model. We then turn to the difficult question of the determinants of advance notification and examine the consequences of endogenizing notice for the single equation estimates provided earlier. The aim here is to provide a method for assesssing the likely effects of mandating notice. That being said, a word of caution is necessary since no study of which we are aware has adequately modeled the costs to employers of providing notice. Pending resolution of this issue, we have only a partial understanding of the diversity of notice across contracts and hence the consequences of recent legislation.

Notice and Unemployment In an "early" study of *publicly announced* shutdowns, Folbre, Leighton, and Roderick (FLR) (1984) examine the impact of plant closings in Maine on unemployment rates within fifteen (out of thirty) of that state's local labor market areas.[11] FLR regress monthly local unemployment rates on the number of workers laid off in major plant closings expressed as a percentage of labor force (current and seven lagged values of the layoff variable are employed), an advance notification dummy (publicly announced closings = 1; 0 otherwise) interacted with the layoff variable, and a set of control variables comprising the overall state unemployment rate and (fourteen) dummies for the local labor market areas.

For the month of closing of an establishment, it is found that, for every worker laid off, 0.814 workers who would otherwise be employed in the local area were unemployed. In the presence of advance notification, however, the coefficient on the layoff variable fell by more than 50% to 0.326 (that is, the reported interaction term is -0.488). In other words, advance notification is estimated to have reduced the effect of a major layoff from approximately 0.8 to 0.3 unemployed workers in the local area for every worker laid off that month. Summing the estimated coefficients on the current and lagged values of the layoff variable and the layoff-advance notification interactions over a six-month interval produces the result that notice lowers *aggregate* months of unemployment per worker laid off from five to somewhat over four months.

Given its aggregative nature, the FLR study cannot address the diversity of factors other than the mere fact of notice of plant closings that may be expected to influence unemployment, more specifically the duration of unemployment, in the wake of displacement. A more complete analysis must be anchored within the framework of an explicit duration model.[12] One such model is offered by Addison and Portugal (1987), who employ data on plant closings from the January 1984 DWS. The model assumes that the notice interval is exogenous and that equally situated individuals engage in the same amount of search to locate an acceptable job offer. The technology of search is further assumed to be the same both on and off the job. In this situation, the density functions describing the relation between job finding and job search duration for two compositionally identical groups of workers—one of which receives prenotification of impending job loss, and the other does not—will be identical. The only difference between the two is that the location of the function for the nonnotified group will be displaced to the right of that for the notified group by the length of the notice interval. It follows that, for a given probability of job finding, the difference in unemployment duration by notification status will yield a (crude) measure of the length of the notice interval. It will be recalled that the latter is not reported in either the 1984 or 1986 DWS.

Addison and Portugal employ an accelerated time to failure model (Kalbfleisch and Prentice 1980) in which the natural logarithm of unemployment duration is regressed on its covariates, including notification of impending displacement, their effect being either to accelerate or decelerate the time of failure (namely, job finding). Note also that explicit account is taken of right-censored unemployment duration data associated with ongoing unemployment or unemployment spells that exceed (or have exceeded) by an unobserved margin the ninety-nine week point at which the duration data are top coded (see chapters 2 and 5). Failure to accommodate incomplete duration data, that is, relying only on completed spells of unemployment, not only results in the loss of valuable information but also imparts severe bias to the regression parameters since those with incomplete spells are likely to suffer greater unemployment than other workers. The authors employ maximum likelihood methods that account for the stochastic nature of the point of censoring.

The Addison-Portugal estimates of the reduced-form unemployment duration model yield the following results. First, in an equation that includes the unemployment insurance (UI) benefits status of the worker, prenotification reduces unemployment by some 27.5%. Evaluated at the sample means of all variables, this translates into a four-week reduction in the median spell of unemployment. Recall that this would also imply that the median period of notice amounts to four weeks. If the intensity of search is greater when the individual is searching full time as opposed to on the job, the median length of notice will exceed four weeks: if search intensity doubles on displacement, the estimate of notice interval will rise to eight weeks, and so on.

Second, the impact of advance notification is considerably reduced when the individual receives UI benefits. This result is not unexpected. It reflects the fact that notified workers who locate jobs quickly will not draw benefits. The advantage of having been notified must be much reduced after the point of layoff: eligible workers who apply for UI benefits presumably have not been able to exploit their informational advantage and are to all intents and purposes in much the same position as those who were not given notice.

Third, Addison and Portugal report that the impact of notice is also sensitive to the inclusion of a variable that identifies those who quit the job at some point between receiving notice and shutdown. The magnitude of the reduction in the coefficient on notice in the presence of this early leaving phenomenon suggests that one very important route through which advance notification "works" is in stimulating quits. The effect of early leaving is to reduce spell length of unemployment by 59.1%, ceteris paribus.

Given that receipt of UI benefits is endogenous (in part, determined by duration of unemployment[13]) and that early leavers are likely to have located jobs, it is more appropriate to exclude both variables in estimating the impact of prenotification on unemployment duration. We therefore reestimated the basic model purged of both variables, for separate samples by source of job loss. In general, the results of this exercise conformed closely with the earlier findings. Thus, for example, married and white workers and those with higher levels of education were again found to have lower unemployment on displacement, while unskilled workers and those with higher tenure on the lost job experienced significantly higher durations. The main result, that advance notification produces significantly shorter spells of joblessness, was also confirmed for laid off workers. Prenotificiation reduced unemployment duration by 22.7% in the case of those dislocated by plant closings and by 13.3% for those losing their jobs by reason of slack work and abolition of shift or position. Implicitly, the smaller effect for the latter group is interpreted as reflecting shorter notice intervals (Addison, 1989a).

In a more general study of postdisplacement worker adjustment, again using the DWS but this time employing a proportional hazards model, Podgursky and Swaim (1987b) also report evidence on the impact of prenotification on joblessness. The authors do not directly model the role of advance notification in the manner of Addison and Portugal, and their duration equations are disaggregated by broad occupational status and gender rather than source of job loss. It is reported that advance notification has a sizably negative effect on female duration, and in particular that of white-collar females whose median spell of joblessness is some 7.9 weeks shorter than their nonnotified counterparts. That being said, insignificantly positive coefficients are obtained in the case of male workers.[14] (Although in a very different analysis, more firmly grounded in a search model, Swaim and Podgursky [1990] suggest that *all* groups, with the exception of blue-collar females, gained significantly from prenotification in terms of substantially reduced unemployment duration.)

The authors also find that workers displaced by plant closings have very much shorter spells of joblessness than those dislocated via slack work or abolition of shift or position. They (p. 219) attribute this result to a waiting for recall phenomenon, arguing that ". . . as long as a plant remains in operation, many workers maintain unrealistically high expectations regarding recall and thus postpone aggressive job search or other long-term adjustment strategies . . . ; or they maintain unrealistically high reservation wages." We shall return to this point below.

While there is reasonable support for the proposition that advance notification works by stimulating on-the-job search in the notice interval, there remains some ambiguity as to the precise mechanism. In other words, does advance notification have a continuing beneficial effect on reemployment prospects or is its impact confined to enabling some workers to locate jobs without any intervening spell of joblessness? Ehrenberg and Jakubson (1989a) state unequivocally that advance notification works solely by increasing the possibility that a displaced worker will not experience *any* unemployment. The presence of an advance notice provision is estimated to increase this probability by some 2.2 to 3.5 percentage points (15% to 24%) in the case of those displaced by reason of slack work or abolition of shift or position, and by between 4.3 and 8.4 percentage points (18% to 31%) in the case of plant shutdowns. By contrast, once an individual experiences any unemployment, prenotification is reported to have no effect on the eventual duration of that unemployment. Pending improved analysis of the distributional shape of unemployment duration, however, the safest conclusion to be drawn from econometric analyses of the determinants of unemployment duration conditional on some positive spell of joblessness is that the benefits of prenotification simply dissipate after the point of layoff. Empirical hazard rates for separate groups of notified and nonnotified workers do of course confirm that the major impact of advance notification occurs within the first week of joblessness (Addison and Portugal 1987).

A closely related issue concerns the treatment of zero spells of joblessness in the duration model. It was argued earlier that the density function describing the reemployment probabilities of notified workers is displaced leftward to that of otherwise equally situated nonnotified workers by the length of the notice interval. Unfortunately, although we have information from the DWS on the associated distribution function of nonnotified workers, that for notified workers is truncated at the point of closure since we are merely told the identity of those notified workers who found work without any intervening spell of joblessness. Specifically, the data points on the density function for such workers over that part of the job search interval delineated by the arrival of notice and actual shutdown/layoff are missing; instead, the observations are massed at the point of layoff.

Most previous studies have failed to accommodate this truncation of the cumulative distribution function for notified workers. The upshot is that estimates of the notice interval will be downwardly biased, because although very short spells of unemployment will be recognized for the nonnotified, correspondingly short search intervals of the notified will be measured differently. It does not necessarily follow that the estimated impact of notice on unemployment duration will be understated since the estimated notice interval picks up the maximum impact of notice (it being less for those subgroups who ordinarily find work after very short search intervals); rather, the main point is that models that ignore truncation will suffer from misspecification.

Portugal and Addison (1988), use an approach that allows explicitly for censoring associated with completed job search in the notice interval, using data from the 1986 DWS and distinguishing between sources of job loss.[15] It is reported that the notice interval ranges from 5.7 to 8 weeks in the case of plant closings and from 4.3 and 5.7 weeks for slack work.[16] Recall that these intervals represent the maximum possible effect of advance notification; namely, where all notified workers who locate jobs without any intervening spell of joblessness do so in an interval that coincides exactly with the notice period. To obtain the actual effects of notice on duration account has also to be taken of the (inferred) distribution of completed job search in that interval. Once this is accomplished, Portugal and Addison obtain estimates of unemployment time saved amounting to between 5.2 weeks (38.1%) and 7.5 weeks (39.4%) in the case of workers dislocated by plant closings. Correspondingly smaller savings are observed for those displaced via slack work; namely, between 4.1 weeks (20.5%) and 5.5 weeks (20.7%). By way of contrast, estimated effects from a model that ignores this form of truncation bias are 3.6 weeks (28.6%) and 2.6 weeks (14.6%) for plant closings and slack work, respectively. It will be recalled that the simple model from which these estimates are constructed equates the saving of unemployment time with the length of the notice interval.

Portugal and Addison also calculate the contribution of advance notification to observing zero spells of joblessness, namely the area

225

under the censored probability density function. This amounts to between 6.8% and 7.9% for plant closings and 1.8% and 2.4% in the case of slack work. These estimates do not deny the proposition that the main impact of notice on duration occurs via an enhanced probability of observing very short spells of joblessness, but they do cast doubt on Ehrenberg and Jakubson's empirical conjecture that notice "works" *only* by allowing displaced workers to find jobs without any intervening spell of joblessness. Unlike these authors, Portugal and Addison do not truncate on the dependent variable but, rather, treat unemployment of whatever duration as the outcome of a continuous search process.

In a final part of their analysis, Portugal and Addison consider the impact of prenotification in the context of the number of jobs held (0, 1, 2, and 3 or more) in the wake of displacement. Separate duration equations are again run for plant closings and slack work. For the former, it appears that advance notification works for those with either one or two postdisplacement spells of employment, and particularly where only one job is held. This result is consistent with the view that advance notification operates by enabling workers to make better job matches. Interestingly, in the case of slack work, the notification parameter is statistically significant only in the case of that group with two jobs following displacement. This latter result is consistent with an (unrealized) expectation of recall. That is to say, notified workers who anticipate recall will be more likely to take up a temporary job in the first instance, in which case we might only expect to discern a significant impact on notice after an interval (in part captured by the lead time) during which the expectation of recall erodes.

Notice and Earnings   Before turning to the vexed question of endogeneity of notice, we briefly review material pertaining to the effect of advance notification on earnings. Here, the evidence is rather more mixed. For example, in an early study of forty-two plant shutdowns dislocating some 9,500 workers, Holen, Jehn, and Trost (1981) report a significantly positive association between (the length of) prenotification and postdisplacement earnings *losses*. No other study of which we are aware obtains this apparently perverse result. More typical is the conclusion reached by Podgursky and Swaim (1987a) that advance notification has no discernible effect on earnings development. The authors report that receiving notice did not improve the probability of reemployment or independently influence earnings in a selectivity-adjusted postdisplacement wage equation. Ehrenberg and Jakubson (1989a) report similar results. Also using the 1984 DWS, they find that inclusion of an advance notification dummy yields an insignificantly negative coefficient in postdisplacement wage equations, with or without controls for selection into re-employment status. Interactions between the notice variable and a broad occupational dummy produced only one significantly positive coefficient; for female white-collar workers displaced by reason of slack work or abolition of shift or position. The interaction terms for this group suggest higher postdisplacement wages in the range 15% to 20%. No such positive effects, however, were detected for other gender/occupational groups.

Although it does appear to be the case that advance notice fails to *directly* influence postdisplacement earnings or earnings losses, the instrument does seem to increase earnings *indirectly* to the extent that it lowers spell length of unemployment following displacement. Addison and Portugal (1989) find that intervening spell of joblessness is a potent source of reduced earnings on the postdisplacement job in an analysis of reemployment earnings that allows for the simultaneity between postdisplacement wages and unemployment duration. It is found that a 10% increase in duration decreases the accepted wage by around 1%. Whatever the positive effects of search on postdisplacement wages, these are evidently swamped by human capital depreciation, stigma effects, and/or a declining reservation wage.

The Endogeneity of Notice We have already traveled some considerable distance in the quest for improved estimates of the impact of advance notification. Yet one major problem still remains to be addressed. We refer to the assumed exogeneity of notice. All of the studies considered thus far, while dealing with problems raised by sample construction, are at root based on single equation models that will produce biased and inconsistent estimates if prenotification is endogenous. For example, if workers who are most likely to experience shorter spells of unemployment sort themselves into jobs that provide notice, then estimates of the effect of notice will be upwardly biased. An opposite result obtains if notice is only given to those who are less likely to quit in the notice interval or who face especial reemployment difficulties. Moreover, the question of selectivity bias gains added currency in an environment of mandated notice. It has to be noted at the outset that our understanding of the endogeneity of notice is fragmentary. Studies examining this question fall into three main categories. First, we have some evidence on the likelihood of observing formal notice provisions, drawing upon the theoretical arguments on contractual failure entered in section III. Second, there is some evidence relating prenotification to the costs of displacement. Finally, and more conventionally perhaps, the determinants of notice may be modeled to derive separate selection arguments for groups of notified and nonnotified workers.

227

Deere and Wiggins's (1988) study of contract endogeneity is to be distinguished from the other material considered here not only because of its methodology but also because of its use of GAO data. Using data on 338 establishments, the authors first regress the presence of an explicit notice contract on corresponding dummy variables identifying union presence, establishment size, and multiplant operation. Of these arguments only the union variable is significant: union presence increasing the likelihood of observing a contractual notice provision by around 30%, which the authors' interpret as consistent with their hypothesis that unionism reduces the cost of an explicit agreement requiring notice (see section III). Deere and Wiggins also consider the determinants of the notice interval, now running separate regressions for blue- and white-collar workers on the reasoning that the reputation effects mechanism is likely to be more a constraint on employment malfeasance for the latter group because of their allegedly superior information networking. Data on length of notice is regressed on the same variables as before plus an additional argument representing the number of days of contractual notice. It is found that the union presence dummy is no longer significant in either regression but that multiplant operation is significantly positive in the white-collar regression and contractual notice is significantly positive in both equations. The authors argue that, although facilitating negotiation of an explicit notice clause, unionism has no additional influence on actual notice length. The significance of multiplant operation in extending notice—by some twenty-three days—is justified in terms of reputation effects, at least for white-collar workers.

In a final part of their analysis, Deere and Wiggins present simple cross-tabulations on length of notice by occupation and the presence or otherwise of an explicit notice contract, for single-plant and multiplant operations. It is reported that single-plant establishments with an explicit notice agreement provide their white-collar (blue-collar) workers with an average notice interval of thirty-three (forty-one) days as compared with fifteen (twenty) days in the case of their counterparts offering no notice. The differences are less pronounced in the case of multiplant firms, where the corresponding mean lengths of notice in the two contractual regimes are forty-three (thirty-six) days and thirty-eight (twenty-four) days, respectively. The conclusion would appear to be that longer notice intervals are provided by establishments that are part of a multiplant entity irrespective of a formal notice contract, and that for single-plant firms the presence of a contract may be of major importance in extending the notice interval.

We have reported the Deere and Wiggins findings in some detail because they are suggestive of variables likely to be of significance in modeling the endogeneity of notice. It is the case, however, that the author's empirical work is only loosely linked to the underlying model, which is geared to explaining the incidence of notice (and not necessarily the presence of a formal contract stipulation) rather than the length of notice per se. (Further elaboration of the marginal costs and benefits of notice is required here.) The authors' length of notice regressions compound two effects, namely the incidence *and* the extent of notice, raising sample selection problems. The simplest empirical strategy would have been to purge those who did not receive notice from the sample, or at least to omit the notice argument from the length of notice regressions (the intercept term providing a crude measure of its importance). The preferred strategy would be to express the dependent variable as length of actual notice *less* period of formal notice.

Other analyses of the endogeneity of notice are somewhat more transparent to the extent that they do not fuse the determinants of notice with those of notice interval. By the same token they lack some of the insights offered by a contract-theoretic model.

Perhaps the most novel treatment is that of Howland (1988), who exploits the suggestion that advance notification is more likely to be given to workers who confront reemployment problems. She models the likelihood of receiving notice as a function of the costs of displacement to the worker and a variety of other variables including the strength of the local labor market, the size of the employee's plant, and the presence of a union. Note that since Howland uses DWS data, the two latter variables are average values for the worker's three-digit industry of displacement.

The displacement cost variable measures the gap between the worker's pre- and postdisplacement earnings over a five-year interval. It is assumed that the worker's wage on the lost job would have continued five years into the future, and the discounted value of this income stream is compared with the corresponding value of worker earnings on the new job, over the same five year interval including zero earnings for that part of the period the worker was unemployed. It is similarly assumed that the wage obtained on reemployment holds at its observed value for the full five years less the interval of unemployment. The wage loss value thus obtained is regressed on an advance notification dummy, the aggregate growth in employment together with that of the worker's two-digit industry of displacement, and a variety of demographic and economic variables specific to the individual.

In estimating the wage loss equation using OLS methods, Howland finds, as did Holen, Jehn, and Trost before her, that prenotified workers appear to suffer greater earnings losses than do nonnotified workers. But joint estimation of the two-equation system produces an abrupt change in the sign on the coefficient of the (predicted) notification variable in the wage loss equation, from negative to positive. In other words, advance notification reduces earnings losses attendant on displacement once account is taken of the endogeneity of notice; notice being given to those who would in the normal course of events be expected to suffer larger earnings losses. Unfortunately, the prenotification equation is poorly determined and the coefficient on the predicted notification variable is statistically insignificant at conventional levels in the costs of displacement equation. Confronted with these rather unsatisfactory results, Howland splits her already small sample ($n = 191$) into two subsamples of blue- and white-collar workers, and disaggregates the cost of displacement argument into its unemployment and earnings "components."[17] Howland's 2SLS estimates suggest that notified blue-collar workers do not gain either in terms of wages or unemployment from notification. White-collar workers, on the other hand, do gain principally via reduced spells of joblessness.

A number of difficulties apart from sample size attach to this study. Perhaps most unsatisfactory of all are the assumptions made concerning wage development, namely the use of fixed pre- and postdisplacement wage values for up to five years. The compounding of wage and unemployment effects is also unsatisfactory, not least because postdisplacement earnings and unemployment duration are jointly determined. The disaggregation of the compound earnings loss variable raises further difficulties, most notably because of the use of OLS methods to estimate the unemployment duration equation. Computation of the wage loss variable also begs some important questions, such as the presence of rents and compensatory differentials in the predisplacement wage. Although each problem must be borne in mind in interpreting her results, Howland's study makes an interesting foray into the hitherto largely uncharted waters of notice endogeneity.

Ehrenberg and Jakubson (1989a) have paid perhaps the closest attention to the endogeneity of notice. For example, the authors' (reduced-form) probit equations estimated over separate samples of male and female workers by source of job loss (layoffs and plant closings) contain no less than forty-six variables. Thus, in addition to conventional individual demographic and economic characteristics, variables measuring a wide range of similar characteristics aggregated over the worker's three-digit industry of displacement are also included. Other variables include

area characteristics (unemployment and employment, also disaggregated by major industry group), whether or not the individual resided in
either Maine or Wisconsin (states with notification laws) at survey date,
the industry of displacement wage premium estimated from regressions
using May 1979 CPS data, and whether or not the displacement job
offered health insurance. Of the 184 coefficients, only 16 are significant
at conventional levels. The main results are that prior coverage in an
employer provided health insurance plan increases the probability of
receiving notice; that the presence of a state notification law does *not*
influence receipt of notice one way or another; and that industries offering a high wage premium are less likely to provide their displaced workers with notice. Note that the latter result, which is significant only for
those workers displaced by plant closings, might be viewed as evidence
of compensation for not receiving notice, although the authors' (OLS)
analysis fails to detect lower wages on the predisplacement job for notified workers.

Although chi-square tests confirm that the probit equations have
explanatory power, the authors are reluctant to place much weight on
using the estimates to control for the endogeneity of notice in their
subsequent analyses of unemployment duration. It will be recalled that
Ehrenberg and Jakubson's duration equations are conditional on there
being some positive spell of joblessness. The probit equations are duly
employed to obtain an instrument for notice and it is found that the
variable entered with a positive coefficient; that is, advance notice actually increased the duration of unemployment experienced by displaced
workers. The significantly positive coefficients on the predicted notice
variable in three out of four cases (the exception being females dislocated by reason of plant shutdown) led the authors to conclude that the
instrument was picking up something spurious.

This is all rather disappointing. The authors use an instrument for
notification status as a control for possible endogeneity. Alternative
methods of controlling for endogeneity are available and, moreover, this
approach does not address the selection into notification status issue. In
what follows we provide results of an inquiry into the selection question.
For the purposes of this inquiry we used data from the 1984 and 1986
displaced worker surveys. In order to simplify the problem of correcting
for selectivity bias in the context of censored unemployment duration
data, a conscious decision was taken to limit data taken from the two
surveys to the first three years of each. It will be recalled that the DWS
unemployment duration measure is top-coded at ninety-nine weeks. By
restricting our attention to the first three years of each survey (1979 to

1981 in the case of the January 1984 DWS and 1981 to 1983 for the January 1986 DWS), we know that at least two years will have passed since the occasion of displacement. Accordingly, the vast majority of unemployment spells will be completed, in effect freeing us from the need to accommodate the right-censoring of the dependent variable.

The arguments employed in the estimating equation are much as before. The probit equation used to construct the selectivity argument(s) includes in addition to the arguments employed in the basic unemployment duration equation just two additional variables; namely, receipt or otherwise of health insurance benefits on the displacement job, and (seven) industry dummies. Regularities across the probits are a negative association between the predisplacement wage and receipt of notice, and positive correlations in the cases of tenure on the previous job and health insurance provision.

In testing for evidence of selectivity bias, we use the standard two-stage procedure suggested by Heckman (1979). The use of maximum likelihood methods to estimate the duration and notice equations simultaneously would have been preferred because of the inefficiency of estimates derived from the Heckman procedure but, despite repeated experimentation with different specifications and the use of alternative algorithms, we failed to achieve an interior solution in situations where the selection coefficient was negative in sign.

The basic difference between our procedure and that employed by Ehrenberg and Jakubson is that they use the probit equation to construct a single instrument for the receipt of advance notification. But since we have information on the unemployment duration of both notified and nonnotified workers, we can proceed further and use the selfsame probit procedure to generate two selection coefficients for duration equations estimated across notification status.

Essentially we seek to answer the following questions. First, on the basis of the selectivity term for the notified worker duration equation, if all workers had been notified of their impending displacement would those currently receiving notice have experienced higher or lower than average unemployment (positive or negative selection). Alternatively put, had the nonnotified been in the notified category would they have experienced lower or higher than average spells of unemployment. Second, now using the nonnotified equation, if all workers had been nonnotified would workers currently in this category experience lower or higher than average unemployment (negative or positive selection). Or, again, had notified workers been in the nonnotified category would they evince higher or lower than average unemployment spells. In this way one can devise estimates of the autonomous effect of advance notice and the likely effects of mandated notice.

It would be comforting if the results of this exercise proved consistent; for example, positive selection in the notified worker duration equation and negative selection in the corresponding nonnotified worker equation, and conversely. Given the former outcome, for example, we could argue that some workers selected into notification precisely to reduce their exposure to market risk while yet others selected into jobs that did not provide prenotification because the costs of notice exceeded the benefits. In short, advance notification works in part by allowing the notified "tortoise" to catch up with the nonnotified "hare." Such evidence would also indicate that the true effect of advance notification on unemployment duration would be greater than observed in extant studies. Opposite coefficients would prove the reverse.

What is the evidence? Results for notified and nonnotified worker samples by source of job loss and broad occupational status are given in table 4. As can be seen there is little to suggest consistency across the 1984 and 1986 displaced worker surveys. The most notable feature of regressions using the 1984 DWS is the general insignificance of the probit equation. Chi-square tests reveal that only in the case of plant closings, for the all-worker and blue-collar samples, is the function endogenizing notification status significant at conventional levels. For these two equations there is evidence of negative selection among notified workers and positive selection among nonnotified workers. An explanation of this phenomenon would proceed along the following lines: notified workers are, in the normal run of events, better suited to cope with displacement and *in addition* enjoy the benefits of notice. Nonnotified workers may be viewed as perhaps queuing for jobs in the notified sector. Alternatively put, single-equation estimates of the effect of advance notification on unemployment duration are upwardly biased. Although similar evidence of negative and positive selection obtains in the case of all workers displaced by slack work, a chi-square test on the probit equation failed to achieve statistical significance. Subject to this latter caveat, no economic sense can of course be made of positive selection in both notified and nonnotified duration equations (namely, white-collar workers displaced via plant closings). Maximum likelihood estimates of the selection coefficients, where convergence was achieved, are not only always lower than those implied by the Heckman procedure but also have larger standard errors.

The results for the 1986 DWS are more encouraging in the sense that each of the probit equations is significant. But note that in contrast to the

Table 4 On the Endogeneity of Notice: Selection Coefficients from the Notified and Nonnotified Unemployment Duration Equations, by Source of Job Loss and Broad Occupational Category

Method/ Equation	1984 DWS						1986 DWS					
	Plant closings			Slack work			Plant closings			Slack work		
	All[a]	BC[a]	WC	All	BC	WC	All[a]	BC[a]	WC[a]	All[a]	BC[a]	WC[a]
Heckman												
Notified	-3.167*	-2.480*	5.404	-1.994*	-.732	-2.063***	1.288	1.542***	-.275	.117	.083	1.270
	(.959)	(.761)	(3.987)	(.737)	(.940)	(1.126)	(.873)	(.872)	(1.457)	(.921)	(1.179)	(1.049)
	[n = 531]	[n = 310]	[n = 221]	[n = 424]	[n = 313]	[n = 111]	[n = 629]	[n = 420]	[n = 209]	[n = 356]	[n = 276]	[n = 80]
Nonnotified	2.553*	.604	.999	1.432**	1.254	.461	-1.113	-1.649**	-.148	-.374	-.375	.482
	(.861)	(.690)	(2.522)	(.677)	(.802)	(.953)	(.755)	(.767)	(1.215)	(.726)	(.873)	(.698)
	[n = 445]	[n = 260]	[n = 185]	[n = 420]	[n = 289]	[n = 131]	[n = 532]	[n = 362]	[n = 170]	[n = 373]	[n = 262]	[n = 111]
Maximum likelihood												
Notified	—	—	.465	—	—	—	.335*	.316*	—	.106	.052	.883***
			(.711)				(.131)	(.133)		(.611)	(.091)	(.460)
Nonnotified	.353	.281	.098	.308	.321	.204	—	—	—	—	—	.276
	(.374)	(.368)	(1.637)	(.353)	(.397)	(.647)						(.182)

Notes: Standard errors given in parentheses.

*, **, *** denote significance at the .01, .05, and .10 levels, respectively.

[a] signifies significance of underlying probit equation.

results obtained for the 1984 DWS we have an abrupt reversal of the "privileged class" phenomenon and the emergence of a "tortoise-and-hare" type of explanation with positive selection in the notified worker regime and negative selection in the nonnotified worker regime. At least this is true for the all-worker sample in the case of plant closings and slack work, and for blue-collar workers in each category. Here, then, the suggestion is exactly the opposite of the dominant result from the 1984 regressions: workers who would ordinarily suffer higher unemployment select themselves into jobs providing notice that limit their exposure to displacement costs. In this case, single-equation estimates *understate* the effect of notice on unemployment duration. We also observe negative selection for notified and nonnotified white-collar workers displaced via plant closings. If the coefficients were significant, which they are not, the suggestion would be that both groups are better off by virtue of their particular notification status: workers sort themselves into sectors where they have the better possibility of being reemployed. Evidence of positive selection is confirmed by the selection coefficients derived using maximum likelihood procedures, at least in the case of all workers and blue-collar workers displaced via shutdowns. Positive selection is also confirmed in the case of notified white-collar workers displaced by reason of slack work, though not for white-collar nonnotified workers.

To repeat, these are disappointing results and one has no explanation for the very different performance of the probit equations as between the 1984 and 1986 surveys. Like Ehrenberg and Jakubson (1989a) we would err on the side of caution and conclude that there is little convincing evidence of endogeneity in the data. What evidence there is *appears* more consistent with a tortoise-and-hare explanation.

Had we more faith in the probit equation and more convincing results we could of course use the selection coefficients from the notified and nonnotified equations to predict the effect of mandating notice. For this purpose we need consider only nonnotified workers since the notified would be unaffected by legislation. (Here we abstract from the usual complications introduced by length of notice.) Again let us assume a positive selection term for the notified worker regression and negative selection for the nonnotified worker regression. Beginning with the former, we know that a regime of notice would mean that nonnotified workers would have a predicted duration of unemployment given by the product of the coefficients in the regression and the mean values of the corresponding variable *less* the positive selection term. This is a gain in terms of reduced unemployment. Turning to the nonnotified worker regression, here negative selection implies that had all workers been notified the nonnotified workers' gain from being nonnotified in a zero notice regime would be lost. Accordingly, the expected unemployment duration of nonnotified workers computed from the nonnotified regression (which, again, is the product of the coefficients and the mean values of the corresponding variables, but this time *plus* the selection term) must be subtracted from the expected duration of the same workers had their duration been given by the notified worker equations. The resulting value would provide a measure of the effect of mandated notice. Given the assumed signs of the selection terms, the effect of notice hinges on their magnitude *and* differences in coefficients in the two equations. If the two selection terms wash out, the effect of mandating notice is simply the true effect of notice.

What, then, are we to conclude from this evidence on the apparent exogeneity of notice? The most obvious conclusion is that the determinants of notice status have proved extremely elusive. The poor explanatory power of the underlying probit equations reflects their tenuous link to a theoretical model. For the future, and abstracting from notions of contractual failure, an important task will be to model explicitly factors that may be expected to influence the parties' decision to bargain over notice. Currently, we do not possess a coherent picture of the factors that are relevant in this calculus, let alone of the determinants of the notice interval conditional on notice being given. The crucial lacuna of existing studies is the costs (to employers) side of the equation. To be sure, some cost elements have received empirical scrutiny. Thus, for example, Ehrenberg and Jakubson (1989a, chapter 6) find that the quit decision is not highly correlated with observed determinants of productivity, such as schooling level, and conclude that quit behavior may be likened to a random process.[18] But such evidence falls far short of an analysis of the costs of prenotification and how they may be expected to vary from firm to firm. A potentially important factor here is the variability in the market environment confronted by the firm.

Of course, even if we succeed in identifying relevant cost factors, the analytical question is whether the private costs borne by employers are to be translated into social costs. The position taken on this issue hinges importantly on one's view of the efficiency of regular markets. And, even if such costs are deemed strictly private, a policy of mandated notice may well have to cope with transitory increases in unemployment.

Our prejudice is that the apparent randomness of notice is perhaps best interpreted as implying that results that have been obtained on the benefits side may be generalized to an environment of mandated notice, subject to the caveat entered by Ehrenberg and Jakubson to the effect

236

that formal communication of notice may not add to the information already possessed by workers. (It will be recalled that the 1984 and 1986 surveys do not permit a distinction to be drawn between the expectation of notice and actual receipt of communicated notice.)

Conclusions

In this essay we have sought to establish what we do and do not know about the effects of advance notification. The currency of the exercise is provided by the February 4, 1989, implementation of a mandatory sixty-day notice standard. Some readers will be disappointed by what we have learned and perturbed by the controversy surrounding estimates of the impact of advance notice. But in a very real sense our knowledge of these effects is incomparably better than just a few years ago. Controversy is in no small part a reflection of continuing inadequacies of the data and hence the assumptions that have to be made in seeking to infer such elements as mean notification period and the duration of unemployment attendant upon displacement. We should also add that our improved knowledge of the effects of prenotification reflects no little ingenuity on the part of researchers. It will be interesting to see whether findings from the 1984 and 1986 displaced worker surveys will be replicated in analysis of the 1988 survey, which, at the time of writing, has only just become available. A further note of caution should be entered: the specific results reported in this chapter hinge not only on choice of distributional form with respect to the duration of unemployment but also, and more importantly, on model specification. In sum, the analysis offered here is not the last word on measurement.

There is a measure of agreement on the effectiveness of *voluntary* notice provisions. The main impact seems to be in reducing the spell length of joblessness of displaced workers vis-à-vis their nonnotified counterparts, although positive wage benefits are also observed once account is taken of the simultaneity between postdisplacement wages and unemployment duration. There is agreement that advance notification "works" by stimulating on-the-job search during the lead time offered by prenotification. Conceptually, while there is no saving in search time per se, there is a clear saving in unemployment time. Controversy attaches to whether advance notification reduces joblessness solely by promoting job finding without any intervening spell of unemployment, rather than having a more continuous effect on unemployment duration. While it is true that the main effects of prenotification occur within the

237

first week of joblessness, we are wary of the claim that notice has no effect once some positive amount of joblessness is experienced. The jury is still out on this question, not least because of statistical difficulties introduced by truncating on the dependent variable.

Advance notification seems to have a bigger payoff for some groups than others. In particular, there are clear signs in the literature that white-collar workers and those displaced by reason of plant shutdown fare better. In both cases, differential notice intervals would seem to loom large. Moreover, if longer notice intervals are positively correlated with the amount of reemployment assistance offered workers, then we have an additional reason for this differential impact. But in the case of plant closings there is also the possibility that the results are produced by (unobserved) worker quality differences (all workers are "canned" in the case of shutdowns) and absence of abortive waiting-for-recall effects. More work is required on the receptivity of different groups to prenotification for both econometric and more practical reasons.

Positive externalities in the form of savings to the public purse clearly accrue if workers find jobs more quickly. Moreover, prenotification, at least in principle, permits enhanced effectiveness of existing manpower instruments. A possible qualification arises here if there is a fixed pool of vacancies such that the unemployment gains reported for notified workers come at the expense of non-notified workers (Ehrenberg and Jakubson, 1989b), although by itself this is hardly an indictment of mandatory notice.

Problems emerge when we come to consider the implications of analyses based on voluntary notice for a regime of mandated notice. We feel much of the discussion of notice endogeneity has been wide of the mark, and have noted a procedure that in principle allows one to calculate the likely effect of mandated notice using selection coefficients for nonnotified workers obtained from selectivity-adjusted regressions run over separate samples of notified and nonnotified workers. We have only just begun to analyze the determinants of notice, and have little understanding of the precise nature of the costs attaching to notice and the trade-offs implied by a voluntary exchange process. Improved knowledge of these costs will yield better estimates of the determinants of notice and consequently address the basic criticism that the legislation will produce parameter shifts. For this reason we must be very wary of generalizing the results of extant notice studies to a regime of mandated notice. We are perhaps entitled to conclude that the benefits we have detected can probably be so generalized and as not being a chimera produced by sample selection. But the costs remain opaque.[19]

Yet these costs may be expected to vary with the length of the notice period and this returns us to the theme of whether or not a sixty-day interval is in any sense "excessive." Judged solely on the basis of voluntary notice contracts, and assumptions having to do with differential search intensity during the notice interval and thereafter, perhaps not. But consideration has also to be given to the (unobserved) interval that would obtain, absent the variety of yet-to-be established constraints on contracting, in no-notice situations. A neat solution to this dilemma would be to allow the parties to negotiate around a legislated standard, such as sixty days, which would then become the default value in the absence of specific contracting to the contrary.

This solution, first suggested by Deere and Wiggins, is preferable to (that is, more flexible than) a mandated standard even with gateways. Yet this strategy did not commend itself to policy makers. Given that we now have a sixty-day standard, it is to be hoped that policy will be experimental in the sense that the costs of the instrument will be carefully monitored. But our prejudice is that the benefits of the current standard could well exceed the costs.

NOTES

1. For details of the international practice, see U.S. Congress, Office of Technology Assessment (1986b), Emerson (1987), and Addison (1989b).

2. Activism has not been restricted to Congress. Thus, between 1975 and 1983, over 125 plant closing bills were introduced in 30 state legislatures (Ehrenberg and Jakubson 1989a). Prior to the passage of WARN, however, just three states—Maine, Wisconsin, and Hawaii—had mandatory legislation on the statute books.

3. An earlier version of the bill reported out of the House Committee on Education and Labor in October 1985 would have required employers of fifty or more workers to give ninety-days' notice of impending redundancy (plant closing or mass layoffs) affecting fifty or more employees at any site during any thirty-day period. Furthermore, employers had to consult "in good faith" with employee representatives for the "purpose of agreeing to a mutually satisfactory alternative to or modification of" a scheduled closing or layoff. Such consultation was to involve giving the employee representative sufficient information to evaluate the circumstances of the closure or to pursue alternatives and modifications to closure. Finally, the Labor Department was to be given a direct investigatory and enforcement role: the Secretary of Labor could petition a U.S. District Court for injunctive relief where the notice and consultation provisions appeared to have been violated. That relief could take the form of an extended period of consultation and even reinstatement of the work force with back pay and benefits.

4. For additional information on the National Employment Priorities Act, see Mc-Kenzie (1982, Appendix A).

5. As before, this legislation was a watered down version of two earlier proposals. In May 1987, the Senate Labor and Human Resources Committee had voted in favor of legislation (S.538) that would have required 90-days' advance notice of a plant closing or permanent layoff involving 50 to 100 workers, 120-days' notice if 101 to 499 workers were involved, and 180-days' notice if over 500 workers were involved. In the following month, the House Education and Labor Committee approved similar legislation (H.R. 1122) that had slightly different notification requirements and also resurrected the good faith consultation clause of H.R. 1616, as originally introduced.

6. We note parenthetically that the conference agreement dealt with a number of inconsistencies in the July Senate bill, most notably with respect to the definition of a mass layoff, and a certain fuzziness about the nature of a layoff deemed to count toward employment loss, both of which stimulated widespread employer opposition. Thus, in outlining penalties for noncompliance, the original Senate bill had omitted the 33% rule, implying that prenotification was required in employment loss situations that could scarcely be considered mass layoffs. Also, employment loss was originally defined in terms of "a layoff of indefinite duration," with the result that there was no clear distinction between temporary and permanent job loss.

7. For a full discussion of the mandated benefits controversy, see McKenzie (1988).

8. Deere and Wiggins's model is cast in terms of individual worker benefits. No account is taken of aggregate worker benefits. These are not merely larger but also hint that number of employees may be an important determinant of notice in the presence of transaction costs.

9. In a recent case study undertaken by the National Center on Occupational Re-adjustment (1985), it was found that UI taxes were considerably lower than had been anticipated by the company because employees were given outplacement assistance before leaving the company, many of whom accepted positions with other employers either prior to being displaced or shortly thereafter. The savings to that company in one month alone amounted to over $500,000.

10. The Dun and Bradstreet data, maintained to determine business credit risk, contain listings on over 5 million establishments.

11. It will be recalled that Maine is one of three states that currently impose a notice obligation on employers (see table 1). But because the time frame of the FLR study is from 1974 to 1982, it is neither an events analysis nor an investigation of compliance. Although Maine's first plant closing law was enacted in 1971 and required all businesses with one hundred or more employees to provide the work force with one month's notice of an intended plant closing, the notice provision was dropped in 1973. The notice requirement was resurrected in 1975 but it was now indirect: to the Director of the State Bureau of Labor, rather than to the workers directly. Only as a result of a further amendment in 1983 was notice once again required to be given to employees. Accordingly, the FLR study compares the impact of publicly announced plant closings with that of unannounced shutdowns.

12. This is not to deny the worth of the FLR analysis. For example, their findings have a bearing on the argument that there is a fixed pool of vacancies for which notified displaced workers compete with their non-notified counterparts, so that all that prenotification achieves is a reshuffling of jobs (Ehrenberg and Jakubson 1989b). We should also note that FLR find that advance notification in Maine was associated with a significant reduction in the size of the local labor force in the month of closing, reflecting an unmeasured mix of labor force withdrawals and outmigration.

13. For a detailed discussion of the endogeneity of UI benefit status, and its implications for analyses of the effects of UI on unemployment duration, see Portugal and Addison (1990).

14. Podgursky and Swaim claim that this result is consistent with research showing that female workers benefit most from job search assistance (Johnson, Dickinson, and West 1985).

15. Swaim and Podgursky (1990) also recognize that jobless weeks is a truncated measure of total search time for notified workers *and* attempt to tackle the differential intensity of search on and off the job.

16. This range is produced by alternately using sample means of all variables and the means of predicted duration for each observation.

17. Howland excludes workers displaced in nonmetropolitan areas because she wishes to merge in variables reflecting *local* labor market conditions. Since she also excludes those with ongoing or otherwise right-censored unemployment duration by focusing on those displaced in just the first three years of the 1984 DWS, her final sample is tiny.

18. We note that case study material consistently fails to indicate evidence of shirking behavior and other sources of productivity loss in the notice interval (Weber and Taylor 1963; Driever and Baumgardner 1984; U.S. Congress Office of Technology Assessment 1986a). But we would caution that few companies are likely to have a reliable measure of productivity over this period: in-process inventories will be drawn down and equipment maintenance reduced, both of which factors could even yield the statistical appearance of productivity gain.

19. For investigations of the unemployment consequences of policies increasing employer adjustment costs, see Hamermesh (1988), Lazear (1987), and Addison (1989b).

REFERENCES

Abowd, John M., and Orley Ashenfelter (1981). "Anticipated Unemployment, Temporary Layoffs, and Compensating Wage Differentials." In *Studies in Labor Markets,* edited by Sherwin Rosen. Chicago: University of Chicago Press (for NBER).

Adams, James D. (1985). "Permanent Differences in Unemployment and Permanent Wage Differentials." *Quarterly Journal of Economics* 100 (February): 29–56.

Addison, John T. (1989a). "The Controversy over Plant Closing Legislation in the United States." *British Journal of Industrial Relations* 26 (July): 235–63.

———(1989b). "The Absence of Job Protection Legislation: A Source of Competitive Advantage for the U.S.?" *Advances in the Study of Entrepreneurship, Innovation, and Economic Growth* 3, edited by Gary D. Libecap. Greenwich, Conn.: JAI Press.

Addison, John T., and Barry T. Hirsch (1989). "Union Effects on Productivity, Profits, and Growth: Has the Long Run Arrived? *Journal of Labor Economics* 7 (January): 72–105.

Addison, John T., and Pedro Portugal (1987). "The Effect of Advance Notification of Plant Closings on Unemployment." *Industrial and Labor Relations Review* 41 (October): 3–16.

————(1989). "Job Displacement, Relative Wage Changes, and Duration of Unemployment." *Journal of Labor Economics* 7 (July): 281–302.

Berenbeim, Ronald E. (1986). *Company Programs to Ease the Impact of Shutdowns.* Report no. 876. New York: The Conference Board.

Brown, Sharon P. (1987). "How Often Do Workers Receive Advance Notice of Layoffs?" *Monthly Labor Review* 110 (June): 13–17.

Deere, Donald R., and Steven W. Wiggins (1988). "Plant Closings, Advance Notice, and Private Contractual Failure." Working Paper 88-39. College Station, Tex.: Texas A & M University.

Driever, L. S., and C. R. Baumgardner (1984). "Internal Company Preparation." In *Managing Plant Closings and Occupational Readjustment: An Employer's Guidebook.* Washington, D.C.: National Center on Occupational Readjustment.

Ehrenberg, Ronald G., and George H. Jakubson (1989a). *Advance Notice Provisions in Plant Closing Legislation.* Kalamazoo, Mich.: Upjohn Institute.

————(1989b). "Advance Notice of Plant Closings: Does It Matter?" *Industrial Relations* 28 (Winter): 60–71.

Emerson, Michael (1987). "Regulation or Deregulation of the Labour Market: Policy Regimes for the Recruitment and Dismissal of Employees in the Industrialised Countries." Internal Paper no. 55. Brussels: Commission of the European Communities.

Folbre, Nancy R., Julia L. Leighton, and Melissa Roderick (1984). "Plant Closings and Their Regulation in Maine, 1971–1981." *Industrial and Labor Relations Review* 37 (January): 185–96.

Hamermesh, Daniel S. (1988). "The Demand for Workers and Hours and the Effects of Job Security Policies: Theory and Evidence." In *Employment, Unemployment and Labor Utilization,* edited by Robert A. Hart. London and Boston: Unwin Hyman.

Hamermesh, Daniel S., and John R. Wolfe (1986). "Compensating Differentials and the Duration of Wage Loss." Mimeographed. East Lansing: Michigan State University.

Heckman, James J. (1979). "Sample Selection Bias As a Specification Error." *Econometrica* 46 (July): 153–61.

Hirsch, Barry T. (1989). *Labor Unions and the Economic Performance of U.S. Firms.* Kalamazoo, Mich.: Upjohn Institute.

Holen, Arlene, Christopher Jehn, and Robert P. Trost (1981). "Earnings Losses of Workers Displaced by Plant Closings." Mimeographed. Alexandria, Va.: The Public Research Institute.

Howland, Marie (1988). "The Impact of Prenotification on the Reemployment Success of Displaced Manufacturing Workers." Mimeographed. College Park: University of Maryland, Institute for Urban Studies.

Johnson, Terry R., Katherine Dickinson, and Richard West (1985). "An Evaluation of the Impact of ES Referrals on Applicant Earnings," *Journal of Human Resources* 20 (Winter): 117–37.

Kalbfleisch, John D., and Ross L. Prentice (1980). *Statistical Analysis of Failure Time Data.* New York: Wiley.

Lazear, Edward P. (1987). "Job Security and Unemployment." Mimeographed. Stanford, Calif.: Stanford University, The Hoover Institute, 1987.

Li, Elizabeth H. (1986). "Compensating Differentials for Cyclical and Noncyclical Unemployment: The Interaction Between Investors' and Employees' Risk Aversion." *Journal of Labor Economics* 4 (April): 277–300.

McKenzie, Richard B. (1982). *Plant Closing: Public or Private Choices?* Washington, D.C.: The Cato Institute.

242

————(1988). "Labor Policy in a Competitive World." Mimeographed. Clemson, S. C.: Clemson University.

Murphy, Kevin M., and Robert H. Topel (1987). "Unemployment, Risk, and Earnings: Testing for Equalizing Wage Differences in the Labor Market." In *Unemployment and the Structure of Labor Markets,* edited by Kevin Lang and Jonathan S. Leonard. New York and Oxford: Blackwell.

National Center on Occupational Readjustment (1985). *Case Studies [on Plant Closings].* Washington, D.C.

Podgursky, Michael, and Paul Swaim (1987a). "Job Displacement and Earnings Loss: Evidence from the Displaced Worker Survey." *Industrial and Labor Relations Review* 41 (October): 17–29.

————(1987b). "The Duration of Joblessness Following Plant Shutdowns and Job Displacement." *Industrial Relations* 26 (Fall): 213–26.

Portugal, Pedro, and John T. Addison (1988). "Advance Notification and the Job Search Process: Notification Interval, Unemployment Time Saved, and Zero Spells of Joblessness." Mimeographed. Columbia: University of South Carolina.

————(1990). "Problems of Sample Construction in Studies of the Effects of Unemployment Insurance on Unemployment Duration." *Industrial and Labor Review* 43 (April): 463–77.

Summers, Lawrence H. (1989). "Some Simple Economics of Mandated Benefits." *American Economic Review, Papers and Proceedings* 79 (May): 177–183.

Swaim, Paul, and Michael Podgursky (1990). "Advance Notice and Job Search: The Value of an Early Start." *Journal of Human Resources* 25 (Spring): 145–78.

Topel, Robert H. (1984). "Equilibrium Earnings, Turnover, and Unemployment: New Evidence." *Journal of Labor Economics* 2 (October): 500–22.

U.S. Congress, General Accounting Office (1987). *Limited Advance Notice and Assistance Provided Dislocated Workers.* GAO/HRD-87-105. Washington, D.C.: U.S. Government Printing Office, July.

U.S. Congress, Office of Technology Assessment (1986a). *Technology and Structural Unemployment: Reemploying Displaced Adults.* OTA-ITE-250. Washington, D.C.: U.S. Government Printing Office.

————(1986b). *Plant Closings: Advance Notification and Rapid Response.* Washington, D.C.: U.S. Government Printing Office.

Weber, Arnold R., and David P. Taylor (1963). "Procedures for Employee Displacement: Advance Notification of Plant Shutdown." *Journal of Business* 36 (July): 302–15.

243

CHAPTER NINE

Public Policy to Retrain Displaced Workers: What Does the Record Show?

DUANE E. LEIGH

I. Introduction

For more than twenty-five years the federal government and individual state governments have provided retraining programs to ease the labor market adjustment required of workers directly or indirectly displaced from their jobs by a mass layoff or plant closure. At the federal level, the first comprehensive attempt to provide adjustment assistance to displaced workers was the Manpower Development and Training Act (MDTA) passed in 1962. MDTA was replaced in 1973 by the Comprehensive Employment and Training Act (CETA), which, in turn, was replaced in 1982 by the Job Training Partnership Act (JTPA). Title III of JTPA is specifically directed at meeting the needs of displaced workers. Most recently, the "Omnibus Trade and Competitiveness Act of 1988" amends JTPA Title III and authorizes the spending of $980 million during fiscal year 1989 on retraining and other displaced worker adjustment assistance services.[1]

The displaced workers focused on by these laws are usually defined as persons on permanent layoff who possess a stable employment history. In addition to their work experience, the main distinction between displaced workers and other laid-off workers is that the displaced have little chance of being recalled to jobs with their old employer or even in their old industry. Thus, displaced workers often experience substantial adjustment costs in the form of lengthy unemployment spells, lost firm-specific skills, and reemployment at considerably lower wages. The need to seek reemployment in a new occupation or industry may require that

244

displaced workers tool up in the vocational skills required to qualify for jobs in expanding industries. A stable work history suggests, moreover, that the job search skills of many displaced workers may have grown rusty because of their lengthy attachment to their prelayoff employer. For both of these reasons, training is defined in this paper to include the enhancement of job search skills as well as vocational training, The principal roles for public retraining programs are to reduce the private and social costs associated with unnecessary delays in the reemployment process and to assist in the replenishment of specific human capital lost when a permanent layoff unexpectedly takes place.

The purpose of this paper is to answer the following research questions involving government training assistance to displaced workers:

1. Do some types of training work better than others?
2. Do some groups of workers benefit more from training than others?
3. To the extent that training improves reemployment prospects, does it work by increasing posttraining wage rates or by reducing the duration of unemployment?
4. Referring specifically to vocational training, how do we know what to train workers to do?

The first of these questions raises the possibility that the major types of training—classroom training (CT), on-the-job training (OJT), job search assistance (JSA), and remedial education—may differ in the benefits they offer displaced workers as well as in their costs. The premise of CT is that the specific skills of displaced workers have been made largely obsolete, but that marketable skills can be developed through intensive, formal training in a classroom setting. OJT, on the other hand, is appropriate in the acquisition of specific skills that can most efficiently be learned on the job. The objective of JSA is basically to assist job-ready workers to develop effective job-seeking skills. Finally, remedial education programs are designed to assist the perhaps 20% of displaced workers who have a deficiency in basic reading or problem solving skills.

Question 2 is posed in recognition of the fact that not all displaced workers may benefit equally from retraining services and, moreover, that not all of these workers are equally in need of adjustment assistance. The analysis of 1984 Displaced Worker Survey (DWS) data by Podgursky and Swaim (1987a) shows that the distribution of completed spells of joblessness is highly skewed to the right. While nearly half of respondents in their sample found jobs within fourteen weeks of

245

displacement, a substantial minority faced a high risk of being jobless for a year or more. It is this minority to whom adjustment assistance efforts should be targeted. Podgursky and Swaim loosely identify these individuals to include workers displaced from blue-collar occupations, workers with below-average levels of education, minorities and women, and residents of communities with above-average unemployment rates. In a parallel paper using DWS data, Podgursky and Swaim (1987b) also report that a sizable minority of displaced workers—mostly workers with substantial specific human capital investments—experienced large and enduring earnings losses upon reemployment.

The distinction made in question 3 is intended to separate the effect of vocational training on labor productivity as measured by a higher posttraining hourly wage from its effect in speeding up reemployment by providing a credential that moves workers up in the queue for vacant jobs. Question 4, finally, fixes attention on the issue of how to identify growth occupations and develop appropriate curricula so that successful program graduates have a reasonable chance of being hired and retained in training-related jobs.

To answer these questions, a logical way to proceed is by examining the existing evidence. Only after the available evidence has been systematically analyzed is it possible to assess what we know and what remains to be learned. The federal government and the states have opted to invest substantial amounts of resources in funding programs and demonstration projects providing different types and mixes of adjustment services to displaced workers. Evaluations of these programs and demonstration projects have generated a large amount of quantitative and qualitative evidence. This paper focuses on the existing quantitative studies in attempting to formulate answers to the four policy questions.

The paper is organized as follows. Section II provides a brief history of federal legislation enacted to assist displaced workers. With this background, the bulk of the paper then deals with available evaluation studies. Section III is an overview of CETA program evaluations. Although CETA was not limited to retraining services or to serving displaced workers, the CETA evaluations are a good starting point for two reasons. First, they provide baseline quantitative estimates to which the impacts of later programs and demonstration projects can be compared. Second, a discussion of the CETA evaluations represents an opportunity to introduce some of the main methodological issues involved in program evaluation.

Section IV is the heart of the paper. It follows up on the CETA evaluations by examining in detail the quantitative evidence generated by four major displaced worker demonstration projects. The Downriver program and the Buffalo program of the Dislocated Worker Demonstration projects were designed to test the effectiveness of alternative services in accelerating the reemployment of displaced workers. The New Jersey Unemployment Insurance Reemployment Demonstration project and the Texas Worker Adjustment Demonstration, in contrast, attempted to evaluate ongoing displaced worker programs. A final section summarizes the evaluation evidence by attempting to answer the four policy questions.

II. Federal Displaced Workers Programs

Going back to the early 1960s, the passage of the Manpower Development and Training Act in 1962 represented the response of Congress to a rising national unemployment rate coupled with a growing concern over the effects of technological change on the employment options of midcareer adult workers. The primary objective of the program was to provide retraining for workers whose skills had been made obsolete by new technology. But by the mid-1960s, an improved labor market and lessened concern over automation led to a shift in interest and funding away from the reemployment problems of displaced workers and toward the employability of disadvantaged young people and welfare recipients.[2] Interest in evaluating MDTA programs increased in the late 1960s and early 1970s, but most of these early attempts at evaluation were hampered by the lack of a comparison or control group and the absence of good information on earnings.

Also passed in 1962, the Trade Adjustment Assistance (TAA) program was created by Congress to provide income support and retraining to a specific category of the displaced: those workers who had lost jobs in industries adversely affected by increased foreign competition arising from the relaxation of import restrictions. For the first twelve years of the program, a very low rate of program participation reflected the stringent requirement that affected workers and firms demonstrate that trade liberalization led to increased imports, which, in turn, were the "major" cause of reduced domestic sales and lost jobs. Most displaced workers who did qualify for TAA assistance during this period received income-maintenance support, with only about 10% of recipients receiving retraining services. Neumann (1978) provides a generally negative appraisal of the TAA program. He reports that the higher income-maintenance benefits received by trade displaced workers tended to

247

increase the duration of their unemployment, and that training and counseling services had little effect on reemployment.

The Trade Act of 1974 liberalized TAA requirements making eligibility easier and providing more generous income support packages over a longer time interval. The combination of easier eligibiliy and improved benefits caused TAA expenditures and the number of workers served to increase rapidly over the next several years peaking at more than $1.6 billion and over 500,000 workers in 1980. Retraining, however, continued to receive relatively little attention. Corson and Nicholson (1981) report that the liberalization of eligibility conditions caused an important shift in the composition of TAA recipients. Rather than primarily benefiting workers formerly employed in older declining industries (e.g., shoemaking) who could not reasonably expect to be recalled to their old jobs, nearly 72% of post-1974 TAA recipients ended their unemployment spells by returning to work for their previous employers.

Congressional concern about the program's high cost and the special treatment of TAA recipients as opposed to regular UI recipients led to new legislation in 1981 that tightened eligibility and reduced income support payments. Authorization for TAA lapsed in 1985, but legislation was passed in 1986 extending a much scaled-back version of the program until 1991. The 1986 legislation includes a requirement that receipt of income support is conditional on participation in a job search program, and that workers are to be encouraged, but not required, to enter a job training program.

Returning to the early 1970s, the next major comprehensive training initiative was the passage in 1973 of CETA, which consolidated nine earlier programs including MDTA. Designed to be federally funded but locally managed, two distinct types of programs were authorized. Title I of CETA provided disadvantaged workers a program mix including CT, OJT, and "work experience" (subsidized public sector jobs emphasizing work habits and skill development designed for individuals with essentially no prior labor market experience). In contrast, Titles II and VI offered public service employment (PSE) programs to workers who had recently lost jobs in high-unemployment geographic areas. Title II was intended to serve the structurally unemployed, while Title VI was strictly a countercyclical job creation program. As unemployment rose during the mid-1970s, CETA expenditures shifted away from Title I training programs toward the provision of PSE jobs primarily funded under Title VI. In particular, a major employment initiative in the early years of the Carter administration was the expansion of PSE from 300,000 to 750,000 job slots in a period of just nine months. As described by Levitan and Gallo (1988, p. 9), "[T]he pressure to quickly fill these jobs resulted in isolated, though highly publicized, cases of careless management and enrollment of ineligible applicants that were to haunt CETA for the rest of its limited life." Amendments to the CETA legislation in 1978 and 1981 first reduced PSE expenditures and finally eliminated PSE funding entirely.

The CETA program expired in 1982 with the economy in the trough of the deepest recession since the 1930s. Once again, the displacement of experienced adult workers became an important national issue. Rather than renewing CETA with its politically unpopular emphasis on PSE, extended negotiations between the Reagan administration and Congress resulted in a broad new program—the Job Training Partnership Act—intended to train and place workers in private sector jobs. The new law had three major titles. Title II of JTPA provided training to disadvantaged youth and adults and summer jobs to disadvantaged youth. Title III funded training and other adjustment assistance services for displaced workers. Under both of these titles, federal dollars are allocated to the states, which are made responsible for program design and implementation. Finally, Title IV authorizes programs that are directly administered by the U.S. Department of Labor (USDOL) including training services for native Americans, seasonal and migrant workers, and veterans. In contrast to CETA and earlier federal programs, the JTPA legislation makes the direction of training programs the responsibility of state governors who are required to issue performance standards for evaluating the success or failure of programs in their states. In addition, JTPA defines a more active role for the business community in program development, and it concentrates resources on training and JSA services rather than PSE and income-maintenance allowances.

To assist Congress in its program oversight role, the U.S. General Accounting Office (GAO) carried out a nation-wide survey of all JTPA Title III projects operating between March 1982 and March 1985. The resulting GAO report (1987) documents the wide range of services provided to Title III participants. JSA was by far the predominant service supplied with over 80% of participants receiving this form of assistance. About 26% of participants received CT, followed by 16% and 6%, respectively, who were provided with OJT and remedial education. The GAO report also estimates that, at most, 7% of eligible workers received Title III assistance through June 30, 1986.

In August of 1985, Secretary of Labor Brock appointed a task force to examine the specific adjustment problems faced by experienced workers displaced from their jobs by plant closings and mass layoffs. After a year of study, the task force issued a well-publicized report recommending a new national program that would incorporate the existing JTPA Title III and TAA programs (see the Secretary of Labor's Task Force on Economic Adjustment and Worker Dislocation 1986). With respect to training services, the report makes three main recommendations. The first is that remedial educational opportunities should be made available to those displaced workers identified as having a severe enough deficiency in basic skills to retard their reemployment or even their acquisition of new vocational skills. Regarding skill training, the report takes the position that customized training to match the needs of a specific employer is the optimal approach to retraining. From this perspective, the report's second recommendation is that OJT is to be preferred to CT as the primary long-term training service to be provided in the new program. For those CT programs included as part of a comprehensive menu of services, finally, the task force suggests that contracts with training institutions be performance based.

The massive trade bill proposed by President Reagan in the fall of 1987 included most of the training-related recommendations in the task force's report, as well as the suggested incorporation of JTPA Title III and TAA into a broad new displaced worker program. In the final version of the trade bill, which became law in August 1988, the title "Economic Dislocation and Worker Adjustment Assistance Act" amends JTPA Title III and authorizes the spending of $980 million for retraining and other adjustment assistance services.[3] This level of spending represents a substantial increase in federal expenditures on displaced worker programs in relation to the $200 million budgeted for JTPA Title III in fiscal year 1987 and the about $30 million budgeted for TAA in 1988. It is considerably less, however, than total expenditures on CETA programs which peaked at $10.3 billion in 1979.

The new displaced worker title specifies that 80% of the $980 million authorized is to be allocated to the states to set up new state agencies called "dislocated worker units" with the capability of reacting quickly in providing on-site services to workers adversely affected by plant closures or mass layoffs. Through these dislocated worker units, permanently unemployed workers are initially to be supplied with "basic" readjustment services such as testing and assessment, career counseling, and job placement assistance. For those workers determined to be likely to benefit from additional services, the basic services are to be followed by retraining services defined broadly to include not only CT, OJT, and remedial education but also relocation assistance, English literacy, and entrepreneurial training. The remaining 20% of the funds appropriated is to go into discretionary federal grants to supplement the funds already allocated to states facing unemployment rates above the national average.

III. CETA Evaluations

An important feature of CETA was that for the first time the USDOL funded the development of a database specifically designed for program evaluation. Termed the Continuous Longitudinal Manpower Survey (CLMS), this database includes the following three components: (1) data for random samples of CETA enrollees collected quarterly beginning in 1975, (2) data for comparison groups drawn from March Current Population Survey (CPS) files, and (3) Social Security earnings records for each CETA enrollee and each member of the CPS comparison groups. Thus, the methodological approach to program evaluation permitted by CLMS data involves the use of an externally selected comparison group—in this case, a sample drawn from the CPS. In the absence of such a comparison group, analysts interested in obtaining net impact estimates for earlier programs were typically limited to using participants as their own control group by comparing postprogram labor-market outcomes like earnings with the level of participants' own preprogram earnings.[4] The basic difficulty with the preprogram/postprogram approach is that the preprogram dip in earnings that causes workers to seek to enroll in the program in the first place may be merely a temporary interruption in the permanent path of earnings. If the preprogram dip is caused by some transitory labor-market phenomenon, the program would receive "credit" for the rebound in earnings that would have happened anyway. In addition, all other events that are time conditional (e.g., an upturn in the economy) are assumed to be constant—an assumption that is patently false.

Although the use of an externally selected comparison group is clearly to be preferred to a preprogram/postprogram comparison, there is still the general problem that differences between the treatment and comparison groups will exist because the two groups are not drawn from the same population. In the particular case of CLMS data, CETA eligibility was generally restricted to individuals in low-income families, so that CETA participants differ from members of the nationally representative CPS sample in terms of such characteristics as previous work experience and education. As will be brought out later in this section, the problem of constructing comparable treatment and comparison groups has absorbed a great deal of attention from users of CLMS data.

251

Table 1   Estimated CETA Net Impacts on Earnings

	Men		Women	
Study	White	Minority	White	Minority
Westat (1981)				
CT	$400	$200	$550	$500
OJT	750	1,150	550	1,200
Overall	200	200	500	600
Bassi (1983)				
CT	—	582–773	63–205	426–633
OJT	—	2,053–2,057	80–382	1,368–1,549
Overall	—	117–211	740–778	426–671
Bloom and McLaughlin (1982)				
CT	300	300	1,300	1,100
OJT	−200	1,500	1,200	800
Overall		200	800–1,300	
Dickinson, Johnson, and West (1986)				
CT		−343	0	
OJT		−363	35	
Overall		−690	13	
Geraci (1984)				
CT		372	1,201	
OJT		612	882	
Overall		—	—	
Finifter (1987)				
CT		−9	507	
OJT		686	723	
Overall		—	—	

Source: Barnow (1987, table 3) for the Westat through Geraci studies, and Finifter (1987, table 1).

Note: Overall refers to the combined impact of CT, OJT, PSE, work experience, and multiple activities; —indicates that an estimate is not reported.

Barnow (1987) provides a useful survey of eleven major CETA evaluations. Table 1 summarizes the net impact estimates presented in the five studies he surveyed that use data for adult workers and that provide some breakdown in the results by sex, race, and type of program service. Also shown are results from a recent CETA evaluation by Finifter (1987). The estimates measure the impact of CETA on the first year of postprogram earnings for participants enrolled in 1975 and/or or 1976 net of the earnings of the CPS comparison group. Since PSE and work experience offered enrollees relatively little training, the table focuses on training opportunities supplied through CT and OJT. Three conclusions appear to be warranted. First, most of the estimates for women are larger than those for men, with the male estimates often being zero or even negative. Bloom and McLaughlin (1982) suggest in this connection that regardless of program activity, the main effect of CETA training was to facilitate labor-market entry. Thus persons who were out of the labor market, primarily women, enjoyed a larger program impact than those with extensive but unsuccessful labor-market experience, primarily men.

The second conclusion is that OJT is typically more effective than classroom training, particularly for minority enrollees. A larger impact for OJT than CT is to be expected since the most job-ready of enrollees are those likely to be selected by employers for OJT slots. Relative to classroom training, OJT may also be anticipated to have a larger impact on earnings in the short run than in the long run because job retention is usually assured for the immediate postsubsidy period.

Finally, the range of CETA net impact estimates shown in table 1 is uncomfortably wide. It might, at first glance, seem odd that studies using the same data set to estimate basically the same treatment effect should arrive at such different estimates. The fundamental problem is that the absence of a classical experiment in which sample members are randomly assigned to either the treatment group or a control group requires CLMS users to make two critical decisions. One of these decisions, as noted above, involves controlling for differences between members of the treatment and comparison groups. The second is deciding how best to cope with the selection bias that arises because program participants both choose to enroll and are selected by program operators.[5]

With respect to the first decision, analysts of CLMS data have proceeded by specifying an earnings function that would prevail for both groups in the absence of the program and/or selecting a subsample of CPS respondents that matches CETA participants on a number of key variables determining earnings. The purpose of drawing a matched comparison sample is to reduce preprogram differences between the CETA and CPS samples so that the regression estimates will be less sensitive to the incorrect specification of the postprogram earnings function. Weighting the observations in the earnings regression is also used to make mean values of the explanatory variables more alike in the treatment and comparison groups.

Approaches used in attempting to overcome the selection bias problem include, in increasing order of complexity, (1) specifying additional explanatory variables in the postprogram earnings equation to capture factors believed to be important in the selection process, (2) making specific assumptions about unobservable variables potentially affecting both program selection and earnings in an attempt (typically using a first-difference estimator) to eliminate correlation in the earnings equation between the error term and the training variable, and (3) explicitly modeling the selection process in a separate participation equation and then jointly estimating the participation and earnings equations. The results reported by different analysts may clearly vary in important respects depending on the specification of the earnings function; the matching technique used; the attempt, if any, to model the selection procedure; the assumptions made about unobservable variables; and the decision reached on whether and how to weight CPS observations.

Among the studies listed in table 1, Dickinson, Johnson, and West (1986) perform the useful service of trying to reconcile their very low and even, for men, negative impact estimates with the more sizable positive estimates reported for both men and women in the influential study by Westat (1981). Their analysis suggests that Westat's results are quite sensitive to the omission of preenrollment earnings in the postprogram earnings regressions and to the decision to include in the comparison sample persons without strong labor market ties. When preenrollment earnings are controlled for and persons without strong labor market ties are excluded from the comparison sample, Dickinson, Johnson, and West report that Westat's methodology would result in the much lower net impact estimates of $-\$529$ for adult men and $\$299$ for adult women. This estimate for men is in roughly the same ballpark as the authors' overall male estimate of $-\$690$ shown in table 1. With respect to female CETA participants, it is interesting to note that Dickinson, Johnson, and West conclude that their overall impact estimate reported in the table of just $\$13$ per year is likely to be on the conservative side, and that an estimate on the order of $\$200$ to $\$300$ is more reasonable.

IV. Evidence from Demonstration Projects

Because the CETA evaluations were perceived as being of limited usefulness in shaping the direction of new JTPA Title III programs, beginning in 1980 a series of demonstration projects were funded to test the effectiveness of alternative services in placing displaced workers in private sector jobs. This section examines the results of four major demonstration projects beginning, in chronological order, with the Downriver displaced worker program. Table 2 is intended to present an overview of the four demonstrations indicating the time periods during

Table 2   **Characteristics of Major Displaced Worker Demonstrations**

Demonstration project	Time period	Targeted workers	Sample size	Evaluation method
Downriver:				
Phase I	July 1980–September 1981	Experienced male workers laid off from particular auto plants	388 treatment; 384 comparison	Comparison group drawn randomly from other auto plants
Phase II	November 1981–September 1983		594 treatment; 341 comparison	
Buffalo:				
Target	October 1982–September 1983	Experienced male workers laid off from 6 steel and auto plants	281 treatment; 516 comparison	Random assignment to treatment and control groups
Nontarget		Experienced male workers laid off from 3 other steel and auto plants or from over 300 other establishments	251 treatment; 470 comparison	Self-selected treatment and comparison groups
Texas WAD:				
Houston	1983–85	Mostly male professional workers laid off from petro-chemical plants	470 treatment; 164 control	Random assignment to treatment and control groups
El Paso		Mostly female Hispanic workers laid off from light manufacturing plants	362 treatment; 312 control	
New Jersey UI project	July–December 1986	Male and female UI claimants with at least 3 years of tenure	3,645 treatment; 978 control	Random assignment to treatment and control groups

which the programs were in operation, the groups of displaced workers to which program services were targeted, sample sizes, and differences in evaluation methodologies.

The Downriver Program

Located in the Detroit metropolitan area, the Downriver program operated in two phases. The first phase, which continued from July 1980 through September 1981, made services available to workers laid off when two BASF and DANA auto supply plants were permanently closed during the summer of 1980. Like the CETA evaluations, the methodological approach to evaluating the Downriver program involved comparing a treatment group consisting of randomly selected former BASF and DANA workers with an externally selected comparison group. To minimize differences between the two groups, the comparison group is composed of workers who were also laid off from two Detroit-area auto industry plants that permanently closed during the summer of 1980. The two plants—termed "comparison plants"—were a Lear-Siegler Corporation plant and the Chrysler Huber Avenue Foundry plant.

Downriver's second phase extended program services to workers displaced from their jobs between November 1981 and September 1983 at the Ford Motor Company's Michigan Casting Company (MCC) plant. Laid-off workers from a Chrysler assembly plant and the Chrysler Foundry served as the comparison group for phase II. In both phases, program-eligible workers were experienced male production workers above the age of twenty-five who earned high wages (about $9.00 per hour) on their pre-displacement jobs. BASF and DANA workers averaged nearly fifteen years of tenure on their pre-displacement jobs, while average tenure for Ford MCC workers was about seven years. Most program-eligible workers were married with family responsibilities, and about 31% were black. It should be emphasized that workers were not randomly assigned to the treatment and comparison groups. Rather, treatment and comparison group members were randomly selected, respectively, from the treatment and comparison plants.

Recruitment for the Downriver program was plant-based with the cooperation of employers and the United Auto Workers union in providing rosters of laid-off workers and signing outreach letters. A quite high rate of participation of about 50% was achieved across both phases of the program, even though workers waited on average about sixteen weeks after their layoff before enrolling in the program. The high-participation rate can be attributed to the targeting of program services to workers laid off from particular plants and the active involvement of employers and unions in outreach and recruitment.

Eligible displaced workers who opted to participate in the Downriver program were first enrolled in an orientation and testing program, followed by a mandatory four-day job seeking skills workshop. After completing the workshops, participants who indicated an interest in retraining were evaluated by staff members in an attempt to refer on to training programs only those likely to benefit. Close to 60% of participants received some form of retraining with the bulk of these individuals enrolling in CT. Only about 13% of trainees were enrolled in OJT, in part because OJT positions with local firms were difficult to secure. CT programs were contracted out to local educational institutions, usually under a performance-based contract. Under this contracting scheme, reimbursement of training costs was based partly or entirely on contractor performance as measured by both the number of trainees completing the course and the number of trainees placed in jobs after training.

Table 3 indicates the three outcome measures used in the Downriver program evaluation carried out by Abt Associates and reported in Kulik, Smith, and Stromsdorfer (1984). Placement rates measure the

Table 3   **Net Impact Estimates for the Downriver Program**

Phase and treatment plant	Outcome measure		
	Placement rate	Employment rate	Weekly earnings
Phase I:			
BASF (1)	21.4%**	20.1%**	$110.9**
(2)	17.0**	18.4**	44.4**
DANA (1)	18.8*	6.1*	121.8*
(2)	8.7*	5.8*	33.1*
Phase II:			
Ford MCC (1)	−38.4**	−9.4	−2.3
(2)	−19.2*	−5.6	−18.9

Source: Kulik, Smith, and Stromsdorfer (1984, tables 3.4 and 3.6).

Notes: For phase I, (1) signifies that Lear-Siegler only is the comparison plant, while (2) signifies that Lear-Siegler and Chrysler Foundry are the comparison plants. For phase II, (1) signifies that Chrysler Assembly only is the comparison plant, while (2) signifies that Chrysler Assembly and Chrysler Foundry are the comparison plants. ** and * indicate that the program effect is statistically significant at the 5% and 10% levels, respectively, using a two-tailed test.

percentages of workers who were ever reemployed during the observation period measured from the date of layoff to the survey interview date. The observation period for Downriver participants was on average about two and one-half years. To capture the stability of employment following layoff, the employment rate measures for each worker the fraction of weeks employed during the observation period. Finally, average weekly earnings is calculated as total earnings from layoff to interview divided by the number of weeks in the observation period. A number of measured variables that differed between the program-eligible and comparison groups and that were thought to influence reemployment experience are controlled for using regression analysis. No attempt was made to control for sample selectivity except for the inclusion in the regression models of explanatory variables likely to affect program participation as well as labor-market outcomes.

For phase I of the program, the net impact estimates in table 3 indicate that program enrollment increased both the placement rate and the employment rate of former BASF workers by about twenty percentage points. These findings are especially noteworthy because of their robustness across comparison groups. With respect to average weekly earnings, participants enjoyed an increase in earnings over the level they otherwise could have expected of $44 and $111, depending on whether Chrysler Foundry is included in the comparison group. This sensitivity to the composition of the comparison group may reflect, in part, the fact that Chrysler workers were the highest paid and BASF workers the lowest paid prior to layoff of those surveyed. The higher estimate implies an annual earnings gain on the order of $5,545 (assuming a fifty-week work year), which is considerably larger than any of the estimates shown in table 1 for CETA programs.

Among former DANA workers, the net impact estimates shown in the table for placement rates and especially for employment rates, while still positive, are much smaller than those obtained for the BASF group. In addition, the DANA estimates for placement rates are much more sensitive to the composition of the comparison group. On the other hand, the estimated net impact of the program on earnings is roughly the same for former DANA workers as for former BASF workers with the same degree of sensitivity to the composition of the comparison group.

Turning to phase II, program participation is seen to have actually reduced the placement rate of former Ford workers during the postlayoff observation period; while participation had a negative but not statistically significant effect on the employment rate and on weekly earnings. To reconcile this dramatic difference in estimates between the two phases, Kulik, Smith, and Stromsdorfer consider the effects of possible changes in program services and the characteristics of eligible workers and of the worsening local labor market situation between 1980–81 and 1983. They conclude, however, that the most likely explanation lies in the existence of unmeasured plant-specific differences that were not completely controlled for by the selection of comparison plants and the observed variables included in the regression models. In particular, important differences in motivation may have existed between DANA and BASF workers and Ford workers. Supporting this conclusion is quantitative evidence indicating a shorter length of program enrollment and a lower rate of training completion for Ford workers. Anecdotal evidence also suggests greater problems of absenteeism and drug abuse in the Ford plant.

The Downriver program also sheds a limited amount of light on the four policy questions posed in section I. In connection with the first of these questions, the only available comparison of program services involves CT and JSA. Kulik, Smith, and Stromsdorfer (1984, pp. 82–92) report that average skill training cost per enrollee was more than twice the average cost of JSA and that the program significantly increased access to training programs. Nevertheless, skill training is found not to have significantly improved participants' reemployment prospects above the assistance provided by JSA. The authors qualify this finding with the caveats that (1) the sample sizes are small and (2) workers were not randomly assigned to the CT and JSA-only treatment groups.

Concerning the next two questions, the Downriver program provides evidence regarding program participation in general rather than the receipt of retraining services only. With respect to question 2, the evaluation results indicate that tenure on the prelayoff job, age, and a black skin color are negatively related to postprogram employment and earnings. Total labor-market experience, on the other hand, serves to enhance employment prospects. Turning to question 3, the results shown in table 3 for phase I (but not, as noted, for phase II) indicate that program participation decreases duration of unemployment and increases weekly earnings, with the impact on earnings for DANA workers being particularly large relative to the impact on unemployment. Without evidence on the effect of the program on weekly hours, however, it is not possible to calculate its impact on average hourly wages.

The approach of Downriver program planners with respect to question 4 is worth discussing in some detail. Staff members first attempted to identify occupations for which demand was expected to grow in the local labor market. This task was accomplished by reviewing economic

259

forecasts and studies conducted by local universities, studying trade jour-
nals, and analyzing labor market data collected by the Michigan Employment Security (ES) commission. Next, the actual demand for labor in
the occupations that survived this scrutiny was verified through interviews with local employers and representatives of trade associations.
Kulik, Smith, and Stromsdorfer (1984, p. 30) emphasize, however, that

> [P]rogram staff were *not* interested in identifying *firm-specific* labor
> needs for which "customized" training would need to be developed, as
> staff considered this a risky investment. Rather, they preferred to train
> for occupations for which there was sufficient demand on the part of a
> number of employers, so that participants' reemployment prospects
> were not tied to the fortunes of only one firm. (Italics in the original.)

Once the decision on occupations was arrived upon, Downriver officials
invited local educational institutions to participate in designing curricula
suitable for class-size training programs. It is interesting to recall from
section II that the Secretary of Labor's Task Force (1986) takes exactly
the opposite approach to designing skill training programs in recommending that training should be customized to match the needs of specific employers.

The Buffalo Dislocated Demonstration Project

The Downriver results are difficult to interpret because of the striking differences between the two phases of the project and the sensitivity
of even phase I impact estimates to the choice of comparison plants. To
provide firmer evidence on the effect of retraining and other services in
assisting displaced workes, the USDOL funded six additional demonstration projects located in Alameda County, California; Buffalo; Milwau-
kee; Lehigh Valley, Pennsylvania; Mid-Willamette Valley, Oregon; and
Yakima County, Washington. Concurrently, a seventh project funded by
state, local, and private sector sources was implemented in the Southgate area of Los Angeles. The six projects plus the Southgate program
served over 10,000 displaced workers between October 1, 1982 and
September 30, 1983.

Early in the evaluation design process it was decided that due to cost
considerations the impact analysis should be limited to one site only.
The Buffalo program was chosen as the impact analysis site, primarily
because it offered a true control group for the majority of the workers
recruited for the program. Buffalo program services were offered to two
groups of displaced workers: (1) mostly steel and auto workers displaced

during 1982 from nine area plants and (2) a more heterogeneous group of workers permanently laid off after 1980 from over three hundred area establishments. About 30% of program slots were reserved for the latter group. For six of the nine target plants, slots were rationed through a formal lottery mechanism. Thus, displaced workers in what is termed the "target-plant sample" who were offered program services (or recruited) are a random sample of all workers from these six plants. Workers from the remaining three plants and from firms other than the nine target plants were offered program services on a first-come, first-served basis as program slots became available. These workers are termed the "nontarget-plant sample." For both samples, labor-market outcomes observed for program participants are compared to those observed for recruited nonparticipants (i.e., workers recruited for the program who chose not to participate) and comparison group members who were not recruited but who are generally similar to recruited workers as a group.

Most of the personal and job-related characteristics of recruited workers in both the target-plant and nontarget-plant samples are quite similar, with recruited workers being predominantly white males between the ages of twenty-five and fifty-five working full time prior to their displacement. In addition, recruited workers in both groups experienced lengthy periods of postdisplacement unemployment prior to program participation. On average, target-plant workers had been laid off more than a year before the start of the program, while those in the nontarget-plant sample had been laid off for about eight weeks. The other major difference between the two samples is that the prelayoff hourly wage of recruited workers in the target-plant sample averaged $10.78 as opposed to an average prelayoff wage of $8.70 for recruited nontarget-plant workers. Length of prelayoff tenure was 10.1 years and 8.5 years, respectively, for recruited target-plant and nontarget-plant workers.

Complicating the evaluation carried out by Mathematica Policy Research are the low take-up rates for workers offered program services in both samples (16% among recruited target-plant workers and 28% among nontarget-plant workers who applied and were offered services). These low participation rates raise the possibility of selection bias due to nonrandom assignment or selection of displaced workers into the participant, recruited nonparticipant, and comparison groups. As described in the evaluation report by Corson, Long, and Maynard (1985), the selection bias problem is dealt with by first explicitly modeling program participation. The resulting parameter estimates of the participation equation are then used to construct a selectivity variable (i.e., the

**Table 4   Estimated Program Impacts for the Buffalo Displaced
Worker Project, by Principal Program Treatment**

Outcome variable and principal program treatment	Target plants	Nontarget plants
Placement rate	31%**	6%
Average weekly hours	13.6**	7.6**
Employment rate:		
Overall	33%**	11%
CT	47**	46**
OJT	18	13
JSA only	33**	−6
Average weekly earnings:		
Overall	$115**	$96**
CT	122	141
OJT	64	136**
JSA only	134**	15

Source: Corson, Long, and Maynard (1985, tables IV.3 and IV.4).

Note: ** and * signify that the program effect is statistically significant at the 5% and 10% confidence levels, respectively, using a one-tailed test.

inverse Mill's ratio), which is included as a regressor in each post-program outcome equation. The results shown in table 4 are calculated using this econometric approach to obtain program effects free of selectivity bias. All four outcome variables displayed in the table are measured for the first six postprogram months.

Beginning with target-plant workers, the results in table 4 indicate that program participation has a statistically significant effect on placement and employment rates as well as on weekly hours and earnings. These effects are quite large, generally equalling or even exceeding in size the Downriver phase I results for the same outcome variables. Expressing the coefficient estimates as percentages of preprogram mean values, participation in the Buffalo project more than doubled the proportion of time spent employed and increased the placement rate by more than one-half. Increases in average weekly hours and average weekly earnings are 135% and 195%, respectively, suggesting that the program may have boosted hourly wages for those reemployed, at least in the short run. For the nontarget-plant sample, the overall estimates shown in table 4 are uniformly smaller than for the target-plant sample; and the main program impacts appear to be increases in weekly hours and average weekly earnings as opposed to improvements in employment opportunities.

262

Corson, Long, and Maynard (1985, pp. 110–17) also report net impact estimates broken down by program treatment and demographic subgroups. With respect to program treatments, the Buffalo site, as was the case for all six sites in the demonstration project, offered participants a full range of services including JSA, CT, and OJT. Following initial orientation and assessment sessions, all Buffalo participants were required to attend a four-day job search workshop. About 45% of program participants were then channeled into either CT or OJT positions. Area employers at each of the six sites were offered a 50% wage subsidy to develop OJT slots, and the Buffalo program provided the highest proportion of OJT positions among the six sites. The 55% of participants who did not receive CT or OJT were assigned to counselors or resource coordinators and offered job development and referral services. The Buffalo program also maintained a resource center to be used by workers in conducting their own job search.

For the employment rate and average weekly earnings, table 4 presents net impact estimates disaggregated by program treatment. Among target-plant workers, the results indicate that JSA and CT had large effects of roughly the same magnitude on both outcome measures. The strong results for CT, but not for JSA, also carried over to the nontarget-plant estimates. Drawing on the more reliable results for the target-plant sample, Corson, Long, and Maynard (1985, pp. 111–13) point out that JSA is the more cost effective of the two treatments. The reason is that the additional effects (if any) of CT above those of JSA are not large enough to compensate for the higher cost of CT services. (Average costs per participants were $851 for JSA only, $3,282 for CT with JSA, and $3,170 for OJT with JSA.) The authors note, however, that many CT participants completed their training near the end of the demonstration period and thus received relatively little placement assistance. Interestingly, OJT is seen not to have much of an impact on either the employment rate or average earnings for the target-plant sample; but it is statistically significant in raising average earnings for nontarget-plant workers. Since OJT was primarily used in the Buffalo program as a placement tool, the absence of an effect on employment opportunities suggests that the OJT treatment was unnecessary.

Net program effects are also available broken down by sex, race, age, education, wages, and tenure on the predisplacement job, and availability of income support from supplemental unemployment benefit (SUB) programs. Focusing on proportion of time employed for the target-plant sample, program impacts are found to be greater for women than men, for individuals under age forty-five than for those older, and

263

for workers with more than ten years of tenure on their prelayoff job than for those with less tenure. Time spent employed did not appear to be strongly affected by race, education, prelayoff wages, and availability of SUB income support. The result for SUB support is important because it suggests, at least for Buffalo project participants, that the availability of income-maintenance support did not affect their response to program services.

Beyond the net impact results appearing in table 4, Corson, Long, and Maynard (1985) present a comparison of the characteristics of the reemployment job with those of the prelayoff job. Their analysis shows that, on average, weekly hours were reduced from 5% to 10%, but that an even larger reduction occurred in weekly earnings, particularly for the relatively high-wage target-plant sample. For the target-plant group, about one-third had weekly earnings of less than 50% of their prelayoff weekly earnings, while less than 20% showed an increase. Considerable occupational shifting also occurred reflecting a substantial movement of workers to new jobs outside manufacturing, the industrial sector in which a majority of the prelayoff jobs were located.

One final note on the Buffalo project relates to the design of CT programs. Corson, Maynard, and Wichita (1984, pp. 75–77) point out in their overview report on all six demonstration sites that the one-year duration of the project severely limited both the careful selection of high-growth occupations and the testing and assessment required to insure that participants possessed the motivation and basic academic skills to benefit from formal classroom training. In general, CT was limited to those occupations and training deliverers amenable to short-duration, high-intensity courses developed on short notice. Local employer involvement in the design of training programs typically took the form of recommendations of Private Industry Council (PIC) committees based on ". . a relatively unsystematic impression of labor-market demand" (Corson, Maynard, and Wichita 1984: 76).

The Texas Worker Adjustment Demonstration (WAD) Projects

Carried out during 1983–85 by the Texas Department of Community Affairs, the WAD program involved some 2,250 JTPA Title III program participants in two projects in El Paso and one in Houston. In comparison to the Downriver and Buffalo projects, an important distinguishing feature of the WAD projects is that they represent an attempt to evaluate a continuing displaced worker program. In addition, WAD program services were provided to groups of displaced workers other than the

264

mostly white male steel and auto workers who were targeted for assistance in the Downriver and Buffalo projects. Perhaps most important, the WAD projects applied a true experimental methodology including random assignment.

As described in the Abt Associates report by Bloom and Kulik (1986), the experimental design of the WAD projects allowed Title III program participants to be assigned randomly to either of two treatment groups or to a control group. The first treatment group (called Tier I) received JSA services only. Core JSA services provided at all three sites included orientation, job search workshops, assessment, and job development and placement. Members of the second treatment group received JSA followed, if necessary, by more expensive classroom or OJT retraining (the Tier I/II sequence). The control group was supplied all non-Title III services available in Texas. As noted earlier, even though a majority of Buffalo project slots were rationed on a random-assignment basis, evaluation of the project was made more difficult by low rates of participation for those workers offered program services. This was not a problem for the WAD projects, with 71% of those assigned to the treatment groups choosing to participate. Bloom and Kulik (1986, pp. 29–31) mention, in particular, that shortfalls between the number of planned and actual participants occurred almost exclusively in connection with Tier II services; and these shortfalls were mainly the result of overestimating provider capacity rather than exaggerating workers' interest. In Houston, in addition, there was an important mismatch between the types of Tier II services supplied and the demand of the client population. This mismatch will be discussed at greater length later in this section.

Beyond the Tier I and Tier I/II distinction, there were also important differences between the WAD sites in Houston and El Paso. In terms of workers' personal and job-related characteristics, over 80% of those recruited and assigned to treatment and control groups in the Houston project were male and about 57% were white. Also represented in Houston were sizable groups of blacks and Asians. In the two El Paso sites, in contrast, approximately 90% of program eligibles were Hispanic and a majority were women. These differences by race and sex primarily reflect the industrial orientation of the projects, with the Houston program targeting its services to highly educated, largely white-collar professional workers laid off from petrochemical plants. By comparison, both El Paso programs focused on workers with much less education displaced from apparel, food processing, and other light manufacturing jobs. Mirroring this difference in industry orientation, the

Table 5   Estimated Program Impacts for the Texas WAD Projects,
           by Sex and Project Site

	Men		Women	
Outcome measure	Houston	El Paso	Houston	El Paso
Earnings for the year after random assignment	$750	$770	0	$1,070*
Weeks worked for postassignment quarters 3 and 4	2.1	.7	1.7	3.1*
Total UI benefits for 30 weeks after random assignment	−$210	−$170	$200	−$130

Source: Bloom and Kulik (1986, Exhibit 7.2).

Note: * signifies that the program effect is statistically significant at the 2.5% level using a one-tailed test.

average hourly wage of Houston's eligibles was slightly over $13.00 as compared to about $5.00 for eligible workers in El Paso. Rather surprisingly, most WAD eligibles in all three sites had been employed in their prelayoff jobs for less than five years—a considerably shorter period of time than the seven to fifteen years of prelayoff tenure reported for Downriver and Buffalo displaced workers. One final difference between WAD sites is that only for the Houston site could the differential effect of the additional services in the Tier I/II sequence be distinguished from Tier I JSA-only services. The program outcome measures available for the El Paso sites are limited to a comparison of the Tier I/II sequence and the control group.

The WAD demonstration yielded three main results. As summarized in table 5, the first is that program participants experienced short-run positive impacts on annual earnings and weeks worked, as well as a decrease in dollars received in UI benefits. (The ambiguous findings for female participants in the Houston site appear to be due to a small sample size.) More important, these impact estimates tend to be larger and more pronounced for women than for men. In particular, female participants in El Paso experienced a program-induced gain in annual earnings of $1,070. The gain in annual earnings for men in Houston and El Paso were $750 and $770, respectively. Since the mostly white male Houston participants earned more than twice as much as the mostly Hispanic female El Paso participants prior to WAD enrollment, the gender difference in estimated earnings gains is even more striking when expressed in percentage terms.

266

Table 6　　　　**Estimated Program Impact on Quarterly Earnings for the Texas WAD Projects, by Sex**

Earnings in postassignment quarter	Men	Women
Quarter 1	$110	$480*
Quarter 2	500*	330*
Quarter 3	40	160
Quarter 4	130	−110
Total	790	890*

Source: Bloom and Kulik (1986, Exhibit 7.1).

Note: * signifies that the program is statistically significant at the 2.5% level using a one-tailed test.

A second result emerges from quarter-by-quarter program impact estimates calculated by sex across all three sites and shown in table 6. Large and statistically significant earnings gains occurred for men only in the second postassignment quarter. For women, similarly, WAD participation increased earnings on average by $480 (relative to a total impact of $890) in the first postprogram quarter, followed by gradually decaying impacts for subsequent quarters. This time pattern in the results for both sexes indicates that the main effect of the program was to enable participants to find jobs sooner than would have otherwise been the case. But ultimately, the employment opportunities of program participants were no better and the wages of participants no higher than for members of the control group.

The final result involves the differential effect of Tier I versus Tier I/II services for males in the Houston program. Average program costs per participant were $1,531 for Tier I and $4,991 for Tier I/II. Consistent with the results of the Downriver and Buffalo projects, retraining (which was almost exclusively classroom training) failed to have a positive incremental effect on earnings and employment over that of JSA-only services. In fact, the earnings gain for the year after random assignment was $860 for Tier I-only participants as compared to only $680 for Tier I/II participants; and calculated net impacts on weeks worked are 4.3 weeks and 0.6 weeks, respectively, for Tier I-only and Tier I/II services. The incremental effect of retraining services on total UI benefits is exactly zero.

Bloom and Kulik (1986, pp. 170–73) take considerable care in interpreting these negative results for skill training. One explanation they offer is that the addition of a retraining program is likely to cause participants to delay undertaking serious job search until after the training period is completed. If, as just indicated, the primary program effect for men is to expedite their reemployment and this effect occurs soon after the receipt of JSA services, a delay in beginning the job search process will reduce reemployment rates.

A second explanation considered more realistic by the authors is the mismatch between the retraining opportunities offered and the interests and backgrounds of the target group. The classroom training programs provided by the Houston Community College were primarily technical/vocational in nature offering retraining in occupations including air conditioning and refrigeration and computer maintenance technology. At the same time, as noted, Houston program participants were well educated, highly paid former white-collar workers. Further complicating matters was a lack of integration of the JSA and CT program components caused by poor communication between the Tier I and Tier II contractors. It is therefore not surprising that the take-up of retraining was low and the payoff limited. In their recommendations for future Title III programming, Bloom and Kulik (1986, pp. 179–82) suggest that (1) JSA should be the core service provided in displaced worker programs and (2) skill training should be offered to fewer, more carefully screened participants who can be better matched to training opportunities that are potentially available in the community. At the same time, however, they conclude that the cost-effectiveness of high-quality, accurately targeted skill training remains open to question.

The New Jersey UI Reemployment Demonstration Project

The fourth and final demonstration project discussed in this section—the New Jersey UI Reemployment Demonstration—was initiated by the USDOL and operated as a joint venture by the USDOL and the New Jersey Department of Labor. Implemented in July 1986, the project had two primary objectives. The first is to assess the feasibility of an "early intervention" strategy. At issue are the questions of whether and how it is possible to use the UI system to identify early in the claim period unemployed workers who are likely to face prolonged spells of unemployment and exhaust UI benefits. "Early" is defined operationally in the demonstration as the fifth week of claiming UI benefits. The second objective is to empirically measure the effectiveness of three alternative packages of reemployment services in accelerating the return to work. The three packages of services—designated treatments 1, 2, and 3, respectively—are JSA only, JSA combined with training or relocation assistance, and

268

JSA combined with a cash bonus for early reemployment. Demonstration services were provided at each of ten demonstration sites.

Concerning the first objective, the basic problem is to distinguish displaced workers from those unemployed for cyclical, frictional, or seasonal reasons so that unneeded services are not be provided to workers reasonably anticipating recall to their old jobs or otherwise expected to have little difficulty in locating new employment. The clearest way to make this distinction is by looking at the length of completed unemployment spells. The longer the spell, the more likely it is that an unemployed worker is truly displaced. Unfortunately, this approach is not of much help in making decisions early in the spell of unemployment on which workers should be targeted for assistance. Assistance might also be restricted to workers displaced from their jobs by a mass permanent layoff or a plant closure. But this approach neglects the needs of job losers adversely affected by the ripple effect of a large plant closure or mass layoff in causing suppliers to the closed plant and local retail and service outlets to lay off employees.

The approach taken by New Jersey program designers to distinguish the displaced from other unemployed workers is to apply five "screens" during the fourth week of claiming benefits. The cumulative effect of these screens defines the displaced to be unemployed workers on permanent layoff who are twenty-five years of age and older and who had at least three years of tenure with their last employer prior to being laid off. About 4,600 claimants passed through these screens during the July–November 1986 period and were randomly assigned to the three treatment groups and the control group.

Turning to the second objective of the demonstration, a full range of JSA services is included as part of treatment 1. These services include orientation, testing, a job search workshop, a resource center, an assessment/counseling interview, and job referral. Following the assessment interview, participants are expected to have a specific job goal, an "employability plan" directed at achieving that goal, and a working knowledge of how to effectively use a resource center. Treatment 2 offers OJT and, more commonly, CT programs at the assessment interview. (Very few participants expressed interest in the offer of relocation.) With respect to CT, two major areas of skill training—(1) business and office and (2) computer and information services—each accounted for 35% of total training. Over half of the OJT slots are in business and sales occupations. The interim evaluation report by Corson and Kerachsky (1987, p. 16) offers little information on how these occupational areas were selected except to note that "it appears that the training that

269

is being provided is directed towards occupations that are in demand."
The average length of training is 19.4 weeks for CT and 14.5 weeks for
OJT. Mean costs are $2,563 and $3,116 for CT and OJT, respectively.

Both treatment 1 and treatment 2 services are provided in addition
to the JTPA Title III retraining programs and ES placement assistance
currently supplied to unemployed New Jersey residents. Thus, the demonstration compares the effect of the alternative treatments with the
existing service environment. The demonstration services differ from
those currently offered in that claimants in the demonstration have a
considerably higher chance of receiving services, and the demonstration
services are generally provided earlier in the unemployment spell. It is
also worth noting that the demonstration is designed to use existing
agencies and vendors to provide program services. Hence, ES staff members provide JSA services and JTPA staff are involved in identifying
appropriate CT and OJT opportunities and placing claimants in them.

The reemployment bonus concept made operational in treatment 3
is directed at the problem that the reemployment of displaced workers is
delayed, not by inadequate job search skills, but by a lack of motivation
to engage in search or by the natural reluctance to accept a new job
offering considerably lower wages and benefits than the prelayoff job.[6]
The New Jersey reemployment bonus treatment works as follows. During the assessment interview, claimants selected for this treatment are
informed of the specifics of the bonus program. If they decide to participate, they can collect the maximum bonus by locating and accepting a
job during the next two weeks. The maximum bonus is specified to be
one-half of the claimant's remaining UI entitlement at the time of the
interview. (The maximum bonus averages about $1,600.) After the two-
week period has passed, the size of the bonus decreases by 10% per
week, reaching zero at the end of the eleventh week after the assessment
interview. A bonus payment is made only to participants who obtained
full-time employment with a new employer lasting four weeks or longer.

The report by Corson and Kerachsky (1987) discusses preliminary
results for the first six months of program operation following its implementation in July 1986. Regarding the demonstration's first objective,
the report notes that it is as yet not possible to determine whether the
five screens satisfactorily identify claimants who, in the absence of
additional employment services, would experience difficulty in becoming reemployed. Nevertheless, the screens do appear to restrict the
demonstration-eligible population to persons whose attributes are usually associated with displaced workers and reemployment difficulty.
Cases in which the screening procedure tended to break down include

individuals from growing industries like services, and claimants who eventually returned to their former employer and presumably did not require program services.

With respect to the second objective, strengths of the New Jersey demonstration are its broad coverage of state residents and its large sample size. Men and women are about equally represented in the eligible population, there are sizable proportions of blacks (19%) and Hispanics (17%) as well as of workers age fifty-five and older (25%), and the industry mix of the eligible population includes workers laid off from jobs in the trade and services industries as well as from manufacturing jobs. As is the case for the Buffalo demonstration project, the assessment of treatment 2 services is made more difficult by the low participation rate in retraining programs. Of those who passed through the assessment interview and were offered training, the participation rate was only 13% to 14% for CT and 14% to 16% overall. Corson and Kerachsky (1987, pp. 16–17) speculate that these lower than expected participation rates may be because (1) the offer of retraining early in the layoff period comes before claimants recognize that they could benefit from training services and (2) potentially inadequate screening means that some individuals offered training simply do not need it.

Since the treatments are intended to lead to more rapid reemployment of participating claimants, it is expected that the amount of UI benefits received by treatment group members will be less than the amount received by control group members. This expectation is borne out in the negative and statistically significant net impact estimates shown in table 7, where the estimates reported are the treatment mean

Table 7 Estimated Program Impacts for the New Jersey UI Reemployment Demonstration, by Program Treatment

Treatment	Outcome measure	
	Weeks of UI	UI benefits paid
JSA only	−.54	−$87.55
JSA plus retraining	−.49	−69.42
JSA plus reemployment bonus	−1.00	−171.72
All treatments	−.64	−102.56

Source: Corson and Kerachsky (1987, table 4).

Note: All impact estimates shown are statistically significant at the 5% level using a one-tailed test.

271

minus the control mean after taking account of differences in claimants' characteristics. (Later reports will include estimates of treatment effects on employment and earnings.) These findings are to be viewed as preliminary because the observation period is truncated at the end of December 1986. This means that many sample members have not stopped collecting UI as of the end of the observation period.

Looking at the estimates for the three individual treatments, table 7 indicates that JSA-only results in a 0.54-week reduction in UI receipt over the six-month observation period. This translates into a reduction in benefits paid per eligible claimant of about $88 for six months—an estimate that is somewhat less than the −$220 calculated over thirty weeks for the WAD projects. The reemployment bonus is expected to have the largest impact of the three treatments because of the substantial reemployment incentive created by the bonus; and the incremental effects of the bonus over those of JSA-only are substantial and statistically significant. It is also expected that the retraining treatment will have the smallest immediate effect on UI receipt since individuals undergoing training continue to receive UI benefits. Table 7 shows, consistent with evidence produced for the Texas WAD projects, that the retraining programs in treatment 2 do not have a positive incremental effect on UI benefits. It should also be noted that all of these impact estimates are likely to understate the ultimate effect of the treatments because the available six-month observation period is shorter than the sample's full UI eligibility period.

V. Conclusion

The four demonstration projects discussed in section IV have the common objective of quantitatively assessing the labor-market effectiveness for displaced workers of public retraining programs. These programs include mixes of JSA, CT, and OJT services. (None of the projects offered training to meet basic skill deficiencies.) Although they have a common objective, the projects differ considerably in terms of geographic location, experimental design, and the target populations of displaced workers served. This concluding section attempts to make sense of the net impact estimates obtained for the different projects (as well as for the CETA evaluations considered in section III) by asking what the results have to say regarding the four policy questions posed in the introduction.

Question 1: Do some types of training work better than others?

The Buffalo, Texas WAD, and New Jersey projects are unanimous in indicating that JSA services strongly affect in the intended direction a variety of labor-market outcomes including earnings, placement and employment rates, and amount of UI benefits. Given the relatively low cost per worker of JSA, this evidence suggests also that JSA services are cost effective. For the other reemployment services, evidence across all four demonstrations indicates that CT fails to have a sizable incremental effect on earnings and employment above that of JSA only. It certainly does not appear to be the case that the additional effect of CT is large enough to compensate for the higher cost of CT services. The authors of the major evaluation reports are plainly troubled by these unexpectedly weak results for CT, and they offer a number of caveats for their findings. To anticipate the discussion of question 4, these caveats include small sample sizes, the problem that participants undergoing skill training have relatively little time left to receive placement assistance (given demonstration periods of fixed length), and the difficulty of finding training providers capable of putting together high-quality, short-duration training courses on short notice.

Regarding OJT, it was noted in section II that the Secretary of Labor's Task Force report (1986, pp. 33–34) recommends that OJT rather than CT be regarded as the primary source of long-term skill upgrading. The CETA evaluations summarized in table 1 support this recommendation by showing generally larger net impact estimates for OJT than for CT. Among the four demonstration programs, the Buffalo project is the only one with enough participants placed in OJT slots to provide reasonably reliable estimates of the net impact of OJT programs. Contrary to the CETA results, OJT is not found to consistently have a positive effect on earnings. Nor does it have much of an effect on employment rates. Since OJT was primarily used in the Buffalo program as a placement tool, it appears that this service was unnecessary.

Question 2: Do some groups of workers benefit more from training than others?

The Texas WAD projects provide the strongest evidence of the four demonstrations regarding differential program effects across groups of workers. In terms of earnings and employment, female participants in the El Paso WAD project are found to enjoy much larger net impact estimates than males in both the El Paso and Houston projects. These

273

gender differences between program sites are particularly striking when it is recognized that a majority of male Houston participants are white, whereas female El Paso participants are largely Hispanic. Reinforcing these WAD results is evidence from the CETA evaluations and the Buffalo project indicating larger program effects for women than men. The Buffalo project also suggests that little difference in net impact estimates exists for blacks and whites, but that workers under age forty-five benefit more from program services than do older workers.

Question 3: To the extent that training improves reemployment prospects, does it work by increasing posttraining wage rates or by reducing the duration of unemployment?

With respect to this question, it would clearly be desirable to disaggregate program services sufficiently to isolate the impact of CT and OJT (as distinct from JSA) on wages versus employment. This is not possible for the demonstration projects. For all program services combined, however, the Buffalo project permits the calculation of short-run program effects on weekly hours and average weekly earnings. The larger percentage effect on average weekly earnings than weekly hours suggests that the Buffalo program boosted hourly wages for those reemployed during the first six postprogram months. Unfortunately, the quarter-by-quarter program impact estimates calculated for the WAD projects indicate that this short-run effect does not persist over time. The time pattern of the WAD results indicates that the program increased quarterly earnings in the first and second quarters, followed by gradually decaying impacts for subsequent quarters. Ulitmately, therefore, the employment opportunities of WAD participants appear to be no better and their wages no worse than those of the members of the control group. There is no evidence, in other words, that program services increase labor productivity.

Question 4: Referring specifically to vocational training, how do we know what to train workers to do?

A valuable contribution of the demonstration projects is to make apparent the difficulty in a short-duration demonstration of developing solid training curricula that meet the market test of providing marketable skills.[7] Corson, Maynard, and Wichita (1984, p. 16) note in the context of all six sites of the Dislocated Worker Demonstration Projects that key lessons learned are that (1) many displaced workers will not be able to adapt to CT and (2) despite attempts to base course selection on labor-market data, many successful program graduates may not be able to locate training-related jobs. The authors go on to recommend the use of performance-based contracting with training vendors as one way to improve participant screening in determining access to CT programs and to increase postprogram placement and job retention rates. The WAD demonstration also emphasizes that one reason for low program take-up rates and modest net impact estimates is that CT curricula may not match the backgrounds and perceived needs of client workers.

Drawing on this information, a policy issue that remains to be addressed involves the ideal mix of adjustment assistance services to meet the needs of displaced workers. The point that comes out most strongly from the empirical evidence is that JSA should be the core service provided in the ideal system. JSA has been convincingly shown to be effective in speeding up the reemployment process, it allows for quick intervention before workers disperse after layoffs or plant closings, and it is relatively cheap. In view of the practical difficulties addressed in the New Jersey demonstration of distinguishing displaced workers from other unemployed workers, the low cost of JSA services is particularly attractive because it makes it feasible to supply assistance even to those unemployed workers who turn out ex post to have little difficulty in locating new jobs or are recalled to their old jobs.

The roles of skill training and remedial education programs are not as clear cut. Skill training programs are substantially more expensive than JSA, and the empirical evidence summarized here indicates that training has little or no impact on labor-market outcomes as typically measured. Nevertheless, the various caveats noted in connection with the skill training programs surveyed leave open the question of whether a high-quality, narrowly targeted skill training program could be cost effective. Given the present state of our knowledge, it seems reasonable to conclude along with Bloom and Kulik (1986, p. 181) that in the ideal system skill training should be offered sparingly for well-specified needs and only where adequate local training resources are present.

Remedial education has received little attention in this paper because none of the demonstration projects provided this service to targeted workers. As indicated in the introduction, however, a typical finding in the empirical literature is that displaced workers with low levels of formal education are much more likely than other displaced workers to experience lengthy spells of unemployment and low earnings upon reemployment; and most analysts agree that at least 20% of the displaced worker population is seriously deficient in basic reading and problem-solving

275

skills. Remedial education thus appears to be an important service to be offered to the minority of displaced workers determined in the assessment and testing phase of JSA programs to lack basic skills.

NOTES

1. At the present time, nearly all states provide funding to subsidize the direct costs of training programs. While states do not typically provide associated income-maintenance benefits to trainees, unemployed workers enrolled in a training program are eligible for Unemployment Insurance benefits if the program is approved by the state's employment security agency. Leigh (1989) presents a comprehensive survey and evaluation of proposed and on-going state initiatives to assist displaced workers. In addition to vocational training and job search assistance, these initiatives include wage subsidies, reemployment bonuses, rapid-response team programs, enterprise zones, employee buy-out assistance, and unemployed entrepreneur programs.

2. The disadvantaged are usually defined to include poorly educated, unskilled workers with unstable work histories and youths with no job experience at all.

3. The final version of the trade bill also includes a highly controversial advance notice provision. Termed the "Worker Adjustment and Retraining Notification (WARN) Act," employers of one hundred or more workers are required to provide written sixty-day notification of a planned plant closing or mass layoff to employees or their unions and to the state dislocated worker unit. Although he had threatened to veto the entire trade bill because of this one provision, President Reagan finally allowed the bill to become law without his signature. WARN is examined in detail in chapter 8 of this volume.

4. An important exception to this statement is Ashenfelter's (1978) study of the impact of MDTA-funded CT programs using as a comparison group a sample drawn from the Continuous Work History Sample maintained by the Social Security Administration. Ashenfelter reports for males that the net impact of training on annual earnings is between $150 and $500 in the year immediately following training, declining to about half these amounts after five years. For females, the net impact estimates are between $300 and $600, with no evidence of a decline in succeeding years.

5. The important advantage of random assignment is that, in principle, the link is broken between program participation and unobservable determinants of earnings so that unbiased net program effects can be obtained. Heckman, Hotz, and Dabos (1987, pp. 421–24) properly emphasize, however, that participation in a training program entails a multistage process of application, selection, continuation in the program until completion, and finally job placement. An experimental assessment of the effect of training conditional on completing each stage of the process would require random assignment at each stage—something that is rarely done in social experiments.

6. The initial test of the reemployment bonus concept in this county took the form of two controlled experiments carried out in Illinois between mid-1984 and mid-1985. In the Claimant Bonus Experiment, a random sample of new UI claimants was told that they would receive a cash bonus of $500 upon reemployment. In the Employer Bonus Experiment, another random sample of new UI claimants was instructed that, once a hiring

commitment was made, the employer of each newly hired claimant would be eligible for a $500 cash bonus. In contrast to the generally insignificant results reported for the latter experiment, Woodbury and Spiegelman (1987) find that, on average, the claimant bonus reduced UI benefits by $158 and duration of insured unemployment by 1.15 weeks, where both outcome variables are measured over the benefit year.

7. Even in the context of a permanent retraining program, the problem of identifying growth occupations and developing appropriate curricula is a difficult one. Indeed, the National Academy of Sciences Panel on Technology and Employment (see Cyert and Mowery 1987, pp. 142–43, 173) recently concluded that it is futile to attempt to forecast the occupational labor demand impact of new technology and structural economic change. The alternative to forecasting occupational demand in choosing program curricula is to permit employers to be more heavily involved in designing curricula and implementing programs, which is the approach taken in most state-funded retraining efforts (see Leigh 1989).

REFERENCES

Ashenfelter, Orley (1978). "Estimating the Effect of Training Programs on Earnings." *Review of Economics and Statistics* 60 (February): 47–57.

Barnow, Burt S. (1987). "The Impact of CETA Programs on Earnings: A Review of the Literature." *Journal of Human Resources* 22 (Spring): 157–93.

Bassi, Laurie J. (1983). "The Effect of CETA on the Postprogram Earnings of Participants." *Journal of Human Resources* 18 (Fall): 539–56.

Bloom, Howard S., and Jane Kulik (1986). "Evaluation of the Worker Adjustment Demonstration: Final Report." Cambridge, Mass. (July).

Bloom, Howard S., and Maureen A. McLaughlin (1982). "CETA Training Programs—Do They Work for Adults?" Joint CBO-NCEP Report.

Corson, Walter, and Stuart Kerachsky (1987). "The New Jersey Unemployment Insurance Reemployment Demonstration Project: Interim Report." Washington, D.C.: Employment and Training Administration, U.S. Department of Labor.

Corson, Walter, Sharon Long, and Rebecca Maynard (1985). "An Impact Evaluation of the Buffalo Dislocated Worker Demonstration Program." *Mathematica Policy Research* (March 12).

Corson, Walter, Rebecca Maynard, and Jack Wichita (1984). "Process and Implementation Issues In the Design and Conduct of Programs to Aid the Reemployment of Dislocated Workers." *Mathematica Policy Research* (October 30).

Corson, Walter, and Walter Nicholson (1981). "Trade Adjustment Assistance for Workers: Results of a Survey of Recipients Under the Trade Act of 1974." In *Research In Labor Economics*, edited by Ronald G. Ehrenberg, pp. 417–69. Greenwich, Conn.

Cyert, Richard M., and David C. Mowery, eds. (1987). *Technology and Employment: Innovation and Growth in the U.S. Economy.* Washington, D.C.

Dickinson, Katherine P., Terry R. Johnson, and Richard W. West (1986). "An Analysis of the Impact of CETA Programs on Participants Earnings." *Journal of Human Resources* 21 (Winter): 64–91.

Finifter, David H. (1987). "An Approach to Estimating Net Earnings Impact of Federally Subsidized Employment and Training Programs." *Evaluation Review* 11 (August): 528–47.

Geraci, Vincent J. (1984). "Short-Term Indicators of Job Training Program Effects on Long-Term Participant Earnings." Report prepared for the U.S. Department of Labor.

Heckman, James J., V. Joseph Hotz, and Marcelo Dabos (1987). "Do We Need Experimental Data to Evaluate the Impact of Manpower Training on Earnings?" *Evaluation Review* 11 (August): 395–427.

Kulik, Jane, D. Alton Smith, and Ernst W. Stromsdorfer (1984). "The Downriver Community Conference Economic Readjustment Program: Final Evaluation Report." Cambridge, Mass. (May 18).

Leigh, Duane E. (1989). *Assisting Displaced Workers: Do the States Have a Better Idea?* Kalamazoo, Mich.

Levitan, Sar A., and Frank Gallo (1988). *A Second Chance: Training for Jobs.* Kalamazoo, Mich.

Neumann, George R. (1978). "The Labor Market Adjustments of Trade Displaced Workers: The Evidence from the Trade Adjustment Assistance Program." In *Research In Labor Economics,* edited by Ronald G. Ehrenberg, pp. 353–81. Greenwich, Conn.

Podgursky, Michael, and Paul Swaim (1987a). "Duration of Joblessness Following Displacement." *Industrial Relations* 26 (Fall): 213–26.

———(1987b). "Job Displacement and Earnings Loss: Evidence from the Displaced Worker Survey." *Industrial and Labor Relations Review* 41 (October): 17–29.

Secretary of Labor's Task Force on Economic Adjustment and Worker Dislocation (1986). "Economic Adjustment and Worker Dislocation in a Competitive Society," December.

U.S. General Accounting Office (1987). "Dislocated Workers: Local Programs and Outcomes Under the Job Training Partnership Act," March. Washington, D.C.

Westat (1981). "Continuous Longitudinal Manpower Survey Net Impact Report No. 1: Impact on 1977 Earnings of New FY 1976 CETA Enrollees in Selected Program Activities." Report prepared for the U.S. Department of Labor. Washington, D.C.

Woodbury, Stephen A., and Robert G. Spiegelman (1987). "Bonuses to Workers and Employers to Reduce Unemployment: Randomized Trials in Illinois." *American Economic Review* 77 (September): 513–30.

CHAPTER TEN

Displaced versus Disadvantaged Workers

DOUGLAS L. KRUSE

Is displacement a good criterion for providing employment and training assistance to workers? A central issue in the policy debates on worker displacement is the harm suffered by displaced workers. Implicit in many expressed views is the idea that those who are displaced are often those who can afford it least—workers who may be disadvantaged in finding other jobs and do not have other resources to fall back upon. However, there has been very little direct analysis of the empirical link between displacement and disadvantage, or of the policy issues involved.[1] The aim of this chapter is to raise such issues and to frame relevant research questions.

As noted by Adam Seitchik in this volume, the term "displacement" has been subject to various definitions; here it will be defined simply as the involuntary separation of a worker from a job due to a plant closing or employment cutback (not individual firings for unsatisfactory work). "Disadvantage" is less easy to define. Customarily, disadvantaged workers are thought of as those who have characteristics that impair them in the labor market: few skills, low quality or quantity of education, low mobility, low family resources, and/or characteristics that serve as criteria for discrimination (particularly female or racial minority status). The disadvantage may be manifested by low wages, involuntary unemployment, and/or lack of access to jobs or programs that upgrade skills. Consistent with common usage, this chapter will not employ a strict definition of disadvantage, but will broadly address the characteristics listed above that are commonly identified with disadvantage.

It is useful to distinguish two broad views on the relationship between disadvantage and displacement. In one view, which could be loosely identified as a standard competitive view of labor markets, there is no necessary reason for displacement and disadvantage to be positively related. To the extent that individuals join firms or industries with higher (ex ante) probabilities of displacement, the individuals should be rewarded with compensating differentials for this risk.[2] Workers choosing the jobs with high probabilities of displacement would have more unemployment over their working lives but also higher wages during employment periods, so that there is no clear implication that they would be "disadvantaged." For individuals joining firms with higher probabilities of displacement, there will be smaller incentives for the individual or the firm to invest in firm-specific training, so that there will be a flatter tenure-earnings profile; again, however, this reflects the choice of the worker and there is no implication that it necessarily reflects any form of disadvantage.

Since risk-aversion is typically assumed to decline with higher incomes, disadvantaged low-skill workers would presumably pick the more stable jobs; therefore, those who actually become displaced would be less likely to be disadvantaged workers. Ex post, the displaced workers may suffer temporary economic losses as they search for new jobs, and permanent losses from the loss of any firm-specific or industry-specific training investments (Hamermesh 1987), and from the decrease in general labor-market experience over the period of unemployment. However, any decrease in lifetime earnings from ex post displacement should be at least partially offset by the positive compensating differential for the ex ante risk of displacement; in addition, in a competitive labor market the losses are minimized by the ability of displaced workers to find new jobs fairly quickly at wages reflecting their personal productivities.

A second broad view, articulated particularly by segmented labor-market theorists, is that there are strong mutually reinforcing links between displacement and disadvantage.[3] A central concept in the segmented and dual labor-market literature is that a substantial portion of the workforce is restricted to a segment of "bad" jobs (the secondary sector), which is characterized by low wages, instability (including both displacement and voluntary turnover due to the "dead-end" nature of the jobs), and little if any returns to education and experience. Workers in these jobs do not have access to the "good" jobs (the primary sector) for a variety of mutually reinforcing reasons, among them that the bad jobs may create bad work habits, provide few skills, and may stigmatize an individual in the eyes of a primary sector employer. One factor that may prevent mobility between the two sectors is the payment of efficiency wages in the primary sector; Bulow and Summers (1986) show how this may generate job rationing in the primary sector.

Therefore, in this view of the labor market, disadvantaged workers are confined to jobs that, among other things, have high probabilities of displacement. In addition, even if workers start out with primary sector employment, displacement and the subsequent unemployment can have a "scarring" effect that can cause a worker to become disadvantaged and prevent access to primary sector jobs.

The issue of displaced versus disadvantaged workers was raised by Bendick and Devine (1982), who were specifically interested in the question of whether "dislocated workers per se should receive high priority in the use of scare federal employment and training resources." Based on their analysis of Current Population Survey (CPS) data, they answer this question in the negative. While the terms "displacement" and "dislocation" are often used synonymously, their measure of dislocation was more restrictive than the definition of displacement given above: a "dislocated" worker was defined as one who (1) was a civilian unemployed worker between ages twenty-two and sixty-four, (2) had been unemployed at the survey date for at least eight weeks (or alternatively, for at least twenty-six weeks), and (3) was associated with either a "declining industry" (negative average annual employment change over 1978–80), "declining occupation" (negative average annual employment change over 1978–80), or "declining region" (Standard Metropolitan Statistical Areas [SMSAs] or balance of state with population decrease between 1970 and 1980 or greater than 8.5% unemployment rate in March 1980). Note that while this definition is more restrictive in terms of the duration of unemployment and the requirement of association with a declining industry, occupation, or region, it does not require that the worker actually lost a job ("dislocated" workers may have been job leavers, labor-market reentrants or new entrants[4]). "Disadvantaged" workers, on the other hand, were defined as unemployed persons who were in "low-income" families (no more than 150% of the federal poverty threshold).

Dislocated workers were found to have—relative to disadvantaged workers—higher education levels, smaller proportions of minorities and women, higher salaries and fringe benefits in the year prior to the survey, a higher rate of home ownership, and higher family incomes while unemployed. In addition, association with a declining region was found to be positively related to long unemployment spells, although association with declining industries and occupations did not have such an association. In their conclusion, Bendick and Devine implicitly invoke both equity and efficiency criteria when they ask whether the "needs" of

281

dislocated workers are "sufficiently urgent, and the potential returns to that investment sufficiently high, to justify serving their needs at the expense of disadvantaged workers who currently are the main focus of [employment and training assistance]?" Due to the relative affluence of dislocated workers, they answer in the negative, but note that short-term "crisis" interventions for dislocated workers may be justified in some circumstances (such as for the auto industry in the early 1980s).

Several of their findings are inherent in the definitions employed. For example, since coming from a low-income family was part of the definition of disadvantage, it is not surprising that current family incomes, last-year incomes, and the rate of home ownership are higher among dislocated workers. Also, one of the criteria for being a "dislocated" worker was a long spell of unemployment at the survey date: this also makes it not surprising that this group would be relatively more affluent than disadvantaged workers, since more affluent workers are more likely to be able to stay unemployed long enough to meet the duration criterion. A minimum level of affluence is practically implied in the criteria for being "dislocated."

While the empirical conclusions are therefore subject to several criticisms, Bendick and Devine nonetheless point out the importance of the question posed above: Should displacement per se be used as a criterion for government assistance, or does this waste resources by providing assistance to many who do not need it? The approach used by Bendick and Devine is to make a cross-sectional comparison of the personal and family characteristics of "dislocated" versus "disadvantaged" workers. Here I will argue, however, that the more salient public policy questions concern the causal links between displacement and disadvantage. If displacement is not likely to cause disadvantage, then the policy case for aiding displaced workers is weakened. If, however, there is a significant likelihood that displacement will cause later disadvantage (through "scarring" or other effects) then there is a stronger policy case for early intervention to assist displaced workers. One salient question, therefore, is whether displacement causes disadvantage.

Another salient question is whether disadvantage causes displacement. If displacement is as likely to occur among nondisadvantaged workers as among disadvantaged workers, then the policy case for focusing on displacement is weakened. However, if disadvantaged workers are more likely to be in jobs that are unstable and likely to disappear, displacement may be a relatively good signal of those who could use adjustment assistance. Even if displacement is not a primary cause of future disadvantage, displacement may still be a useful focal point for assistance to move disadvantaged workers into better and more stable jobs. In addition, as will be explained later, if programs targeted to disadvantaged workers defeat themselves by stigmatizing the assisted workers, making aid available to all displaced workers may improve the employment prospects of disadvantaged workers.

Does Displacement Cause Disadvantage?

It is apparent that some loss is suffered by almost all workers who are displaced, which in itself may provide some justification for adjustment assistance. An argument can be made on efficiency grounds that such assistance promotes labor-market flexibility by reducing the political and social impediments to economic change, and on equity grounds that the costs of economic change should be widely shared by the public.[5] The case made by Bendick and Devine is that workers who are relatively affluent at the time of displacement do not have such urgent needs for assistance as the disadvantaged workers who do not have resources to fall back upon. However, even if workers are relatively affluent at the time of displacement, the displacement experience may diminish their affluence and cause them to become disadvantaged in the labor market through stigmatizing by employers or personal effects (alcoholism, divorce, etc.) of unemployment. If this occurs, a case can be made that assistance should be given to workers shortly after displacement to arrest the process by which they become disadvantaged.

Evidence on this casual link is sparse. Three types will be covered here. One form of evidence comes from studies that attempt to identify changes in the probability of reemployment throughout unemployment spells. If unemployment has a stigmatizing or scarring effect, the probability of reemployment would decline as the unemployment spell progressed ("negative duration dependence"). Several studies have in fact found declining hazard rates for unemployed workers (e.g., Podgursky and Swaim 1987a; Lynch 1986). An alternative interpretation, however, is the heterogeneity or sorting hypothesis: given a distribution of unmeasured worker skills and preferences that produce a distribution of hazard rates, the workers with long unemployment spells may simply be those with constant low reemployment probabilities (Heckman and Borjas 1980). Another alternative interpretation is that hazard rates vary according to the reason for displacement: Katz (1986) finds constant hazard rates for those who were not put on temporary layoff, and a declining hazard rate for those who were told they were on temporary layoff (reflecting a declining probability that employers will recall the workers); studies that fail to separate these categories may find an overall declining hazard rate due simply to the latter group.

A second area of inquiry has been the effect of unemployment spells on future employment experiences. Ellwood (1982) looks at teenage employment using longitudinal data (from the National Longitudinal Survey, or NLS), to control for constant unobserved heterogeneity. He found that an early employment experience has a positive effect on weeks worked in the following year, but very little effect beyond the first year or two. Two studies use data from the Panel Survey of Income Dynamics (PSID) to attempt to control for unobserved heterogeneity. Corcoran and Hill (1985) restrist their sample to adult men with employment status data over the 1967–76 period. While the simple conditional probabilities showed strong relationships among unemployment (not restricted to involuntary separations) in adjoining periods, controlling for constant individual differences (and statistical problems associated with interval sampling) led the authors to conclude that "past unemployment does not increase adult men's chances of current unemployment" (p. 176). Using the same data set but a different procedure, Ruhm (1987a) attempts to control for heterogeneity by comparing the employment experiences over a five-year period of those laid-off in the first year with those laid off in the fifth year. While unemployment was about twenty weeks higher over the five-year period for those laid off in the first year, this was concentrated in the first two years after layoff and there were no differences in weeks of unemployment in years four and five. This led him to conclude that the effects of involuntary separations were transitory.

While these studies cast doubt on the idea that there is any strong causal relation leading from current unemployment spells to future unemployment spells (beyond one or two years), the negative effects of unemployment spells may show up as effects on wages and/or the quality of jobs obtained in the future. The previously cited study by Ellwood (1982) found that although early work experience has little impact on future employment beyond the subsequent year, it does have a substantial impact on wages in the first four years out of school (whether the effect increases or diminishes beyond that time could not be tested). Evidence on this link has also been obtained from the Displaced Workers Survey. Podgursky and Swaim (1987b) find that among workers displaced over 1979–83 who were reemployed in January 1984, only 32.5% of blue-collar and 38.0% of white-collar workers had (wage-inflation-adjusted) weekly earnings in their new job that equalled or

exceeded the weekly earnings in the job from which they were displaced. Those who had current weekly earnings that were less than 75%
of their previous earnings comprised 37.0% (30.9%) of blue-collar
(white-collar) workers. The median ratio of current earnings to previous
earnings was 0.87 (0.93) for blue-collar (white-collar) workers. Greater
years of education led to smaller earnings losses, while greater years of
tenure on the previous job and higher area unemployment rates led to
larger earnings losses.

Therefore a large portion of displaced workers do suffer large earnings losses; it is possible, however, that this is simply a transitory adjustment as workers invest in a new set of firm- or industry-specific skills, or
as they "experiment" with new jobs in order to find the one in which
they will be the most productive.[6] Ruhm (1987b) looks at the persistence
of wage changes following involuntary separation, and finds that 42–
68% of the initial wage changes (from the year preceding separation to
the year following separation) continue through the third and fourth
years following separation. Also, wages in the third and fourth years are
lower for the involuntarily separated workers who later change jobs
(table 6), arguing against a simple story of "experimentation" with new
jobs to find the most productive. The pattern of displacement year
dummy coefficients in Podgursky and Swaim (1987b) showed no general
tendency of greater earnings recovery for those displaced in earlier
years, suggesting that the wage effects last at least four years.[7]

In summarizing the piecemeal evidence, to the extent that displacement may cause "disadvantage" lasting beyond one or two years, the
disadvantage is more likely to be in the form of wage effects rather than
future unemployment effects. It should be noted that even if evidence
indicates that displacement has no *general* effect on long-term unemployment, it may still have an effect for a portion of workers. Depending on
the costs to workers and society of long-term unemployment, even this
subgroup effect may justify assistance designed to curtail the negative
effects.

Does Disadvantage Cause Displacement?

As noted earlier, the segmented labor-market literature views disadvantaged workers as being restricted to the secondary sector in which,
among other things, the jobs are unstable (due to both displacement and
voluntary turnover).[8] This raises the question of a causal link opposite of
that considered in the last section: Whether or not displacement causes

285

disadvantage, does disadvantage restrict one to jobs with a high probability of displacement? If so, is displacement a useful focal point for assisting disadvantaged workers?

Two theoretical arguments can be put forward in favor of aiding displaced workers as a way of helping disadvantaged workers. First, if a high proportion of displaced workers are disadvantaged, then displacement may be a relatively efficient signal of those who could use assistance (particularly compared to the more intrusive and more manipulable indicators such as personal or family income and wealth). This argument is strengthened if a minimum number of postdisplacement weeks of unemployment is used as a criterion: advantaged workers will select out of assistance programs by becoming quickly reemployed, leaving a higher proportion of disadvantaged workers.

Second, programs in which one must be formally defined as disadvantaged in order to participate may have a stigmatizing effect that counters the intent of the programs. For example, Burtless (1985) reports on an experiment in which some disadvantaged workers applied for jobs with vouchers entitling their employers to tax credits or deductions (equivalent to 50% of the worker's first-year wages), while the control group of disadvantaged workers applied for jobs without such vouchers. While employer cost-minimizing behavior would seem to favor hiring those with vouchers, the hiring rate was actually significantly higher within the control group. Burtless' explanation for this is that the vouchers had a stigmatizing effect: in the absence of perfect information about the characteristics of applicants, those with vouchers were viewed as "damaged goods."

If stigma is an important factor in the labor market, programs for which only the disadvantaged are eligible (and which employers know about) may do more harm than good to their labor-market prospects. However, the substance of the program may do more good than harm if there is a less stigmatizing criterion for eligibility. Displacement is potentially such a criterion, given that the reasons for displacement (particularly for large-scale layoffs or plant closings) are generally perceived as outside the control of an individual displaced worker, and therefore less likely to be stigmatizing.

One empirical question, then, is whether disadvantaged workers comprise a high proportion of those who are displaced. The answer to this question obviously depends on one's definition of "disadvantage." To the extent that low-skill levels are used as one of the criteria of disadvantage, one might expect that disadvantaged workers would be prone to displacement by technological change and/or imports (due to the higher substitutability of low-skill labor with capital and foreign labor). While there has been continuing concern about "technological unemployment," the degree to which it primarily affects low-skill or otherwise "disadvantaged" workers has not been quantified.[9] There has also been very little study of the relative effects of imports on different groups of workers. One study found that increasing import shares were associated with blue-collar work, lower pay levels, and lower education among displaced workers, suggesting that imports were more likely to displace low-skill workers than high-skill workers (Kruse 1988).

One theme of segmented labor-market literature is that an important manifestation of racial and gender discrimination is the restriction of women and racial minorities to unstable secondary sector jobs. An interesting comparison, then, is the representation of women and minorities among displaced workers relative to their representation in the workforce as a whole. Simple comparisons of this sort, using the Displaced Workers Survey, show virtually no difference in proportion of blacks between displaced workers and all those in the labor force, while women are less represented among displaced workers than in the labor force as a whole (Seitchik, this volume).[10] However, women and blacks do have longer postdisplacement spells of joblessness than do white males, suggesting that displacement is a more serious problem for these groups (Podgursky and Swaim 1987a; Kruse 1988).

Another feature of secondary sector jobs is the low pay. As noted previously, a compensating differentials view would predict higher wages for those in jobs with a high probability of displacement, while segmented labor-market theory views high displacement probabilities as being linked to lower wages. Limited evidence tends to indicate that the predisplacement wages of displaced workers do not differ much from those of nondisplaced workers. Simple comparisons indicate that 57% of displaced (full-time) workers had predisplacement weekly earnings that were lower than median weekly earnings for all employed workers in the same broad occupation; however, this comparison does not take account of education, experience, and other characteristics that may differ among displaced and nondisplaced workers.[11] Hamermesh (1987) reports average wages conditional on experience for heads of households in the PSID; his results indicate that, relative to all workers, those subject to plant closings have higher average wages, while those subject to involuntary layoffs have lower average wages (table 4) (since this was not the focus of the paper, these differences were not formally tested).

An additional piece of rough evidence on this point comes from comparing the predisplacement wages of men displaced in 1983 with their predicted wages based on regression coefficients for all employed men in 1983 (using labor-market experience and its square, years of education, and race, marriage, and SMSA dummies as independent variables).[12] If workers about to be displaced have lower unobserved quality, or are in low-paying jobs that do not reward education and experience as much as for other workers, then the actual predisplacement wages should be generally lower than the predicted wages; in fact, relative to predicted wages, the sample was evenly split between those with higher actual wages and lower actual wages.[13] A fuller test of earnings differentials between workers about to be displaced and other employed workers would be quite interesting.

A third characteristic of disadvantaged workers is the lack of family resources; this may take the form of inadequate wealth or inadequate income from other members of the household. Very little evidence exists on the family resources of displaced workers. No available evidence could be found on the predisplacement wealth or other-family-member incomes of displaced workers. Some suggestive evidence is presented in table 1, which gives the postdisplacement distribution of total family incomes in 1983 for workers who were full-time reemployed in January of 1984 and had been displaced in 1979–80 (to minimize the probability that the initial unemployment spell extended into 1983). For comparison, the distribution of total family income for all families is also presented. As can be seen, the families of displaced workers are more likely to be in the low-income categories than are families as a whole (almost two-thirds of families in the displaced sample had incomes less than $25,000; the national median was $24,580).[14]

Finally, a feature of secondary-sector jobs that may represent disadvantage is the lack of significant on-the-job returns to education and experience. In a test of dual labor-market theory, Dickens and Lang (1985) find that two wage equations fit the data much better than one, and that the coefficients are consistent with the patterns predicted by dual labor-market theory (the "secondary sector" wage equation had effectively no returns to education and experience; on the basis of observable characteristics these workers would have done much better in the jobs defined by the "primary" wage equation). Their results do not deal with the question of displacement. Are displaced workers and nondisplaced workers similar in their experience-earnings and education-earnings profiles for predisplacement wages, and if not, are the differences consistent with the idea that displaced workers are concentrated in a secondary labor market?

One study on this topic (Hamermesh 1987) looked at experience-

Table 1   Total Family Income in 1983, Cumulative Frequencies

Income Category	Full-time Reemployed Displaced Workers*	All Families**
≤4,999	3.4%	5.7%
5,000–9,999	15.1	15.9
10,000–14,999	32.5	27.5
15,000–19,999	48.9	39.3
20,000–24,999	64.2	50.8
25,000–34,999	84.3	70.3
≥35,000	100.0	100.0

*1983 family income of workers displaced in 1979–80 who were full-time reemployed in January 1984 (weighted estimates based on sample of 1,005) (calculated from January 1984 Displaced Worker Survey).
** Taken from the March 1984 CPS as reported in *Statistical Abstract of the United States, 1985* (Washington, D.C.: Bureau of the Census, 1985), p. 446.

earnings profiles for workers prior to displacement. Experience, its square, and tenure were all significant predictors of wages prior to displacement, which is consistent with the existence of returns to both general and firm-specific experience. These profiles changed little as displacement approached, making it appear that workers were surprised by the displacement. No formal comparison was made between the profiles of displaced workers and those who remained employed.

As a preliminary test of the differences in experience-earnings and education-earnings profiles between displaced workers and all employed workers, the predisplacement wage equations for men reporting displacement in 1983 (separately for the 1984 and 1986 surveys) were compared with similar wage equations for all employed men in 1983 (from Dickens and Lang 1985). While the predisplacement wage equations tend to show slightly lower returns to education and higher returns to experience than for employed men as a whole, the data do not reject constraining all coefficients to be identical to those found for employed men as a whole. The implication is that, at the time of displacement, the population of displaced men looked fairly similar to all employed men in terms of returns to education and experience. An interesting project would be to complement Hamermesh's study of predisplacement experience-earnings profiles by doing a full comparison of wage equations between all employed workers and those about to be displaced.

Future Research

In exploring the relationship between disadvantage and displacement, this chapter has argued that policy-relevant research should focus on the causal links. One broad question addressed is whether displacement causes disadvantage. If displacement and the subsequent unemployment cause long-lasting disadvantage for workers, a policy case can be made that government assistance should be given to workers soon after displacement to arrest the process by which they become disadvantaged. The sparse available evidence tends to indicate a transitory impact of current unemployment on future unemployment: the probability of future unemployment is increased in the following one or two years, but not after. However, more sparse evidence indicates that the negative impact on wages may be more long lasting.

More research on the long-term effects of displacement would clearly be useful for policy making. In particular, if "scarring" does operate to decrease the employment prospects of displaced workers, it would be especially important to know the point at which this may begin so that assistance programs could start prior to that time. The difficulty in looking at the long-term effects of displacement is the paucity of longitudinal data that allow one to separate state-dependence from heterogeneity. While good use has been made of the PSID and NLS, their usefulness is limited in many cases by small sample sizes. The Displaced Workers Survey provides larger samples, but with very little longitudinal capability (subsets of the workers in the DWS can be matched across months to other CPS datasets, but a particularly serious bias is introduced by the fact that displaced workers have a high probability of moving, which will cause them to drop out of the household-based CPS). A difficult but potentially very rewarding project would be to use the Unemployment Insurance (ES202) and/or Social Security files to follow over a long time period the workers identified as displaced by plant closings or employment cutbacks.

The second broad question identified in this chapter is whether disadvantage causes displacement. According to standard competitive theory, the workers who are most likely to be displaced are those who are least risk-averse (implying higher income and/or wealth) and who gained a positive compensating differential for the acceptance of the risk of displacement. In contrast, segmented labor-market theory views disadvantaged workers as being confined to the unstable secondary sector in which separations are more prevalent. If it is true that disadvantage leads to a higher risk of displacement, an important question is whether there are macroeconomic or microeconomic policies that can break this link by lessening the overall risk of displacement and/or providing nonstigmatizing assistance to displaced workers to move into more stable jobs.

Again, evidence on this question is spotty. The rough comparisons presented in this chapter indicate that the population of displaced workers is not greatly different than the population of employed workers in demographic makeup, predisplacement wages (conditional on education and experience), or predisplacement returns to education and experience. (No evidence exists on predisplacement family incomes, although simple statistics presented here indicate that family incomes for reemployed displaced workers tend to be lower than for all families). If it is true that displaced workers are representative of employed workers, there would not seem to be a strong case for assisting all displaced workers as a means of aiding disadvantaged workers.

A potential criticism of this conclusion may be related to the liberal definition of "displacement" used here—defining it broadly (as any involuntary separation due to a plant closing or employment cutback) may mask greatly different consequences for different groups. For advantaged workers displacement may simply mean a quick job change, while for disadvantaged workers displacement may signify a difficult adjustment and large personal costs. One implication would be that adjustment assistance to all displaced workers may still be a relatively efficient way of aiding disadvantaged workers, since many advantaged workers will tend to opt out by becoming quickly reemployed. Also, as noted before, programs that are formally targeted to disadvantaged workers may cause stigmatization of these workers by employers; in this case displacement may be a relatively nonstigmatizing criterion for assisting disadvantaged workers (the benefits of using this nonstigmatizing criterion would have to be weighed against the costs of aiding nondisadvantaged workers in the program).

Much better information is needed on the displacement risks and costs faced by workers identified as disadvantaged in the labor market. If these risks and costs are fairly small, the question of displacement might be seen as mostly tangential to the problems of disadvantaged workers. If, however, they are substantial, policy interventions for displaced workers may be one element of the war on disadvantage.

Clearly we know too little about the relationship between displacement and disadvantage. Are they largely separate problems, or are they part of a cycle that public policies have the potential to break? Following is a summary of the most important research questions identified in this chapter:

1. Does displacement lead to long-term unemployment problems (if not for all workers, then for a subgroup of workers)?
2. Does displacement lead to long-term earnings losses (again, perhaps for a subgroup of workers)?
3. Do workers identified as disadvantaged by low skill, education, or other criteria face larger risks and costs of displacement than advantaged workers?
4. What is the distribution of family income and wealth among displaced workers, and do family resources have a large effect on unemployment and access to jobs and training for displaced workers?
5. Do returns to education and general labor-market experience differ among workers according to risk of displacement, and if so, does this represent a form of disadvantage for workers in unstable jobs?

NOTES

1. Osterman (1988) provides a useful discussion of displacement and disadvantage in the U.S. labor market, without directly addressing the question posed in this chapter.

2. As applied to temporary layoffs, evidence for this is provided in Abowd and Ashenfelter (1981).

3. See Edwards et al. (1975) and Berger and Piore (1980); for a neoclassical perspective on segmented labor markets see Taubman and Wachter (1986).

4. To be associated with an industry or occupation, one must have worked in that industry or occupation within the previous five years, which excludes new entrants to the labor force. However, a new entrant could still be counted as "dislocated" in this definition through association with a declining region.

5. Both the efficiency and equity arguments are seen most clearly in the rationale for the Trade Adjustment Assistance program. The "efficiency" argument is that the program was necessary to buy support among labor unions for free trade policies, while the "equity" argument is that the costs of free trade policies should be shared throughout society (Richardson 1983).

6. A one-year follow-up on the 1984 displaced workers sample is reported in Devens (1986). His numbers indicate an improvement from January 1984 to January 1985 in the distribution of the ratio of current earnings to previous earnings; however, there appears to be no adjustment for wage inflation so these numbers are not reported here.

7. The year dummies pick up macroeconomic factors as well as length of time since displacement. Macroeconomic effects on wage changes are partially controlled through the inclusion of area unemployment rates in the year of displacement.

The conclusion of this paragraph is also supported by Mincer and Ofek (1982), who find that wage growth following a interruption in working is "relatively rapid," but is not sufficient to recapture the wage losses associated with the interruption.

8. It should be noted that displacement may not be the most important component in the instability of secondary sector jobs; voluntary turnover in "dead-end" jobs may be more important, and may deserve equal emphasis in addressing the problems of the disadvantaged. Another problem that is not addressed here is the shifting location of secondary sector jobs: Wilson (1987) argues that the number of jobs with low education requirements in inner cities is declining, which shuts down a major mobility path for disadvantaged inner-city residents.

9. For an overview of the problem and recent trends see chapter 8 of Office of Technology Assessment, 1986.

10. Also see table 1 of Hamermesh, 1989, where he finds that women are less likely than men to be displaced, but that nonwhites are somewhat more likely than whites to be displaced.

11. For this calculation, predisplacement weekly earnings (from the 1984 Displaced Workers Survey), were divided by median weekly earnings of full-time workers in the same one-digit occupation and year (taken from CPS data, as reported in the *Statistical Abstract of the United States, 1984*, p. 434; and *Statistical Abstract of the United States, 1985*, p. 419). Of the workers displaced by plant closings (layoffs), 59% (55%) had weekly earnings below the median for full-time workers in their occupation.

12. Regression coefficients for the predicted wages are based on table 1, column 1, of Dickens and Lang (1985). Such a comparison must be regarded as rough because no account is taken of differences in industry and occupation distributions, union status, and other variables affecting earnings.

13. Fifty-one percent of workers had log of actual weekly earnings higher than log of predicted weekly earnings.

14. Insufficient information existed to control for family size, marital status, family head, region, and other variables affecting family income in this comparison. However, males and married persons (characteristics associated with higher earnings) comprise higher proportions of displaced workers than of all employed workers (Seitchik, this volume), so that these factors are unlikely to explain the lower incomes. On the other hand, displaced workers tend to be younger than all employed persons, which could account for some of the differences.

REFERENCES

Abowd, John M., and Orley Ashenfelter (1981). "Anticipated Unemployment, Temporary Layoffs, and Compensating Wage Differentials." In *Studies in Labor Markets*, edited by Sherwin Rosen. Chicago, Ill.: University of Chicago Press.

Bendick, Marc, and Judith R. Devine (1982). "Workers Dislocated by Economic Change:

Do They Need Federal Employment and Training?" In *National Commission for Employment Policy, Seventh Annual Report.* Washington, D.C.: U.S. Government Printing Office.

Berger, Suzanne, and Michael Piore (1980). *Dualism and Discontinuity in Industrial Societies.* New York: Cambridge University Press.

Bulow, Jeremy I., and Lawrence H. Summers (1986). "A Theory of Dual Labor Markets with Application to Industrial Policy, Discrimination, and Keynesian Unemployment." *Journal of Labor Economics* 4 (July): 376–414.

Burtless, Gary (1985). "Are Targeted Wage Subsidies Harmful? Evidence from a Wage Voucher Experiment." *Industrial and Labor Relations Review* 39 (October): 105–14.

Corcoran, Mary, and Martha S. Hill (1985). "Reoccurrence of Unemployment Among Adult Men." *Journal of Human Resources* 20 (Spring): 165–83.

Devens, R. M. (1986). "Displaced Workers: One Year Later." *Monthly Labor Review* 109 (July): 40–43.

Dickens, William T., and Kevin Lang (1985). "Testing Dual Labor Market Theory: A Reconsideration of the Evidence." NBER Working Paper No. 1670, July.

Edwards, Richard C., Michael Reich, and David M. Gordon, eds. (1975). *Labor Market Segmentation.* Lexington, Mass.: D.C. Heath and Company.

Ellwood, David T. (1982). "Teenage Unemployment: Permanent Scars or Temporary Blemishes?" In *The Youth Labor Market Problem: Its Nature, Causes, and Consequences,* edited by Richard B. Freeman and David A. Wise. Chicago, Ill.: University of Chicago Press.

Hamermesh, Daniel (1987). "The Costs of Worker Displacement." *Quarterly Journal of Economics* 102 (February): 51–75.

———(1989). "What Do We Know About Worker Displacement in the U.S.?" *Industrial Relations* 28 (Winter): 51–59.

Heckman, James J., and George J. Borjas (1980). "Does Unemployment Cause Future Unemployment?: Definitions, Questions, and Answers, and Answers from a Continuous Time Model of Heterogeneity and State Dependence." *Economica* 47 (August): 39–77.

Katz, Lawrence (1986). "Layoffs, Recall, and the Duration of Unemployment." NBER Working Paper Number 1825, February.

Kruse, Douglas (1988). "International Trade and the Labor Market Experience of Displaced Workers." *Industrial and Labor Relations Review* 41 (April): 402–17.

Lynch, Lisa (1986). "The Youth Labor Market in the 80's: Determinants of Reemployment Probabilities for Young Men and Women." Discussion paper. Cambridge, Mass.: Industrial Relations Section, Sloan School of Management, July.

Mincer, Jacob and Haim Ofek (1982). "Interrupted Work Careers: Depreciation and Restoration of Human Capital." *Journal of Human Resources* 17 (Winter): 3–24.

Office of Technology Assessment (1986). *Technology and Structural Unemployment: Reemploying Displaced Adults.* Washington, D.C.: U.S. Government Printing Office, February.

Osterman, Paul (1988). *Employment Futures: Reorganization, Dislocation, and Public Policy.* New York: Oxford University Press.

Podgursky, Michael, and Paul Swaim (1987a). "Duration of Joblessness Following Displacement." *Industrial Relations* 26 (Fall): 213–26.

———(1987b). "Job Displacement and Earnings Loss: Evidence from the Displaced Workers Survey." *Industrial and Labor Relations Review* 41 (October): 17–29.

Richardson, J. David (1983). "Worker Adjustment to U.S. International Trade: Programs

294

and Prospects." In *Trade Policy in the 1980's,* edited by William R. Cline. Washington, D.C.: MIT Press.

Ruhm, Christopher J. (1987a). "The Extent and Persistence of Unemployment Following Permanent Quits and Layoffs." Discussion paper. Boston: Boston University Dept. of Economics, January.

————(1987b). "The Economic Consequences of Labor Mobility." *Industrial and Labor Relations Review* 41 (October): 30–42.

Taubman, Paul, and Michael Wachter (1986). "Segmented Labor Markets." In *Handbook of Labor Economics,* edited by Orley Ashenfelter and Richard Layard. Amsterdam: North-Holland.

Wilson, William J. (1987). *The Truly Disadvantaged.* Chicago: University of Chicago Press.

Author Index

Subject Index

301